The ROSE EXPERT

Dr. D.G. Hessayon

1st Impression	300,000

Previous Edition:
BE YOUR OWN ROSE EXPERT
9 Impressions   *2,075,000*

Other Books in the EXPERT Series:
THE HOUSE PLANT EXPERT
BE YOUR OWN GARDENING EXPERT
BE YOUR OWN LAWN EXPERT
BE YOUR OWN HOUSE PLANT SPOTTER
BE YOUR OWN GARDEN DOCTOR
BE YOUR OWN VEGETABLE DOCTOR
VEGETABLE PLOTTER

Acknowledgements
The author wishes to acknowledge the painstaking work of
Jane Jenks and Peggy Easterling. Grateful acknowledgement is
also made to Angela Pawsey (Rose Growers Association),
Len Turner (Royal National Rose Society), Joan Hessayon and
Angelina Hessayon. John Woodbridge provided both artistry
and design work; Henry Barnett and Norman Barber prepared
the paintings for this book.

A rose book without full-colour illustrations is like a beautiful bloom without perfume.
Many people and organizations have provided photographs, and thanks are due to
Cants of Colchester, Dickson Nurseries Ltd., Fryer's Nurseries Ltd., R. Harkness & Co. Ltd.,
E.B. LeGrice (Roses) Ltd., John Mattock of Oxford, Meilland Star Roses Ltd.,
Brian J. Tysterman, Wheatcroft Roses Ltd., A-Z Botanical Collection, Bernard Alfieri,
Floracolour, Robert Harding Picture Library, Royal National Rose Society and
Harry Smith Horticultural Photographic Collection.

pbi PUBLICATIONS

pbi PUBLICATIONS · BRITANNICA HOUSE · WALTHAM CROSS · HERTS · ENGLAND

Contents

Printed and bound in Great Britain by Severn Valley Press Ltd.

ISBN 0 903505 14 2   © D G HESSAYON 1981

CHAPTER 1
LOOKING AT YOUR ROSES

Roses seem to have been with us for ever. We know Nero loved them, the Ancient Greeks wrote myths about them and the Tudor Kings adopted them as our national emblem. The rose came to us early as a source of perfume, as a cure for ills and as a symbol of beauty... but it came to us late as a popular bush for the garden.

The first National Rose Show met with little interest from the general public. It was not until 1900 that the National Rose Society managed to increase its membership to 500. The simple truth is that Victorian gardeners regarded it as a plant for the shrubbery or the house wall, but not for the flower bed where the beloved geranium reigned supreme.

And they were right. In the first half of the 19th century roses were large shrubs, or climbers which bloomed for only a few weeks. But everything changed during Queen Victoria's reign. Before she died the old roses of Europe, tough and hardy with red, white and pink flowers had been bred with the repeat flowering beauties from China. The blood of the Persian roses had been added, bringing bright yellow and orange to the beauty of our roses. All the ingredients were there for breeders to produce the ideal bedding plant.

Repeat flowering is linked with winter hardiness. A breathtaking array of colours is linked with vigorous growth, and it has been Britain's favourite flower since the First World War. Eight out of 10 gardens have one, and each year in this country about 35 million new ones are bought.

The choice is vast — there are thousands of varieties on sale. Nearly all are grown for the beauty or fragrance of their flowers, but there are also roses which bear decorative hips, leaves and even beautiful thorns. The plant you select may reach a height of 4 or 5 in., or it may tower 40 ft into the sky. The purpose of this book is to show you how to choose, plant and care for the fairest of all flowers.

Using rose catalogues

More roses are purchased over the counter than are ordered by post from growers, but for countless rose lovers one of the joys of the gardening year is studying the new catalogues.

New varieties get the largest photographs and the most alluring descriptions, but this does not always make them the best choice. For the ordinary gardener who just wants a few reliable bushes it is sometimes better to wait a year or two to see how the new ones succeed.

Many reliable favourites will, of course, be listed and they are the grower's own selection from the world's top roses. Read the descriptions carefully, but do not expect to find all the faults listed. Don't pay too much attention to the photographs — they give little idea of size or appearance in the garden, and printing cannot capture all flower colours. Yellows and oranges are usually quite accurate, but reds can be distinctly poor. Never reject a rose just because there is no photograph.

More than 80 per cent of rose sales are H.T.s or Floribundas. The Shrub, Miniature and Climbing Rose descriptions are therefore usually briefer and the photographs smaller, but do not neglect them on that account.

Using this book

For most readers, the main purpose of this book will be to learn more about the roses in their garden and about other varieties they may wish to buy.

For them the A–Z section (pages 7–72) provides information on the important properties of each rose, together with an overall assessment of its value for garden or exhibition use. There are two important features of these 332 descriptions — first of all, there has been no attempt to choose the "best" roses. The chosen ones have been included solely on the basis of their popularity and the probability of finding them in garden centres, stores, catalogues and the Royal National Rose Society Analysis of reliable varieties.

Secondly, catalogue-type descriptions have been avoided. Bad points have been listed as well as good ones, and in some cases the drawbacks outweigh the advantages.

Apart from information on varieties, the general reader will need guidance on planting (Chapter 5), upkeep (Chapter 6) and troubles (Chapter 7). For some, however, roses are more than just a flower — they are an absorbing hobby. For them Chapter 8 provides more specialised information on such topics as propagation, exhibiting, famous rose gardens, rose history and rose classification.

PLANT PARTS

BLIND SHOOT

TRUSS (FLOWER CLUSTER)

PEDICEL (FLOWER STALK)

STIPULE

LEAF STALK

LEAFLET

LATERAL BRANCH

HIPS (HEPS) produced after flowering

MAIN STEM (BASAL SHOOT or CANE)

NEW WOOD stem of current year's growth

LEAF

BREAKING BUD

NODE

DORMANT GROWTH BUD (EYE)

OLD WOOD stem of a previous year's growth

SNAG

SUCKER

NECK

BUD UNION

ROOTSTOCK

FLOWER PARTS

FILAMENT

PETAL

ANTHER

STYLE

STIGMA

OVARY

SEPAL

BRACT

RECEPTACLE matures into a HIP

ROOTSTOCKS

Modern roses are not grown on their own roots. They are budded on to the roots of wild roses or their close relatives. Rootstocks commonly used by nurserymen are:

Rosa laxa Now the most popular of all. Reliable, transplants well and rarely suckers. Almost thornless for easy budding.

Rosa canina Produces the hardiest plants. Selected varieties used — a good choice for heavy soils. Suckers freely — popularity has declined.

Rosa multiflora Produces the most vigorous plants. Good choice for Climbers, but hard to bud and can be short-lived.

Rosa rugosa Popular for standards. Not recommended for bushes — suckers freely and is not suitable for heavy soils.

GROWTH TYPES

The four basic growth types are ground cover, bush, standard and climbing (see chart below). A bush may be a Hybrid Tea, Floribunda or Shrub Rose (see page 7).

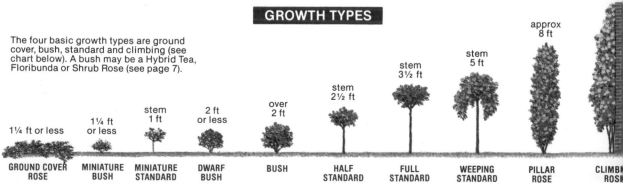

GROUND COVER ROSE	MINIATURE BUSH	MINIATURE STANDARD	DWARF BUSH	BUSH	HALF STANDARD	FULL STANDARD	WEEPING STANDARD	PILLAR ROSE	CLIMBING ROSE
1¼ ft or less	1¼ ft or less	stem 1 ft	2 ft or less	over 2 ft	stem 2½ ft	stem 3½ ft	stem 5 ft	approx 8 ft	

FLOWER TYPES
Number of Petals

SINGLE

less than 8 petals
Examples: Mermaid
Fred Loads
Ballerina
Eye Paint
Dortmund

SEMI-DOUBLE

8-20 petals
Examples: Topsi
Paprika
Joseph's Coat
Masquerade
Frensham

DOUBLE

MODERATELY FULL
21-29 petals
Examples: Pascali
Mojave

FULL
30-39 petals
Examples: Circus
Queen Elizabeth

VERY FULL
40 petals and over
Examples: Peace
Alec's Red

Flower Colours

SINGLE COLOUR
Petals similarly coloured throughout, although some changes may occur as blooms get older.
Examples: Iceberg
Super Star

BI-COLOUR
Colour of the outside of each petal distinctly different from the inside hue.
Examples: Piccadilly
Rose Gaujard

MULTI-COLOUR
Colour of the petals changes distinctly with age. Flower trusses have several colours at the same time.
Examples: Charleston
Masquerade

BLEND
Two or more distinct colours merge on the inside of each petal.
Examples: Peace
Peer Gynt

STRIPED
Two or more different colours on each petal, one of which is in the form of distinct bands.
Examples: Rosa Mundi
Harry Wheatcroft

HAND PAINTED
Silvery petals with red blotched and feathered over the surface, leaving a white eye at the base.
Examples: Picasso
Priscilla Burton

Petal Shapes

The petals of many roses are **plain**, but those of Hybrid Teas and some Floribundas are **reflexed**. A feature of a few roses is a wavy or **ruffled** edge to the petals, and in the *Grootendorst* varieties the petals have a carnation-like **frilled** edge.

PLAIN
Examples: Paprika
Nevada

REFLEXED
Examples: Alec's Red
Fragrant Cloud

RUFFLED
Examples: Just Joey
Dr A. J. Verhage

FRILLED
Examples: F. J. Grootendorst
Pink Grootendorst

Flower Shapes

HIGH-CENTRED
Classical shape of the Hybrid Tea — long inner petals forming a regular central cone.

SPLIT-CENTRED
Inner petals confused, forming an irregular central area.

BLOWN
Normally well-shaped bloom past its best — opened wide to reveal stamens.

GLOBULAR
Bloom possessing many petals forming a ball-like arrangement with a closed centre.

OPEN-CUPPED
Bloom possessing many petals forming a cup-like arrangement with an open centre.

QUARTERED
Inner petals folded into 4 distinct sections rather than forming a cone.

FLAT
Flat, low-centred bloom with a small number of petals.

ROSETTE
Flat, low-centred bloom with many short petals regularly arranged.

POMPON
Rounded bloom with many short petals regularly arranged.

FOLIAGE TYPES

Leaf Surfaces

The typical rose leaf has a smooth surface and is made up of five or seven leaflets. This standard pattern applies to nearly all garden varieties, but the shininess of the surface varies greatly. Some are highly polished as if they have been recently treated with oil — others are distinctly dull. Many varieties have leaves between these two extremes, so the three basic groups are **glossy**, **semi-glossy** and **matt**.

Not all roses have five or seven leaflets — a few such as *Rosa willmottiae* have attractive ferny foliage composed of many small leaflets. Also the surface of the foliage is not always smooth — the Rugosa group of Shrubs have leaves which are deeply ribbed (**rugose**), giving them a characteristic-ally wrinkled effect.

GLOSSY
Examples: Peace
Evelyn Fison

SEMI-GLOSSY
Examples: Redgold
Fred Gibson

MATT
Examples: Tip Top
National Trust

RUGOSE
Examples: Scabrosa
Rosa rugosa alba

Leaf Colours

Nearly all mature rose leaves are green, varying from the insipid pale green of *Fred Loads* to the very dark green of *Cornelia*. As illustrated below, the three basic groups of rose leaf colours are **light green**, **medium green** and **dark green**. Some varieties have green foliage which is **bronze-tinted**, giving the leaves a coppery sheen.

There are exceptions to this general picture, especially amongst the Shrub Roses. Young foliage is sometimes distinctly purplish or crimson, and in some varieties such as *Rosa rubrifolia* and *Buff Beauty* this red coloration persists in the mature leaves. At the other end of the colour spectrum, the leaves of the Alba group are grey-green with a bluish tinge. Several varieties have attractive autumn tints — the Rugosa group is outstanding.

LIGHT GREEN
Examples: Kim
Yellow Pages

MEDIUM GREEN
Examples: Blessings
Ena Harkness

DARK GREEN
Examples: Gavotte
Korona

BRONZE-TINTED
Examples: Bettina
Marlena

HIPS

After the flowers have gone, the coloured and fleshy fruit cases of some Shrub Roses are an extra bonus in the autumn garden. The bottle-shaped red hips of *Rosa moyesii* and the large tomato-like fruits of *Frau Dagmar Hartopp* are well-known but there are many other varieties to choose from.

ROUND: LARGE & RED
Example: Scabrosa

ROUND: SMALL & RED
Example: Rosa virginiana

ROUND: SMALL & BLACK
Example: Rosa spinosissima

ELONGATED
Example: Rosa moyesii Geranium

PRICKLY
Example: Rosa roxburghii

FLOWERING PERIOD

Repeat flowering Roses produce two or more flushes of blooms during the flowering season. Modern roses generally produce blooms at intervals throughout the summer months and into the autumn — one of the main reasons for the unrivalled popularity of Hybrid Teas and Floribundas. Repeat flowering varieties, also known as recurrent and remontant varieties, may produce some flowers between the main flushes. When this feature is strongly marked the descriptions perpetual and continuous flowering are sometimes used, but they are not strictly correct.

Once flowering Roses produce a single flush of blooms which usually last for several weeks. Occasionally a few flowers may appear in autumn, but this flowering is far too sporadic to be considered a second flush. The once flowering varieties most frequently bloom in June/July (**summer flowering**), but there are varieties of Shrubs and Ramblers which bloom in late spring, early summer or late summer.

FRAGRANCE

People will always smell an open bloom if they are trying to decide on its merits. Because of the importance of this feature, the descriptions in the A–Z Guide (pages 7–72) include an indication of the strength of the perfume of each variety — **no fragrance**, **slightly fragrant**, **fragrant** or **very fragrant**.

These statements, however, cannot be taken as a universally agreed assessment. Fragrance depends on many factors —

- **Personal taste**: Some people like heavy sickly smells, others prefer spicy or fruity aromas.
- **Personal sensitivity**: Some people have a deficient sense of smell, which unlike poor eyesight or deafness may go unnoticed.
- **Stage of growth**: Some roses are most fragrant in early flower, others when fully open.
- **Weather**: Warmth and high air humidity enhance fragrance.

Fragrance is, of course, associated with flowers but there are a few varieties with fragrant foliage — see *Lady Penzance* (page 67).

CHAPTER 2

ROSES A~Z

Each rose can be placed in one or other of the five classes listed below. In most cases placing a rose into its proper class is a simple matter, but in recent years the dividing lines have become increasingly blurred. The result is that the classification of some roses depends on which book or catalogue you are reading — you can find *Joseph's Coat* listed under Shrub, Large-flowered Climber or Floribunda!

A new method of classification (see page 108) has been adopted and is expected to replace the present simple system during the next few years. It has the advantage of removing the blurred boundaries, but it has the disadvantages of complexity and the abandonment of household words such as Hybrid Tea and Floribunda.

HYBRID TEA ROSES

see pages 8 — 29

The most popular class, available in both bush and standard form. The flower stems are long and the blooms are shapely. The typical Hybrid Tea bears blooms which are medium-sized or large, with many petals forming a distinct central cone. The blooms are borne singly or with several side buds.

FLORIBUNDA ROSES

see pages 30 — 46

Second only to Hybrid Teas in popularity. The Floribunda bears its flowers in clusters or trusses, and several blooms open at one time in each truss. This class is un-rivalled for providing a colourful, reliable and long-lasting bedding display, but in general the flower form is inferior to that of the Hybrid Tea.

MINIATURE ROSES

see pages 47 — 50

A class which is increasing in popularity due to its novelty and versatility. Miniatures can be used for edging beds, growing in tubs and rockeries or taking indoors as temporary pot plants. Both leaves and flowers are small, and under normal conditions the maximum height does not exceed 15 in. Many varieties are considerably shorter.

CLIMBERS & RAMBLERS

see pages 51 — 60

A class of roses which if tied to a support can be made to climb. There are two groups: Ramblers with long pliable stems, bearing large trusses of small flowers as a single summer flush, and Climbers with stiff stems, bearing flowers which are larger than Rambler blooms and may be repeat flowering.

SHRUB ROSES

see pages 61 — 72

A large class of bush roses with only one feature in common — they are neither Hybrid Teas nor Floribundas. The typical Shrub is taller than a bedding rose, and is a Species variety (related to a wild rose), an Old-Fashioned variety (dating back to pre-Hybrid Tea days) or a Modern Shrub Rose.

HYBRID TEA ROSES

There are five classes of roses, as described on page 7, but when planting time comes around the average gardener looks no further than the Floribundas and the Hybrid Teas. And it is the Hybrid Tea which usually wins the day, because it is the aristocrat of roses.

Each flower on the bush or standard is a thing of beauty in itself. Here is the "classic" rose — a long, pointed bud which opens to reveal many velvety or satin-like petals, neatly reflexed and regularly arranged to form a high central cone. The range of colours is bewildering, the fragrance is usually moderate or strong. It is the prime choice for the show-bench and the flower vase. It is the flower which brings forth the comment "Now that's what I call a rose!"

But it was not always so. When Florence Nightingale tended her sick, the "classic" rose was unknown. It was a chance cross, a hybrid between a delicate Tea Rose and a Hybrid Perpetual, which gave rise to the first Hybrid Tea — *La France*. This event in 1867 is well-known to the keen rose grower—less well known is the lack of interest aroused by the discovery.

Nearly 20 years passed before the first lists appeared in catalogues, but then the popularity of the Hybrid Tea began. In 1900 the first yellow (*Soleil d'Or*) appeared and a steady stream of innovations, noted on page 111, has led to the thousands of different varieties which grace the gardens of the world.

The glowing descriptions in catalogues and the features of the H.T. bloom outlined above sometimes give the impression that this class represents the **ideal** rose. This is certainly not true — many H.T. bushes are upright and rigid and many H.T. blooms are ruined by wet weather. In general, Hybrid Teas bloom less frequently and provide less garden colour than Floribundas. They will not put up with bad conditions like many Shrubs and Floribundas, and the number of blooms produced by some Exhibition H.T.s is disappointing.

So choose carefully. As you will see in the following pages, not all Hybrid Teas are suitable for garden display — some are designed to be cossetted for appealing to show judges rather than the neighbours. The Hybrid Tea is quite rightly regarded as the Queen of Roses — shapely blooms on long stems appearing in flushes throughout the summer and autumn . . . but it is not always divine.

KEY TO THE ROSE GUIDES

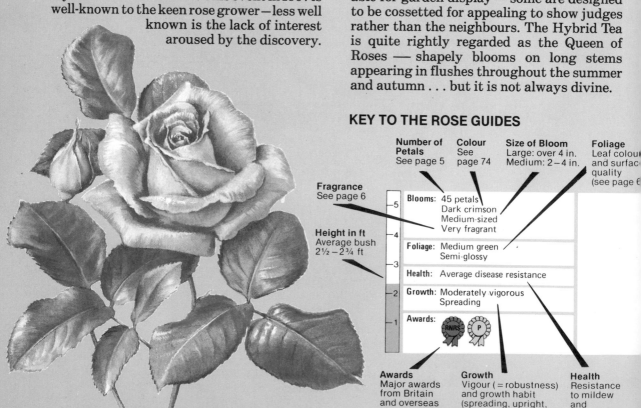

Number of Petals See page 5

Colour See page 74

Size of Bloom Large: over 4 in. Medium: 2 – 4 in.

Foliage Leaf colour and surface quality (see page 6

Fragrance See page 6

Height in ft Average bush 2½ – 2¾ ft

Blooms: 45 petals
Dark crimson
Medium-sized
Very fragrant

Foliage: Medium green
Semi-glossy

Health: Average disease resistance

Growth: Moderately vigorous
Spreading

Awards:

Awards Major awards from Britain and overseas (see page 105)

Growth Vigour (= robustness) and growth habit (spreading, upright, bushy, etc.)

Health Resistance to mildew and black spot

ADMIRAL RODNEY

Blooms:	45 petals
	Pale rose pink; pink reverse
	Large
	Very fragrant
Foliage:	Light green
	Glossy
Health:	Good disease resistance
Growth:	Vigorous
	Upright
Awards:	

The experts agree that *Admiral Rodney* is one of the best roses you can buy for exhibition purposes. The pink blooms with their pale pink centres are exceptionally large and well-shaped —a frequent sight amongst the prize winners at major rose shows. The flowers are strongly scented and the rather tall bushes bear large, healthy leaves. However, it is not free-flowering enough for ordinary garden display; this variety is best left to the exhibitor.

ADOLF HORSTMANN

Blooms:	25 petals
	Bronze yellow, edged pink
	Large
	Fragrant
Foliage:	Medium green
	Semi-glossy
Health:	Good disease resistance
Growth:	Very vigorous
	Upright
Awards:	

An all-purpose variety which is remarkably disease resistant for a yellow rose. It is not in the major league of exhibition varieties but the large blooms can be used on the show-bench if well-grown. It is excellent as a cut flower, with long straight stems and good keeping qualities in water. As a bedding variety it is tall and robust with moderately fragrant blooms borne singly or in small clusters. Unfortunately it occasionally fails to flower freely.

ALEC'S RED

Blooms:	45 petals
	Crimson
	Large, globular
	Very fragrant
Foliage:	Medium green
	Glossy
Health:	Good disease resistance
Growth:	Vigorous
	Upright
Awards:	

Many experts consider this to be the best red rose you can buy today — choose it for bedding, cutting or exhibition. Fragrance is an outstanding quality — very rich and sweet. It has an impressive list of virtues — vigorous healthy growth, strong flower stalks and abundant large blooms throughout the season. The flowers have good rain resistance and hold their colour well with age, but the rather pale crimson petals do not appeal to everyone.

ALEXANDER
Other Name: *ALEXANDRA*

Blooms:	22 petals
	Orange vermilion
	Medium-sized
	Slightly fragrant
Foliage:	Dark green
	Semi-glossy
Health:	Good disease resistance
Growth:	Very vigorous
	Upright
Awards:	

Brilliant flower colour is the outstanding feature — the vermilion is much more luminous than in its famous parent *Super Star* and the blooms have good rain-resisting properties. This tall bush is ideal for a large bed or for hedging, but it is not a good choice if you like large, full blooms with lots of petals or if space is limited. Young flowers have pointed centres and the long stalks make them excellent for cutting.

ALPINE SUNSET

Blooms:	30 petals
	Creamy yellow, flushed peach pink
	Large, globular
	Very fragrant
Foliage:	Medium green
	Glossy
Health:	Good disease resistance
Growth:	Vigorous
	Upright
Awards:	

An English-bred rose which bears large, fragrant blooms suitable for general garden display and exhibition. It is a sturdy, tolerant variety which reaches the average height for Hybrid Teas, and the flowers are recommended for cutting. It comes from a good family (*Grandpa Dickson* is one of its parents), the bush is free-flowering and the colour is attractive. A minor drawback is its tendency to produce blooms in distinct flushes rather than continually.

HYBRID TEA ROSES

Height in

APRICOT SILK

A well-named rose — the petals are an unusual shade of apricot with a surface which has a silky sheen. It is a must for the keen flower arranger — the elegant buds are borne on long stems and have excellent keeping qualities in water. In the garden it is a tall-growing bush with bronzy leaves which are purple when young. It will require spraying to protect it from mildew and black spot, and it needs careful pruning — hard pruning will spoil the display.

Blooms:	20 petals Apricot; reddish orange reverse Large Slightly fragrant
Foliage:	Bronze-tinted Glossy
Health:	Prone to disease
Growth:	Moderately vigorous Upright
Awards:	

BARONNE E. DE ROTHSCHILD
Other Name: MEIGRISO

A splendid rose for the bi-colour enthusiast — large, well-formed, high-centred and unfading. It has the vigour you would expect with *Peace* as a parent, and the shiny, leathery foliage has above-average resistance to both mildew and black spot. It has a strong, sweet fragrance and the growth is bushy rather than upright. Do not confuse this variety with the old Shrub Rose Baroness Rothschild.

Blooms:	40 petals Ruby red; silver reverse Large Fragrant
Foliage:	Dark green Glossy
Health:	Good disease resistance
Growth:	Very vigorous Bushy
Awards:	B L R

BEAUTE

A rather low bedding rose with an abundance of dark green foliage. This variety is best known for its buds — long and shapely, beautifully coloured in orange-yellow and freely produced. Not surprisingly, this variety is popular with flower arrangers. The buds open into golden apricot blooms which have good rain resistance. The drawbacks are a lack of strong fragrance, rather loose flowers and the need for regular spraying against mildew.

Blooms:	25 petals Golden apricot Medium-sized Slightly fragrant
Foliage:	Dark green Semi-glossy
Health:	Prone to disease
Growth:	Moderately vigorous Branching
Awards:	RNRS

BELLE BLONDE

For many years this variety has maintained its reputation as one of the finest yellow Hybrid Teas for bedding. The colour of its blooms is a rich golden yellow which does not fade as the petals begin to age. The bush is compact and free-flowering, with fragrant blooms which are rather larger than average. Unfortunately it is particularly susceptible to black spot, and is not really suitable for areas where this disease is a serious problem.

Blooms:	35 petals Golden yellow Medium-sized Fragrant
Foliage:	Dark green Glossy
Health:	Prone to disease
Growth:	Vigorous Upright
Awards:	

BETTINA

This variety is one of several yellow and orange Hybrid Teas bred in France during the 1950s with *Peace* as one of the parents. *Bettina* is quite distinct from the others because of the dark bronze veins which cover the orange petals. It has long been a favourite for use as a cut flower, and the bush is a good choice if your garden is in an area which does not suffer from black spot. It is vigorous and free-flowering, with blooms which are resistant to rain.

Blooms:	35 petals Orange, veined red or bronze Medium-sized Fragrant
Foliage:	Bronze-tinted Glossy
Health:	Prone to disease
Growth:	Vigorous Branching
Awards:	RNRS

▼

Blooms:	30 petals Deep crimson Large No fragrance
Foliage:	Dark green Semi-glossy
Health:	Average disease resistance
Growth:	Vigorous Upright
Awards:	

BIG CHIEF

A joy on the show-bench — huge crimson blooms of perfect exhibition form. These flowers are long-lasting but they have no perfume. Unfortunately these beautiful roses with their leathery leaves are not suitable for ordinary garden display — *Big Chief* is not free-flowering and the blooms need protection from the rain. It is a popular choice for exhibitors, but as it is not a bedding rose you will not find it listed in many catalogues.

Blooms:	30 petals Coral pink Medium-sized Fragrant
Foliage:	Medium green Glossy
Health:	Good disease resistance
Growth:	Vigorous Upright
Awards:	

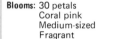

BLESSINGS

Blessings has been described as the ideal bedding variety, and yet it is neither exceptionally fragrant nor are the blooms exceptional in size or shape. The colour is attractive, but it is the sheer number of blooms on the bush which makes this rose so outstanding. From very early in the season until late in the autumn the pink flowers appear in great numbers, borne either singly or in clusters, maintaining their attraction even in rainy weather.

Blooms:	35 petals Silvery lilac Medium-sized Very fragrant
Foliage:	Medium green Glossy
Health:	Average disease resistance
Growth:	Moderately vigorous Upright
Awards:	

BLUE MOON

Other Names: MAINZER FASTNACHT, SISSI

Although it is generally agreed to be the best of the so-called 'blue' roses, this variety is distinctly pale lilac and not blue. Many people dislike the washed-out appearance of the petals in the garden, but indoors the blooms make excellent cut flowers. The buds are tall and pointed, the stems long and the fragrance exceptionally strong. *Blue Moon* used to have a good reputation for disease resistance, but nowadays spraying is often necessary.

Blooms:	35 petals Deep pink; silver reverse Large Fragrant
Foliage:	Dark green Semi-glossy
Health:	Average disease resistance
Growth:	Vigorous Upright
Awards:	

BOBBY CHARLTON

A popular choice for gardeners who dream of winning a prize at the flower show. It is an excellent exhibition variety — large, high-centred blooms of classic shape and with good keeping qualities on the show-bench. For garden display it forms a strong-growing and generally healthy bush with blooms having a spicy fragrance. Unfortunately the flowers appear later than with many other varieties and the number of blooms can be disappointing.

Blooms:	70 petals Peach pink Large Fragrant
Foliage:	Dark green Glossy
Health:	Average disease resistance
Growth:	Vigorous Upright
Awards:	

BONSOIR

A fine variety for the exhibitor and the flower arranger. The blooms are large, well-shaped, pleasantly perfumed and very full. They usually grow in small clusters which means that some disbudding is necessary to produce flowers of exhibition size and quality. *Bonsoir* is a medium-sized bush in the garden, bearing large and glossy leaves. It has one major drawback — the blooms often ball and fail to open in wet weather, so protection is vital for show-bench roses.

HYBRID TEA ROSES

BUCCANEER

An upright easy-to-grow bush which can look attractive in a border but which is too tall and willowy for a small formal bed. The long pointed buds are borne in profusion and turn into shining yellow flowers. They don't have a strong scent but they do hold their colour when fully open and they are not spoilt by rain. The blooms are borne in trusses rather than singly, so the variety is sometimes classed as a Grandiflora (see page 30).

Blooms:	30 petals Buttercup yellow Medium-sized Slightly fragrant
Foliage:	Dark green Matt
Health:	Average disease resistance
Growth:	Vigorous Upright
Awards:	

CHAMPION

A good multi-purpose variety which is becoming increasingly popular. For the exhibitor it has extra large, well-shaped blooms, although there are better varieties to choose from if showing is your main interest (see page 75). For the flower arranger there are long, pointed buds and for the gardener the compact bushes are sufficiently free-flowering to provide a good display of colourful blooms with a pronounced fragrance.

Blooms:	50 petals Creamy gold, flushed pink and red Large Very fragrant
Foliage:	Light green Glossy
Health:	Good disease resistance
Growth:	Vigorous Bushy
Awards:	

CHESHIRE LIFE

The outstanding feature of this rose is its ability to withstand cold and rainy conditions. The vermilion colour of its blooms will appeal to lovers of *Super Star*, but this new variety has the great advantage of outstanding resistance to disease. The bush is short or medium in height, bearing thick leathery leaves and an abundance of blooms which are brightly coloured. The main drawback of *Cheshire Life* is the absence of a strong fragrance.

Blooms:	35 petals Vermilion orange Medium-sized Slightly fragrant
Foliage:	Dark green Semi-glossy
Health:	Good disease resistance
Growth:	Vigorous Upright
Awards:	

CHICAGO PEACE

A colour sport of *Peace*, with all the great qualities of its famous parent plus the virtue of more attractive blooms. Copper and pink dominate the petal surface and the reverse is tinged with coppery yellow. An excellent general purpose rose reaching 3½–5 ft, depending on pruning. It can be used for bedding, hedging and exhibiting. Lack of strong scent is its only vice, and it is now less resistant to black spot than it used to be.

Blooms:	45 petals Pink, copper and yellow Large Slightly fragrant
Foliage:	Dark green Glossy
Health:	Good disease resistance
Growth:	Very vigorous Bushy
Awards:	

CHRISTIAN DIOR

Introduced in 1959, *Christian Dior* provided gardeners for many years with large, very full blooms of velvety red petals. For exhibition purposes the buds and blooms are well-shaped with long stems; in the garden the tall bushes are well-clothed with leathery leaves and almost thornless stems. This variety still has some admirers but its scentless blooms and susceptibility to mildew does not make it a good choice.

Blooms:	45 petals Cherry red; dull scarlet reverse Large No fragrance
Foliage:	Medium green Semi-glossy
Health:	Prone to disease
Growth:	Vigorous Upright
Awards:	

ght in feet

ght in feet

Blooms:	45 petals Deep crimson Large Very fragrant
Foliage:	Dark green Semi-glossy
Health:	Prone to disease
Growth:	Moderately vigorous Upright
Awards:	

CHRYSLER IMPERIAL

Chrysler Imperial used to have a good reputation as an exhibition rose. The highly fragrant, vivid red blooms are tall and pointed, and the stems are stiff and upright. The number of flowers produced is about average for a Hybrid Tea. It is, however, a poor choice these days — the attractive red blooms soon turn to an ugly purple with age and the leaves are highly susceptible to mildew. Choose a modern red variety instead.

Blooms:	35 petals Saffron yellow, shaded gold Large No fragrance
Foliage:	Medium green Matt
Health:	Average disease resistance
Growth:	Vigorous Upright
Awards:	

CITY OF GLOUCESTER

The flowers of this British-bred rose are not exceptionally large, but in the 1970s it became one of the outstanding exhibition varieties. The blooms, borne singly or in groups, are full and beautifully shaped. For garden display the bush is rather taller than average and well-covered with leaves. It is sometimes recommended as a good bedding variety but the foliage is rather dull and the flowers, though colourful, are unscented.

Blooms:	50 petals Orange salmon; yellow reverse Large, globular Slightly fragrant
Foliage:	Dark green Glossy
Health:	Good disease resistance
Growth:	Vigorous Upright
Awards:	

COLOUR WONDER
Other Name: KÖNIGIN DER ROSEN

The blooms of this compact offspring of *Super Star* and *Perfecta* offer an unusual colour combination — petals which are orange on the inside and yellow on the outside. The short, prickly stems are densely clothed with rather small, glossy leaves. The flowers are for garden display rather than the show-bench — the petals are too short and the shape too globular for winning prizes. A reasonably good rose for a small bed or front of the border.

Blooms:	30 petals Deep velvety crimson Medium-sized Very fragrant
Foliage:	Medium green Semi-glossy
Health:	Prone to disease
Growth:	Vigorous Spreading
Awards:	

CRIMSON GLORY

An old pre-war favourite, once the most popular red rose of all. Unfortunately it has become increasingly susceptible to mildew, and so newer varieties have taken its place in most catalogues. *Crimson Glory* is no longer considered to be an exhibitor's rose, but it is still chosen by some gardeners as a bedding variety. The blooms are shapely, velvety, deep red and endowed with a real rose fragrance. The bush is low-growing and spreading. Light pruning (see page 91) is recommended.

Blooms:	30 petals Coral, tinged pale gold Large Very fragrant
Foliage:	Dark green Semi-glossy
Health:	Good disease resistance
Growth:	Vigorous Bushy
Awards:	

DEKORAT
Other Name: FREUDE

This Kordes-bred rose appeared in 1977 and has proved to be very hardy under a wide variety of conditions. Its blooms are large and shapely, but it has not become really popular with exhibitors. It does have some good properties as a bedding variety — the blooms are attractive, the fragrance is very strong and the bush is well clothed with attractive leaves. One drawback is that the first blooms appear rather late in the season.

HYBRID TEA ROSES

Height in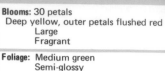

DIORAMA

One of the best yellow roses for the garden bed or border. The flowers appear early in the season and you can expect an attractive display throughout the summer even if the weather is rainy. The free-flowering nature of *Diorama* in the autumn is one of its most outstanding features. The blooms are large and high-centred, which makes them popular with flower arrangers, but even highly recommended varieties have drawbacks — the blooms blow quickly and the leaves need black spot protection.

Blooms:	30 petals Deep yellow, outer petals flushed red Large Fragrant
Foliage:	Medium green Semi-glossy
Health:	Average disease resistance
Growth:	Vigorous Branching
Awards:	

DORIS TYSTERMAN

An English-bred rose which was introduced in 1975 and soon became popular as a bedding variety. Its free-flowering nature and good performance in autumn ensure a pleasing display throughout the season, and the well-shaped, orange-red blooms on long, straight stems are excellent for cutting. There are no major drawbacks, although the blooms are only average in size, the leaves need mildew protection and the fragrance is not strong.

Blooms:	30 petals Tangerine, darker at edges Medium-sized Slightly fragrant
Foliage:	Bronze-tinted Glossy
Health:	Average disease resistance
Growth:	Vigorous Upright
Awards:	

DOUBLE DELIGHT

This American-bred rose aroused a great deal of interest when it was introduced in 1976 and its popularity has now spread to Europe. The main attractions are its strong fragrance and the novel colour of its petals — "like a vanilla ice dipped in strawberry juice" according to the Harkness catalogue. The ratio of cream to red on the petals is highly variable. The bush is strong-growing, freely producing elegant blooms of exhibition size.

Blooms:	40 petals Creamy white, rimmed red Large Very fragrant
Foliage:	Medium green Semi-glossy
Health:	Good disease resistance
Growth:	Vigorous Upright
Awards:	

DR A. J. VERHAGE
Other Name: GOLDEN WAVE

A Dutch-bred variety which is outstanding for cutting. The blooms are high-centred, delightfully perfumed and attractively coloured in yellow and orange. The foliage is small and glossy. It is one of the best choices you can make for cultivation under glass, but it is a poor choice for bedding outdoors in Britain. This low-growing rose is susceptible to frost, which means that it can only be expected to succeed in a warm and sheltered garden.

Blooms:	25 petals Golden apricot, flushed yellow Medium-sized Fragrant
Foliage:	Dark green Glossy
Health:	Average disease resistance
Growth:	Moderately vigorous Upright
Awards:	

DUKE OF WINDSOR
Other Name: HERZOG VON WINDSOR

For many years a favourite with gardeners who have wanted blooms possessing the same luminous vermilion as *Super Star* but on a bush with a more compact growth habit. *Duke of Windsor* has very thorny stems which are densely clothed with large, leathery leaves and the flowers are borne in small clusters throughout the season. These blooms open rather quickly. The major problem is mildew — regular spraying with Benlate is essential.

Blooms:	30 petals Orange vermilion Medium-sized Very fragrant
Foliage:	Dark green Semi-glossy
Health:	Prone to disease
Growth:	Moderately vigorous Branching
Awards:	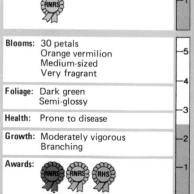

HYBRID TEA ROSES

Blooms:	35 petals
	Golden yellow
	Large
	Very fragrant
Foliage:	Medium green
	Glossy
Health:	Good disease resistance
Growth:	Vigorous
	Upright
Awards:	

DUTCH GOLD

Within a year or two of its introduction in 1978 this outstanding variety was listed in many catalogues. Obviously a new yellow rose which was strongly perfumed and large enough for the show-bench was bound to be a success. The blooms are well-shaped and freely produced, the colour not fading as they mature. Both its parents, *Peer Gynt* and *Whisky Mac*, are more compact in growth habit and the flowers they produce are smaller with a tendency to be open-cupped.

Blooms:	35 petals
	Creamy white, shaded buff and pink
	Large
	Fragrant
Foliage:	Medium green
	Semi-glossy
Health:	Average disease resistance
Growth:	Upright
	Bushy
Awards:	

ELIZABETH HARKNESS

One of the best cream-coloured Hybrid Teas you can buy. The colour of the large, high-centred flowers is hard to describe — the pale, creamy buff shades deepen in autumn. It is an early-blooming variety, continuing to flower freely throughout the season. The blooms are sweet smelling, although the perfume is not particularly strong, and they are excellent for cutting. *Elizabeth Harkness* does well in a good season, but like so many pale-coloured varieties it does not like rain.

Blooms:	30 petals
	Crimson scarlet
	Large
	Very fragrant
Foliage:	Medium green
	Semi-glossy
Health:	Average disease resistance
Growth:	Moderately vigorous
	Branching
Awards:	

ENA HARKNESS

A great old favourite — the most popular red rose planted in Britain for many years. These days its faults are often highlighted — the need for good cultivation, the lack of vigour which is found in modern varieties and above all the weak necks which cause the blooms to hang their heads. But it is still widely grown because the beauty of its form and the richness of its colour have few rivals. It is free-flowering, especially in autumn, and there is little or no fading of colour.

Blooms:	30 petals
	Rich turkey red
	Large
	Very fragrant
Foliage:	Dark green
	Semi-glossy
Health:	Good disease resistance
Growth:	Vigorous
	Upright
Awards:	

ERNEST H. MORSE

Red roses may come and go, but *Ernest H. Morse* was introduced in 1964 and is still in the best-seller lists. It has proved to be thoroughly reliable, but it now needs some protection from mildew in a bad season. It is almost ideal as a bedding rose — large, fragrant flowers in glowing red which stand up to rain. They are borne prolifically throughout the season and the best of them can be used for exhibition and floral decoration. Grow this variety if you want a red-flowering standard.

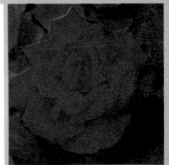

Blooms:	25 petals
	White
	Large
	Fragrant
Foliage:	Dark green
	Semi-glossy
Health:	Good disease resistance
Growth:	Vigorous
	Upright
Awards:	

EVENING STAR

The number of scented white roses is strictly limited, so this recent American-bred variety is well worth considering. The bush is strong and hardy, growing taller than the average Hybrid Tea. The blooms are borne freely and are well-shaped; they are reasonably capable of withstanding rain — a great advantage over many white roses. Although not as good as *Pascali* as a cut flower, the blooms are long-lasting and if disbudded can be used for exhibition.

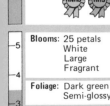

HYBRID TEA ROSES

Height i

FRAGRANT CLOUD
Other Names: DUFTWOLKE, NUAGE PARFUME

One of the all-time greats which needs little description. Its crowning glory has remained untarnished since its introduction in 1964 — an intense perfume which is unmatched by any other modern variety. The blooms appear very early and are well dispersed on the bush, making it an excellent bedding as well as an exhibition variety. But its reputation has declined — mildew as well as black spot can now be a problem and the colour soon fades with age.

Blooms:	30 petals Geranium red Large Very fragrant
Foliage:	Dark green Glossy
Health:	Average disease resistance
Growth:	Vigorous Upright
Awards:	

FRED GIBSON

As a specimen flower for exhibition *Fred Gibson* is in the top ten. The flowers are large, beautifully shaped and high-centred. Some text-books and catalogues recommend it as a garden rose for general display, and it does have some good points. The flowers are borne freely and the autumn display is well above average; it is also excellent for cutting. Unfortunately the bush has a narrow and somewhat gaunt appearance and it is not really satisfactory as a bedding rose.

Blooms:	30 petals Amber yellow Large Slightly fragrant
Foliage:	Dark green Semi-glossy
Health:	Average disease resistance
Growth:	Vigorous Upright
Awards:	

GAIL BORDEN

The outstanding feature of this bi-coloured variety is its exceptionally large, very full blooms. These flowers are often globular but they are sometimes high-centred and suitable for the show-bench. *Gail Borden* is still recommended in some catalogues after nearly 30 years, but it is now prone to black spot and has been overtaken by newer varieties. The bush is attractive and well-clothed with large, leathery leaves. The blooms are borne reasonably freely.

Blooms:	50 petals Rose pink; pale gold reverse Large Slightly fragrant
Foliage:	Dark green Glossy
Health:	Average disease resistance
Growth:	Vigorous Upright
Awards:	

GAVOTTE

You will no longer find this variety in many rose catalogues, but it is still highly recommended for both exhibiting and cutting. Its large, pink blooms are high-centred and they keep their shape for a long period. For show purposes some rain protection is necessary and disbudding is usually required. It is a free-flowering variety with attractive foliage, but it is not a particularly good bedding rose — growth is straggly and black spot protection is needed.

Blooms:	45 petals Warm pink; silver reverse Large Slightly fragrant
Foliage:	Dark green Semi-glossy
Health:	Average disease resistance
Growth:	Vigorous Spreading
Awards:	

GAY GORDONS

If you are looking for a compact, low-growing bush with bi-coloured blooms then *Gay Gordons* would be a reasonable choice. The flowers are similar to those of the much more popular *Piccadilly*, but the yellow is much richer. This variety has good rain resistance, the leaves are attractive and the medium-sized blooms are borne with remarkable freedom, but it has never really caught the fancy of the public. Black spot can be a problem; spray early with Benlate.

Blooms:	25 petals Orange-yellow and red Medium-sized Slightly fragrant
Foliage:	Dark green Glossy
Health:	Prone to disease
Growth:	Vigorous Bushy
Awards:	

HYBRID TEA ROSES

Blooms: 35 petals Very deep yellow Large Slightly fragrant	
Foliage: Dark green Semi-glossy	
Health: Average disease resistance	
Growth: Vigorous Upright	
Awards:	

GOLD CROWN
Other Names: GOLDKRONE, COURONNE D'OR

A sturdy, tall-growing rose for the large bed or border. It has the good points of both its parents — the vigour and large flowers of *Peace* and the colour, high-pointed buds and long stems of *Spek's Yellow*. The blooms are well-formed and suitable for exhibition, but split centres can be a problem. It suffers from a major drawback — the early growth is often blind and so the display at the start of the season can be disappointing.

Blooms: 50 petals Golden yellow Large Fragrant	
Foliage: Medium green Matt	
Health: Average disease resistance	
Growth: Vigorous Upright	
Awards: 	

GOLDEN TIMES

A taller than average variety which has no unique features but possesses many good points. The red-tinged pointed buds open into large blooms of pure pale gold. The fragrance is good (*Fragrant Cloud* is one of its parents) and the floral display lasts until well into the autumn. The foliage is large and leathery and the bushes strong and upright. *Golden Times* is a bedding rose for garden display — the blooms are excellent for cutting but it is not popular with exhibitors.

Blooms: 35 petals Lemon yellow, sometimes edged pink Large Slightly fragrant	
Foliage: Dark green Glossy	
Health: Good disease resistance	
Growth: Vigorous Upright	
Awards:	

GRANDPA DICKSON
Other Name: IRISH GOLD

The best pale yellow Hybrid Tea you can buy. It appears in most catalogues and all rose books sing its praises. Superbly formed blooms with long petals — the star of countless shows. In addition, its good rain resistance, freedom of flowering and late-season blooming make it an excellent bedding variety. But even an "ideal" rose can have a drawback or two. The bush sometimes has a gaunt appearance, and good soil plus feeding are necessary.

Blooms: 25 petals Scarlet, striped yellow Large Slightly fragrant	
Foliage: Medium green Glossy	
Health: Average disease resistance	
Growth: Vigorous Bushy	
Awards:	

HARRY WHEATCROFT

Fittingly named after one of the great characters of the rose world, you will either love this sport of *Piccadilly* for its flamboyant novelty or you will hate it for its garishness. Each large, pointed bloom is a riot of colour, and this variety is excellent for bedding — compact, free-flowering and rain-resistant. Unfortunately it has little perfume and it will need spraying against black spot. The blooms are long-lasting and recommended for flower arranging.

Blooms: 25 petals Apricot, flushed pink Large Very fragrant	
Foliage: Dark green Semi-glossy	
Health: Average disease resistance	
Growth: Vigorous Bushy	
Awards:	

HELEN TRAUBEL

Beautiful buds and beautiful fragrance are the hallmarks of this American variety. Unfortunately the long and shapely buds open into rather loose, open flowers which tend to hang their heads on flexible stems. These drawbacks have prevented *Helen Traubel* from becoming a popular garden rose, but it does have its good points — vigorous growth which produces both flowers and leathery leaves abundantly. The blooms have good rain resistance and it is a strong grower which succeeds anywhere.

HYBRID TEA ROSES

JOHN WATERER

The failure of this reliable variety to reach the top twenty illustrates the popular demand for strong fragrance in red roses. *John Waterer* has so many good features — large and deep red petals, full shapely blooms which stand erect and foliage which is attractive and healthy. It flowers reasonably freely and the blooms are borne singly or in small groups. The major drawback is the absence of a strong scent; another fault is the blackening of the petal edges with age.

Blooms:	40 petals Deep crimson Large Slightly fragrant
Foliage:	Dark green Matt
Health:	Good disease resistance
Growth:	Vigorous Upright
Awards:	

JOSEPHINE BRUCE

Dark red, velvety roses are rare, so the old favourite *Josephine Bruce* still keeps its place in the catalogues. The average-sized bushes have a sprawling growth habit which can be controlled to some extent by pruning to inward-pointing buds. This variety is particularly good when grown as a standard. The early-season display is best — well-shaped blooms which are good enough for the show-bench. In late summer the petals tend to be ragged and there is a constant fight against mildew.

Blooms:	25 petals Deep velvety crimson Medium-sized or large Very fragrant
Foliage:	Dark green Semi-glossy
Health:	Prone to disease
Growth:	Vigorous Spreading
Awards:	

JUST JOEY

This English rose, bred by Cants, is quite unmistakeable with its unique colouring and ruffled petals. It has become one of the most popular of all the bedding roses introduced in the 1970s, combining novelty with beauty and reliability. The buds are attractive and excellent for cutting, appearing with great freedom throughout the season. Not one for the show-bench, but the open blooms are colourful and rain-resistant. It blooms well into the autumn.

Blooms:	30 petals Coppery orange, paler at edges Medium-sized Fragrant
Foliage:	Dark green Matt
Health:	Good disease resistance
Growth:	Moderately vigorous Bushy
Awards:	

KING'S RANSOM

Many roses come and go, but this American-bred variety first appeared in 1961 and is still recommended as the best pure yellow Hybrid Tea for garden display. Its popularity and high reputation are based on a number of features — non-fading blooms which are high-centred and rain-resistant, bushes which produce canes, flowers and leaves abundantly, and buds which are beautifully shaped and excellent for cutting. It is not completely reliable in all soils — choose another rose if your soil is sandy or chalky.

Blooms:	40 petals Rich pure yellow Medium-sized Fragrant
Foliage:	Dark green Glossy
Health:	Good disease resistance
Growth:	Vigorous Branching
Awards:	

KORP
Other Name: PROMINENT

A rose with brilliant red blooms and an identity problem. Some catalogues call it *Prominent*, others refer to it as *Korp*. Half the rose books class it as a Floribunda, because the flowers are often borne in large flower-heads, but the remainder regard it as a Hybrid Tea, as the blooms are sometimes carried singly on long stems. *Korp* is a favourite with many flower arrangers; the buds are superbly shaped and the flowers last well in water.

Blooms:	45 petals Signal red; scarlet reverse Medium-sized Slightly fragrant
Foliage:	Medium green Matt
Health:	Good disease resistance
Growth:	Vigorous Upright
Awards:	

HYBRID TEA ROSES

Blooms:	45 petals Crimson; old gold reverse Large Slightly fragrant
Foliage:	Dark green Glossy
Health:	Average disease resistance
Growth:	Very vigorous Bushy
Awards:	

KRONENBOURG
Other Name: FLAMING PEACE

A sport of *Peace*, with the growth habit and shape of its parent. The blooms are much brighter — even more eye-catching than the colourful *Chicago Peace* (see page 12). It has not become a popular rose as one might have expected because the flowers discolour badly with age. The attractive young blooms soon turn dull and purple, and must be dead-headed regularly. Like *Peace*, it is no longer resistant to black spot.

Blooms:	35 petals Rose pink Medium-sized Very fragrant
Foliage:	Medium green Semi-glossy
Health:	Average disease resistance
Growth:	Vigorous Branching
Awards:	

LADY SETON

A pink, sweet-smelling rose with no serious faults and no special virtues. It has almost disappeared from the catalogues and is now not easy to find. It started out with great promise, winning a RNRS award as the most fragrant new British seedling of its year. The well-shaped flowers are reasonably resistant to rain but they open quickly in warm weather. The attractive bushes bear abundant foliage and are free-flowering, especially in the autumn.

Blooms:	30 petals Pale pink; yellow at base Medium-sized Very fragrant
Foliage:	Medium green Matt
Health:	Average disease resistance
Growth:	Moderately vigorous Upright
Awards:	

LADY SYLVIA

An old favourite, still widely grown for the cut flower trade and as a bedding rose. The blooms are classically shaped, making up in fragrance for what they lack in size. An outstanding feature is the abundance of blooms which appear during late summer and autumn, each flower being borne on a long stem. The bushes are rather tall, but as you might expect from an old variety the stems may be rather sparsely covered. A good choice for the keen flower arranger.

Blooms:	35 petals Soft shell pink Large Fragrant
Foliage:	Medium green Semi-glossy
Health:	Good disease resistance
Growth:	Vigorous Branching
Awards:	

LAKELAND

One of the new varieties which might not have won any awards but has caught the public fancy. Its large, pale pink blooms have been described as old-fashioned roses brought up to date. The flowers are fragrant and the bushes vigorous and free-flowering which is what you would expect from the offspring of *Fragrant Cloud* and *Queen Elizabeth*. It is one of the new breed of triple-purpose roses — weather-resistant enough for bedding, large enough for showing and long-stemmed enough for cutting.

Blooms:	30 petals Coppery gold Medium-sized Fragrant
Foliage:	Dark green Matt
Health:	Good disease resistance
Growth:	Vigorous Upright
Awards:	

LOLITA
Other Names: LITAKOR, KORLITA

A hardy, reliable variety which should be high on any list of roses recommended for cutting. The blooms of perfect form are borne on long, stiff stems and they last extremely well in water. The bushes are well-covered with healthy foliage, making *Lolita* a good bedding rose. The flowers are not large enough for exhibition, but it is a variety well worth considering if you want a rather tall, upright rose with golden flowers.

HYBRID TEA ROSES

MALA RUBINSTEIN

The perfect answer to the claim that modern roses never have the fragrance of the old fashioned varieties, *Mala Rubinstein* is a popular choice as a bedding and cutting rose where a strong scent is required. The number of blooms produced is well above average, and the flowering season extends throughout the autumn. The blooms are well-shaped and pointed, but rather small for exhibition. It is prone to rust and is best avoided where this disease is a problem.

Blooms:	50 petals Coral pink; deep pink reverse Medium-sized Very fragrant
Foliage:	Medium green Matt
Health:	Average disease resistance
Growth:	Vigorous Upright
Awards:	

MESSAGE

Other Name: WHITE KNIGHT

The catalogue description of this offspring of *Virgo* makes it sound most desirable — shapely, greenish buds opening into pure white, high-centred blooms which are large for a rose of this colour. The flower stems are long and straight and the bushes are free-flowering. Unfortunately this is not a rose to choose unless you actually like spraying regularly with a fungicide. It is very susceptible to mildew, and the blooms are damaged by rain.

Blooms:	35 petals White Medium-sized Slightly fragrant
Foliage:	Light green Matt
Health:	Prone to disease
Growth:	Moderately vigorous Upright
Awards:	

MICHELE MEILLAND

It is hard to believe that this delicate rose, with its rather small flowers on rather compact bushes is actually an offspring of the majestic *Peace*. Introduced in 1945, it is no longer widely available as so many bigger and brighter varieties have been introduced in recent years. But there are a few growers who keep it in their catalogues for those who want to grow roses for cutting. The slim blooms with their subtle pastel shades are borne on almost thornless stems.

Blooms:	40 petals Salmon, flushed pearly pink Medium-sized Slightly fragrant
Foliage:	Light green Matt
Health:	Good disease resistance
Growth:	Moderately vigorous Branching
Awards:	

MISCHIEF

Introduced in 1961, *Mischief* remains one of the most popular of bedding roses. Its great appeal lies in the remarkable profusion of beautifully shaped and rain-resistant flowers which appear throughout the season. Flower colour is "cut strawberry" in summer but turns more orange in autumn. Flower size is variable —small blooms may appear, but disbudding can produce large blooms fit for exhibition. Not a good choice for gardens where rust is a problem.

Blooms:	30 petals Coral salmon Medium-sized Slightly fragrant
Foliage:	Light green Semi-glossy
Health:	Average disease resistance
Growth:	Vigorous Bushy
Awards:	

MISS HARP

Some professional rose growers expected this variety to become a winner. Its long-lasting, elegant buds made it an excellent choice for the flower arranger. The Royal National Rose Society listed it as a reliable rose for beginners and for unfavourable positions, and its flowers are both long-lasting and reasonably rain-resistant. But despite its favourable features it never really challenged *King's Ransom* for the deep yellow Hybrid Tea crown.

Blooms:	40 petals Deep bronze yellow Medium-sized Fragrant
Foliage:	Dark green Glossy
Health:	Average disease resistance
Growth:	Vigorous Bushy
Awards:	

Blooms:	25 petals Coral salmon; peach reverse Medium-sized Slightly fragrant
Foliage:	Medium green Matt
Health:	Prone to disease
Growth:	Vigorous Upright
Awards:	

MISS IRELAND

A McGredy rose which attracted a good deal of attention when it was introduced in 1961. The colour combination was unique, and the blooms were freely produced on the neat, compact bushes. Now it has fallen from grace and you will have to search to find it in the rose catalogues. It has little fragrance and the colours fade with age, but the main drawbacks are its proneness to die-back and its lack of resistance to both mildew and black spot. This means that regular spraying is necessary.

Blooms:	35 petals Dark red Large Very fragrant
Foliage:	Medium green Matt
Health:	Average disease resistance
Growth:	Very vigorous Upright
Awards:	

MISTER LINCOLN

A good choice if you want a velvety, deep red rose for cutting — the flowers are borne on long stems and last well in water. *Mister Lincoln* is also a fine variety for garden display in a large bed — it is less prone to mildew than the old dark reds such as *Chrysler Imperial*, and the blooms are less likely to turn purple with age. There are drawbacks — the attractive buds quickly turn into open-cupped blooms and the tall, unbranched canes make it an unsuitable bush for a small bed.

Blooms:	30 petals Pale pink; yellow at base Medium-sized Very fragrant
Foliage:	Medium green Matt
Health:	Average disease resistance
Growth:	Moderately vigorous Upright
Awards:	

MME BUTTERFLY

An old favourite introduced over 60 years ago, but still capable of keeping its place in many catalogues. The charm of *Mme Butterfly* lies in flower colour and form, not size. The flesh pink blooms are not large, but they are perfectly formed with pronounced high centres. They are borne very freely, and some disbudding is necessary. This variety has long been a favourite for cutting and in the garden it is grown as a neat bush in the rose bed or left lightly pruned in the border.

Blooms:	45 petals Dark crimson Medium sized Very fragrant
Foliage:	Medium green Semi-glossy
Health:	Average disease resistance
Growth:	Moderately vigorous Spreading
Awards:	

MME LOUIS LAPERRIERE

One of the better deep red roses — not a new variety but still an excellent choice if you want a low-growing bush which will come into flower early and stay in bloom until late autumn. The flowers are strongly scented and shapely, with good rain resistance, but they are not large. The small leaves are reddish when young and distinctly healthier than most other dark reds such as *Chrysler Imperial* and *Josephine Bruce*. Another plus point is the good colour stability of the blooms.

Blooms:	25 petals Deep orange, veined red Medium-sized Slightly fragrant
Foliage:	Medium green Glossy
Health:	Average disease resistance
Growth:	Vigorous Upright
Awards:	

MOJAVE

A strong and hardy rose, which many consider to be the best of the deep orange Hybrid Teas. The blooms are plentiful, and it is easy to see its appeal to the flower arranger — long slim buds, straight stems and practically no thorns. Its appeal as a bedding rose is less easy to justify — the bushes appear gaunt and leggy, the buds quickly open to produce loose blooms in which the stamens can be seen and the scent is insignificant.

HYBRID TEA ROSES

Height in

MRS SAM McGREDY

Old *Mrs Sam*, dearly loved for 50 years, is nearing the end of its commercial life. Few growers offer it for sale as the bushes have lost their vigour and are very susceptible to black spot. In its time it was a great favourite — beautiful coppery red buds opening into large fragrant blooms of salmon pink. Another famous feature is the foliage — purplish when young, bronze green when mature. To enjoy *Mrs Sam McGredy* again, plant the climbing form which has retained the earlier vigour.

Blooms:	40 petals Coppery orange, flushed red Large Fragrant
Foliage:	Bronze-tinted Glossy
Health:	Prone to disease
Growth:	Moderately vigorous Upright
Awards:	

MULLARD JUBILEE
Other Name: ELECTRON

An excellent bedding rose, for expert and beginner alike. It grows strongly and will tolerate poor conditions, but when treated properly it produces a profusion of pointed buds, either singly or in small groups, throughout the season. These buds open rather quickly into loose flowers, which are not often suitable for the show-bench. In the garden, however, they can be spectacular — exceptionally large, rain-resistant and fragrant.

Blooms:	40 petals Deep rose pink Large Fragrant
Foliage:	Dark green Semi-glossy
Health:	Average disease resistance
Growth:	Vigorous Bushy
Awards:	

MY CHOICE

This bi-colour was expected to become a best-seller after its Gold Medal award by the Royal National Rose Society. Its list of virtues is indeed impressive — profuse flowering, strong growth, superb scent, large blooms and above-average disease resistance. What went wrong? Nobody can be really sure, but the following faults might be the cause — the flowers are rather globular and open quickly (which means they must be cut at a young stage for exhibition) and the foliage is rather dull.

Blooms:	35 petals Pink; pale yellow reverse Large Very fragrant
Foliage:	Light green Matt
Health:	Good disease resistance
Growth:	Vigorous Branching
Awards:	

NATIONAL TRUST
Other Name: BAD NAUHEIM

You will not find it in the list of roses to grow for fragrance nor for exhibiting, yet *National Trust* is one of the outstanding red Hybrid Teas of our time. The bushes lack height and the blooms lack the size of the show varieties, but it is an excellent choice for the front of the bed or border. The blooms are held erect, their shape is impeccable and their colour unfading. The free-flowering bushes are well-clothed with foliage which is coppery red when young.

Blooms:	60 petals Crimson Medium-sized No fragrance
Foliage:	Dark green Matt
Health:	Good disease resistance
Growth:	Vigorous Upright
Awards:	

OPHELIA

Keen rosarians sometimes grow the very early Hybrid Teas as museum pieces but *Ophelia*, the oldest of all in general cultivation, is still planted by ordinary gardeners for the beauty and fragrance of its flowers. Petals of palest pink, sometimes almost white, are arranged in classic form on blooms which appear in large clusters. Avoid this senior citizen of the rose world if the site is exposed or is subject to late frosts; keep an eye out for thrips in summer.

Blooms:	30 petals Pale pink; yellow at base Medium-sized Very fragrant
Foliage:	Medium green Matt
Health:	Average disease resistance
Growth:	Moderately vigorous Upright
Awards:	

HYBRID TEA ROSES

Blooms:	35 petals Dark crimson Large Very fragrant
Foliage:	Dark green Glossy
Health:	Prone to disease
Growth:	Moderately vigorous Upright
Awards:	

PAPA MEILLAND

This variety demonstrates the need to consider both the flower *and* the plant before deciding to buy. If you were guided by the flower alone then *Papa Meilland* would be one of the finest Hybrid Teas available. Nearly black buds open into large, dark red blooms, velvety-petalled and with a scent which is unsurpassed. Unfortunately the plant does not live up to the blooms — in the garden it is unreliable, it is not a prolific bloomer and it is extremely prone to mildew.

Blooms:	25 petals White, shaded cream Small or medium-sized Slightly fragrant
Foliage:	Medium green Glossy
Health:	Average disease resistance
Growth:	Vigorous Upright
Awards:	

PASCALI

Introduced in 1963, *Pascali* remains the best white H.T. rose. It is much less prone to mildew and much more resistant to rain than other varieties of this colour, and the blooms hold their shape longer than most other roses. It is one of the best of all varieties for cutting — the stems are long and straight, and the flowers last well in water. Despite the bouquets it is not the ideal white rose — the bushes are spindly, the blooms are rather small for a Hybrid Tea, the petals are not pure white and the scent is faint.

Blooms:	45 petals Pale or dark yellow, edged pink Large Slightly fragrant
Foliage:	Dark green Glossy
Health:	Good disease resistance
Growth:	Very vigorous Bushy
Awards:	

PEACE

Other Names: GLORIA DEI, MME A.MEILLAND

Quite simply, the world's favourite rose. Always vigorous, always reliable, the 5–6 in. blooms remain attractive from bud to the full-blown stage. It is not a rose for every location — it must have adequate space. It will reach 3½–6 ft high and should never be hard pruned. Nowadays it is sometimes susceptible to black spot so spraying is necessary. Its drawbacks are few — the lack of fragrance, the late start to flowering and the occasional blind shoot.

Blooms:	40 petals Canary yellow, flushed pink Large Slightly fragrant
Foliage:	Light green Matt
Health:	Prone to disease
Growth:	Vigorous Bushy
Awards:	

PEER GYNT

Peer Gynt possesses the basic ingredients of a successful bedding rose — attractive blooms which appear early in the season and continue to appear throughout the summer and autumn. The compact bush is taller than average and well-clothed with large leaves. The edges of the petals turn pink with age, providing a colourful garden display, but this variety is not really for the show-bench as the blooms are open-cupped. Hardy and easy to grow, with weak mildew resistance as the only serious problem.

Blooms:	65 petals Cream, edged and flushed crimson Large Slightly fragrant
Foliage:	Dark green Glossy
Health:	Average disease resistance
Growth:	Vigorous Upright
Awards:	

PERFECTA

Other Name: KORDES' PERFECTA

The name of this rose describes the form of the flower — large and high-centred with a multitude of petals; when skilfully grown under glass it is as near perfection as the rose breeder has yet achieved. A wise and popular choice for the exhibitor but definitely not recommended for general garden display. The buds and early flowers are distinctly unattractive and the large midsummer blooms can droop or even snap off in windy weather.

HYBRID TEA ROSES

Height in

PICCADILLY

Piccadilly remains the most popular of the bi-colours. To see it at its best, look at young blooms in cool weather; with age and in hot sunshine the vivid reds and yellows merge and fade. It is a splendid bedding variety — very early and remarkably free-flowering bushes which bear attractive coppery foliage. There are a few drawbacks — petals are not numerous and so the blooms open wide rather quickly and disease resistance, although still good, has decreased in recent years.

Blooms:	25 petals Scarlet; pale yellow reverse Medium-sized Slightly fragrant
Foliage:	Bronze-tinted Glossy
Health:	Good disease resistance
Growth:	Vigorous Upright
Awards:	

PICTURE

A pre-war favourite which could be found in countless tiny front gardens, where its compact shape and dainty flowers were in keeping with the surroundings. It has now lost its vigour and is near the end of its commercial life, but search the catalogues for it if you want a fine button-hole rose. The low-growing bush starts to flower early in the season and there are several distinct flushes. The small shapely blooms have reflexed petals which are a unique shade of pink. Mildew is no worse than average.

Blooms:	30 petals Clear rose pink Small Slightly fragrant
Foliage:	Light green Matt
Health:	Average disease resistance
Growth:	Vigorous Upright
Awards:	

PINK FAVORITE

This American-bred rose tops the list of disease-resistant varieties; mildew and black spot are almost unknown. Excellent for bedding — the shiny foliage is attractive and the pink blooms appear throughout the summer on top of sturdy stems. The high-centred flowers, darker on the outside of the petals than on the inside, start to appear rather late but this is its only draw-back as a bedding rose. It is also a very popular exhibition variety, but you must disbud to produce a single large bloom.

Blooms:	30 petals Deep pink Large Slightly fragrant
Foliage:	Dark green Glossy
Health:	Good disease resistance
Growth:	Vigorous Branching
Awards:	

PINK PEACE

Like its famous parent *Peace*, this rose bears large blooms, up to 6 in. across, on vigorous bushes which are taller than average. However, there is no other similarity between the two varieties so the name *Pink Peace* is distinctly misleading. Growth is upright, not bushy; foliage is bronze-tinted, not dark green, and the loose, open-cupped flowers are strongly scented. The bushes do not reach the height of *Peace* and the foliage is susceptible to rust, but this pink offspring is more free-flowering.

Blooms:	55 petals Deep pink Large Fragrant
Foliage:	Bronze-tinted Semi-glossy
Health:	Good disease resistance
Growth:	Vigorous Upright
Awards:	

PRECIOUS PLATINUM
Other Names: RED STAR, OPA POTSCHKE

This rose from N. Ireland has won no awards in Britain, has blooms which are not high-centred classic beauties and its fragrance is sweet but not strong. Yet it has become increasingly popular as a bedding rose since its introduction in 1974. The reason is its colour — dazzling red which can be seen from afar. These blooms are borne very freely in small clusters, and they are resistant to, rain. Disease resistance is above average, but watch for mildew.

Blooms:	35 petals Bright crimson Medium-sized Fragrant
Foliage:	Medium green Glossy
Health:	Good disease resistance
Growth:	Vigorous Branching
Awards:	

HYBRID TEA ROSES

ft in feet

Blooms:	25 petals Cherry pink Medium-sized Very fragrant
Foliage:	Dark green Semi-glossy
Health:	Average disease resistance
Growth:	Vigorous Upright
Awards:	

PRIMA BALLERINA
Other Name: PREMIERE BALLERINE

You will find this rose in nearly all the catalogues. The glowing descriptions are justified as far as they go — *Prima Ballerina* is indeed a vigorous bedding variety, taller than average, with beautiful buds and shapely flowers which are outstandingly fragrant. Unfortunately it is now less free-flowering than it used to be and there can be quite long flowerless gaps in late summer. Also it is now susceptible to mildew so that regular spraying may be necessary.

Blooms:	45 petals Vermilion Large Slightly fragrant
Foliage:	Dark green Matt
Health:	Average disease resistance
Growth:	Moderately vigorous Bushy
Awards:	

PRINCESS

An exhibitor's rose, although the blooms are rather globular. It is not popular, and few growers offer it in their catalogues. The reason for this lack of popularity is the absence of any strong advantages — the vermilion flowers lack the brilliance of *Alexander* or *Super Star* and the bushes, although hardy and well-covered with leaves, do not produce many flowers. This latter drawback makes it unsuitable as a bedding rose — choose it if you want a low-growing bush which will produce a few show blooms.

Blooms:	70 petals Scarlet; pale scarlet reverse Large Fragrant
Foliage:	Dark green Glossy
Health:	Good disease resistance
Growth:	Vigorous Upright
Awards:	

RED DEVIL
Other Name: COEUR D'AMOUR

One of the most popular and successful exhibition varieties, which deserves all the praise it has received. The form of the blooms is perhaps the closest yet achieved to the perfect Hybrid Tea shape, and by disbudding, even a beginner can produce prize-winning flowers which are extremely large and fragrant. It is also a good bedding rose — the bush is large, vigorous and the flowers are borne freely. There is one serious drawback — the blooms are damaged by rain.

Blooms:	40 petals Deep cerise pink Large Fragrant
Foliage:	Bronze-tinted Glossy
Health:	Good disease resistance
Growth:	Vigorous Upright
Awards:	

RED LION

Many experienced rose growers consider *Red Lion* to be an outstanding variety for exhibition — the blooms are high-centred and frequently exceptionally large; the fragrance is occasionally intense. It is highly recommended for cultivation in pots under glass and it appears in the Royal National Rose Society Analysis of recommended Hybrid Teas. But it is sold by very few suppliers, since it is not recommended for bedding in the garden — freedom of flowering is only average and the bushes are slender.

Blooms:	30 petals Rose red; silvery reverse Large Slightly fragrant
Foliage:	Dark green Glossy
Health:	Good disease resistance
Growth:	Very vigorous Branching
Awards:	

ROSE GAUJARD

It may seem surprising that such a well-known and well-loved rose should have its faults. The purists frown on the garishness of its colour, the tendency of its blooms to split and the absence of any worthwhile fragrance. But for the ordinary gardener it is a good choice for bedding — the bushes are vigorous, hardy, long-lasting and remarkably easy to grow in poor conditions. It stands up to rain and the blooms are borne very freely. The leaves are large and quite healthy, but watch for black spot.

HYBRID TEA ROSES

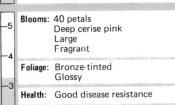

Height in

ROYAL HIGHNESS
Other Name: KÖNIGLICHE HOHEIT

The catalogue description could make you rush out and buy one. Long pointed buds open into large and fragrant classically-shaped blooms with reflexed petals, each one on top of its tall stem like a delicate porcelain flower. Do buy one if you are interested in exhibiting, and if you can provide protection against rain. But it is not a good choice for ordinary garden display, especially if you live in a rainy area. It suffers badly in wet weather and is prone to mildew.

Blooms:	40 petals Flesh pink Large Fragrant
Foliage:	Dark green Glossy
Health:	Prone to disease
Growth:	Vigorous Branching
Awards:	

SHOT SILK

A pre-war favourite which still keeps its place in some rose catalogues. Its main claim to fame is the unique colour combination of its blooms, still unmatched after more than half a century. The flowers, high-centred at first but soon opening wide, are freely borne on the neat bushes. The foliage is bronze-tinted when young. Unfortunately this old variety has now lost its vigour and is likely to be a disappointing selection. Choose the climbing sport which has retained the original vigour.

Blooms:	30 petals Salmon pink, shaded gold Medium-sized Very fragrant
Foliage:	Medium green Glossy
Health:	Average disease resistance
Growth:	Moderately vigorous Bushy
Awards:	

SILVER JUBILEE

The only sad note in the story of this rose was the death of its breeder shortly before its introduction in 1978 — Alex Cocker did not live to see the universal acclaim given to *Silver Jubilee*. No newcomer in recent years has gained such instant popularity, and there are several reasons. Shapely blooms on short stems, unusually long petals which do not lose their colour in hot weather, remarkably dense foliage and an outstandingly free-flowering habit combine to make it a splendid bedding variety.

Blooms:	25 petals Coppery salmon pink, shaded peach Large Fragrant
Foliage:	Medium green Glossy
Health:	Good disease resistance
Growth:	Vigorous Bushy
Awards:	

SILVER LINING

The elegant blooms of *Silver Lining* can be seen at flower shows and they sometimes win prizes, but there are better varieties nowadays for exhibition. It is a useful variety for flower arrangers, as it is strongly scented and the blooms keep well in water. It is sometimes recommended as a bedding variety for general garden display, but it can be distinctly disappointing. It has lost its original vigour, flowering is no longer prolific and the display can be ruined by wet weather.

Blooms:	30 petals Silvery pink; silver reverse Large Very fragrant
Foliage:	Dark green Glossy
Health:	Average disease resistance
Growth:	Moderately vigorous Branching
Awards:	

STELLA

This variety can easily be mistaken for a large-flowered Floribunda — the blooms are borne in clusters of five or more on top of tall stems which are usually unbranched. The main virtue of *Stella* is its ability to resist the effect of heavy rain, but its popularity has declined in recent years as it has become increasingly susceptible to black spot. It is still a good bedding rose — the large flowers, somewhat globular in shape, are long-lasting and can be used for exhibition if the truss is disbudded to leave a single bloom.

Blooms:	35 petals Creamy pink, edged carmine Large Slightly fragrant
Foliage:	Dark green Glossy
Health:	Average disease resistance
Growth:	Vigorous Upright
Awards:	

HYBRID TEA ROSES

Blooms:	50 petals Vermilion; pale vermilion reverse Large Slightly fragrant
Foliage:	Medium green Semi-glossy
Health:	Good disease resistance
Growth:	Vigorous Spreading
Awards:	(RNRS)

SUMMER HOLIDAY

You will not find *Summer Holiday* in many catalogues, but it is well worth looking for if the vermilion colour of its famous parent *Super Star* appeals to you. This variety has flowers which are deeper and brighter than *Super Star*, and it has retained some of the robust good health its parent used to possess. A good bedding rose, free-flowering and rain-resistant. The flowers are borne in small clusters on bushes which are a little taller than average.

Blooms:	35 petals Deep yellow Medium-sized Slightly fragrant
Foliage:	Dark green Semi-glossy
Health:	Average disease resistance
Growth:	Moderately vigorous Upright
Awards:	

SUMMER SUNSHINE
Other Name: SOLEIL D'ETE

The demand for *Summer Sunshine* continues because of its colour — the deepest of all the yellow Hybrid Teas. The purity and brilliance remains from the bud stage to open flower and these blooms are freely produced and reasonably rain-resistant. They are borne singly on long stems. Unfortunately the constitution of the plant does not match the quality of the flower. It is an unreliable and indifferent grower, dying out quite quickly in some areas.

Blooms:	30 petals Golden yellow Medium-sized Slightly fragrant
Foliage:	Medium green Semi-glossy
Health:	Average disease resistance
Growth:	Vigorous Upright
Awards:	(RNRS)

SUNBLEST
Other Name: LANDORA

There are very few pure yellow Hybrid Tea varieties and this one is highly recommended for bedding. It is not a great rose — its blooms are not large and its scent is slight — but it has no serious drawbacks. The shape of the blooms is good, the petals hold their colour and the tall bushes bear abundant flowers. It is an excellent variety for cutting — the slender buds are borne on long straight stems.

Blooms:	35 petals Orange vermilion Medium-sized Fragrant
Foliage:	Medium green Semi-glossy
Health:	Average disease resistance
Growth:	Vigorous Upright
Awards:	(RNRS) (RNRS) (RHS) (US) (H)

SUPER STAR
Other Name: TROPICANA

This variety was the super star of the 1960s with world-wide acclaim for the beautifully shaped blooms which seem almost fluorescent. It is found in countless gardens as a rather tall bedding rose, and its long stems make it excellent for cutting. It was never perfect — flowering begins rather late and the petals turn purple with age. Nowadays it has distinct drawbacks — the foliage is susceptible to mildew and old bushes tend to produce few flowers.

Blooms:	40 petals Fuchsia pink Large Fragrant
Foliage:	Medium green Matt
Health:	Good disease resistance
Growth:	Vigorous Upright
Awards:	

SUSAN HAMPSHIRE
Other Name: MEINATAC

Susan Hampshire appears in some catalogues under its unattractive 'official' name — *Meinatac*. It was bred in France by Meilland and was introduced in 1974. This variety has a number of good points — the petals are an unusual shade of pink and the blooms are full enough and large enough for the show-bench. The fragrance has an old-fashioned quality and the leaves do not succumb easily to mildew. Despite its virtues, it has not become a popular rose.

HYBRID TEA ROSES

SUTTER'S GOLD

An old favourite, but still the most fragrant of all the yellow roses. The tall pointed buds appear very early in the season, and flowering is prolific. The long stems, pleasant perfume and attractive colouring make *Sutter's Gold* an excellent variety for flower arranging, but there is a list of drawbacks. New bushes are slow to establish, and the growth habit is often lanky with sparse foliage. A disadvantage in both garden and vase is the speed with which the buds open and the petals fade.

Blooms:	30 petals Pale orange yellow, shaded pink Large Very fragrant
Foliage:	Dark green Glossy
Health:	Average disease resistance
Growth:	Moderately vigorous Upright
Awards:	

SWEET PROMISE
Other Name: SONIA MEILLAND

This is the pink rose of the cut flower world, sold in florist shops everywhere. The slim blooms, borne on long stems, are amongst the most highly acclaimed roses for flower arrangers. Unfortunately, *Sweet Promise* is distinctly unhappy outdoors in a wet, cool summer and is therefore best grown under glass. But if your garden is in a mild part of the country and if you are keen on roses for cutting then *Sweet Promise* is well worth trying.

Blooms:	30 petals Rosy salmon Small Slightly fragrant
Foliage:	Dark green Glossy
Health:	Average disease resistance
Growth:	Moderately vigorous Upright
Awards:	

TENERIFE

This rose was bred by an amateur from two famous parents — *Fragrant Cloud* provided the sweet perfume and *Piccadilly* provided the bi-colour effect. It is not a rare variety, but it has not reached the popularity one might have expected from its parentage. The colour of the blooms is variable, and there are some doubts about its claim to be free-flowering. Rain resistance is only average, and perhaps its major fault is its susceptibility to black spot.

Blooms:	35 petals Deep coral salmon; peach reverse Large Very fragrant
Foliage:	Medium green Glossy
Health:	Average disease resistance
Growth:	Vigorous Upright
Awards:	

TROIKA
Other Name: ROYAL DANE

If you like copper-coloured roses then this is the one to choose. There is none of the die-back and disease which plague the older varieties in this colour group. The blooms are large enough for exhibition and the buds are long and shapely enough to make them excellent for cutting. But *Troika* is best considered as a bedding rose — the blooms appear early, rain resistance is good and the petals do not fade with age.

Blooms:	30 petals Orange bronze, shaded red Large Fragrant
Foliage:	Medium green Glossy
Health:	Good disease resistance
Growth:	Vigorous Upright
Awards:	

TYPHOO TEA

If you are looking for a compact bush or if a red and cream bi-colour is too garish for your taste then *Typhoo Tea* is not for you. The stems can reach 5 ft or even more and the large flowers are borne singly. There are good points — the perfume is strong and the bush is free-flowering. It has been recommended as a beginner's rose because it will tolerate poor conditions, but it has never reached the top twenty. It is too vigorous for the average plot and the blooms blow rather quickly.

Blooms:	50 petals Red; cream reverse Large Very fragrant
Foliage:	Medium green Glossy
Health:	Average disease resistance
Growth:	Very vigorous Upright
Awards:	

HYBRID TEA ROSES

in feet

Blooms:	35 petals Pink and copper; yellow base Large, rather globular Fragrant
Foliage:	Medium green Semi-glossy
Health:	Good disease resistance
Growth:	Vigorous Branching
Awards:	

TYPHOON
Other Name: TAIFUN

An excellent bedding variety, with large open blooms. Each petal is a blend of orange, salmon and yellow — appealing to some but unfortunately not liked by people who expect their rose blooms to be a single pure colour. The compact bush generally produces plenty of blooms throughout the season and the display is especially good in autumn. The fragrance is variable — usually slight but occasionally strong.

Blooms:	30 petals White Medium-sized Slightly fragrant
Foliage:	Dark green Matt
Health:	Prone to disease
Growth:	Moderately vigorous Branching
Awards:	

VIRGO
Other Name: VIRGO LIBERATIONEM

One of the best loved white roses. Since the 1940s it has provided free-flowering bushes for garden display and beautiful long buds for cutting. The white flowers, occasionally tinged with pale pink, are best grown under glass. It is a poor choice nowadays for bedding — the bush is usually unattractive and sparse, and the foliage mildews badly. The blooms spoil badly in wet weather and today there are much better white varieties to replace this old favourite.

Blooms:	35 petals Deep reddish pink Large Very fragrant
Foliage:	Dark green Glossy
Health:	Good disease resistance
Growth:	Vigorous Branching
Awards:	

WENDY CUSSONS

This British-bred variety is almost the perfect bedding rose. Its list of star qualities is most impressive — outstanding perfume, large well-shaped blooms on large handsome bushes, a prolific flowering habit and above average resistance to rain and mildew. *Wendy Cussons* has an excellent reputation for longevity and reliability, but it is still not quite the perfect bedding rose — the strong cerise pink clashes badly with the colours of many other varieties. Grow it as a standard or give it a bed of its own.

Blooms:	30 petals Golden apricot Medium-sized Very fragrant
Foliage:	Bronze-tinted Glossy
Health:	Average disease resistance
Growth:	Vigorous Bushy
Awards:	

WHISKY MAC

Much has been written about the *Whisky Mac* phenomenon. Experts have often described the drawbacks of this variety — unreliability when grown in average or poor soil, susceptibility to mildew, blooms which quickly become open-cupped and the loss of the free-flowering habit after a few years. Yet *Whisky Mac* has proven to be one of the most popular of all Hybrid Teas in recent years and is listed in nearly all rose catalogues. The reason is simple — a unique colour plus an attractive and unusual scent.

Blooms:	45 petals Golden yellow, flushed pink Large Slightly fragrant
Foliage:	Light green Semi-glossy
Health:	Good disease resistance
Growth:	Moderately vigorous Bushy
Awards:	

YELLOW PAGES

Yellow Pages has earned the reputation of being one of the easiest yellow Hybrid Teas to grow. It is nearly always in flower during the season and the blooms stand up to rain remarkably well. The compact bushes are reliable for bedding and the blooms are suitable for cutting, but this is not a good exhibition variety. The blooms often have confused centres which makes them unacceptable for the show-bench. Never in the best-seller list, the popularity of *Yellow Pages* has continued to decline.

HYBRID TEA ROSES

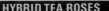

FLORIBUNDA ROSES

A Danish hybridist, Svend Poulsen, once dreamt of producing a new race of roses, with modern flowers borne in large trusses continually throughout the season. He crossed Polyanthas (pompon roses) with Hybrid Teas and his first hybrid, *Else Poulsen*, appeared in 1924. This was followed by other Poulsen roses and the Floribundas were born, but it was not until 1952 that this term was generally adopted.

An expert wrote recently that if he had to begin again, he would plant more Floribundas than Hybrid Teas. At first this may seem surprising, because the basic drawbacks of the typical Floribunda remain from the days when he planted his first rose garden. The blooms lack the size, beauty and fragrance of their more elegant rivals — the Hybrid Teas.

If the drawbacks remain, so do the advantages. Above all, there is continuity of bloom — varieties in this class flower almost continually throughout the summer and autumn, whereas Hybrid Teas tend to bloom in distinct flushes. And it is not only frequency of blooming, it is also quantity of flowers — the Floribunda trusses generally provide a much larger splash of colour on the bush than is found on a Hybrid Tea. The benefits do not stop there. The average Floribunda is hardier, easier to care for and more reliable in wet weather than its Hybrid Tea counterpart.

The increase in popularity amongst expert and ordinary gardener alike has been due to the flood of new varieties in recent years. These have maintained the benefits, introduced new colours and have started to overcome the drawbacks listed above. *Margaret Merril* and *Fragrant Delight* rival the sweet-smelling Hybrid Teas for fragrance ... *Paddy McGredy* and *Violet Carson* rival the Hybrid Teas for elegance. These latter roses (Floribunda-H.T. type) have blurred the dividing lines and made classification difficult — you will find *Sunsilk* classed as a Floribunda in one book and as a Hybrid Tea in another. Large Floribundas with shapely H.T. blooms, such as *Queen Elizabeth*, are called Grandifloras in the U.S.

The Floribunda is the rose *par excellence* for providing colour in the garden. It can be grown as a bush or standard, in both formal and informal settings. There are tall varieties for providing hedges, and there are dwarf varieties (known as Patio or Cushion Roses in the U.S.) for providing neat 1½ ft bushes for the front of the border.

KEY TO THE ROSE GUIDES

Number of Petals
See page 5

Colour
See page 76

Size of Bloom
Large: over 3½ in.
Medium: 2 – 3½ in.

Folia
Leaf
and s
quali
(see

Fragrance
See page 6

Height in ft
Average bush
2½ – 3 ft

Blooms: 40 petals
Orange scarlet
Medium-sized
No fragrance

Foliage: Medium green
Semi-glossy

Health: Good disease resistance

Growth: Moderately vigorous
Bushy

Awards:

Awards
Major awards
from Britain
and overseas
(see page 105)

Growth
Vigour (= robustness)
and growth habit
(spreading, upright,
bushy, etc.)

Health
Resistance
to mildew
and
black spot

Blooms: 20 petals
Buttercup yellow
Small
Slightly fragrant

Foliage: Medium green
Glossy

Health: Good disease resistance

Growth: Moderately vigorous
Branching

Awards:

Blooms: 10 petals
Light vermilion
Large
Slightly fragrant

Foliage: Medium green
Matt

Health: Average disease resistance

Growth: Vigorous
Spreading

Awards:

Blooms: 35 petals
Vermilion
Small
No fragrance

Foliage: Medium green
Semi-glossy

Health: Average disease resistance

Growth: Vigorous
Upright

Awards:

Blooms: 25 petals
Pinkish apricot; golden at base
Large, cupped
Fragrant

Foliage: Medium green
Semi-glossy

Health: Average disease resistance

Growth: Vigorous
Bushy

Awards:

Blooms: 20 petals
Golden yellow
Large
Very fragrant

Foliage: Medium green
Glossy

Health: Good disease resistance

Growth: Vigorous
Upright

Awards:

ALLGOLD

Although it won its Gold Medal in the 1950s, *Allgold* is still recommended as one of the best yellow Floribundas you can buy. Flowering begins early, and goes on almost continually until late autumn. Even in rainy weather the colour of the blooms remains pure and unfading until the petals fall. The compact bushes rarely succumb to mildew or black spot, and finding fault isn't easy. The blooms are rather short of petals and the foliage may be rather sparse, but these are minor drawbacks.

ANNA WHEATCROFT

You will probably have to search through many catalogues before you find *Anna Wheatcroft* these days, but this orange-red rose still retains many good points. The shapely buds open into large flat blooms which deepen in colour as they age. The trusses are sometimes extremely large, especially in autumn, and flowers are borne quite freely. It also has a good reputation for hardiness, but its advantages are overshadowed by the distinct drawback of having only ten petals per bloom. Black spot can be a problem.

ANNE COCKER

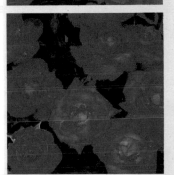

All catalogue and textbook descriptions of *Anne Cocker* highlight its outstanding feature — the length of time its flowers stay fresh on the bush or in a vase. Obviously it is popular with both exhibitors and flower arrangers, but it is also a fine bedding rose. The large trusses are bright and colourful, and the individual blooms are borne on unusually long stalks. The quality of each bloom is excellent, rounded and full of petals, but the flowering season begins rather late and there is no fragrance.

APRICOT NECTAR

This excellent Floribunda won top honours and popular acclaim in the U.S. but it has never reached the best-seller lists in Britain. Its large paeony-like blooms possess a delicate fruity fragrance and the imposing trusses are borne on top of strong stems. If you like unusual pastel shades and if you require a taller than average Floribunda for bedding or hedging, then *Apricot Nectar* is a good choice. In America it is claimed to be very healthy but in Britain you will have to keep watch for mildew.

ARTHUR BELL

Arthur Bell well deserves its reputation and popularity. The tall bush is well-clothed with an abundance of leathery leaves and the flowers are large and weather-resistant. The strength of the fragrance is rarely matched by any other Floribunda and it has a good record for mildew and black spot resistance. Flowering starts very early in the season and continues well into the autumn. Its failing is well known — the golden blooms fade to pale cream as they age.

FLORIBUNDA ROSES

Height

BABY BIO

This dwarf Floribunda is a fairy story rose. Bred by an engine driver (Mr Smith of Sandiacre) in his small greenhouse, it was awarded a Certificate of Merit by the Royal National Rose Society in 1976. Masses of flowers are borne freely and continually throughout the season, and it has been called the best of the dwarf yellows. Disease resistance is very good, but despite its high award and the many glowing reports from the experts it remains a rarity, restricted to the Wheatcroft catalogue.

Blooms: 40 petals
Golden yellow
Small
No fragrance

Foliage: Dark green
Semi-glossy

Health: Good disease resistance

Growth: Vigorous
Bushy

Awards:

BONFIRE NIGHT
Other Name: BONFIRE

Floribunda— H.T. type

Bonfire Night keeps its place in the catalogues because of the brightness of its flowers. When the bush is in full bloom there is a medley of reds, yellows and orange, reminiscent of the universal favourite *Masquerade*. For many gardeners this colour mixture is too garish, but if you find it appealing then *Bonfire Night* is a good choice. The blooms are beautifully formed, like Hybrid Teas, and the trusses are large.

Blooms: 20 petals
Orange, splashed scarlet and yellow
Medium-sized
Slightly fragrant

Foliage: Dark green
Semi-glossy

Health: Average disease resistance

Growth: Vigorous
Upright

Awards:

CHANELLE

The peaches-and-cream Floribunda, much loved by gardeners who favour pastel colours in their roses. The bushes bear abundant glossy foliage which is exceptionally disease resistant. The blooms are nicely formed in bud, looking like miniature Hybrid Teas, but they open into flat, open blooms. These flowers have good rain resistance, and the flowering season carries on well into autumn. *Chanelle* has a good reputation as a thoroughly reliable and prolific Floribunda.

Blooms: 20 petals
Cream, flushed buff and pink
Medium-sized, cupped
Fragrant

Foliage: Dark green
Glossy

Health: Good disease resistance

Growth: Vigorous
Branching

Awards:

CHARLESTON

A multi-coloured rose with blooms which range in colour from chrome yellow in bud to rich red when full blown. The mature open flowers bear both colours, but in *Charleston* the red and yellow splashes on the petals remain distinct, not blended as in the much more popular *Masquerade*. The bush is sturdy with shiny dark foliage and the flower trusses are large, but this variety is not recommended for sites where mildew and black spot are common problems.

Blooms: 20 petals
Yellow and crimson
Medium-sized
Slightly fragrant

Foliage: Dark green
Glossy

Health: Prone to disease

Growth: Vigorous
Bushy

Awards:

CHORUS
Other Name: MEIJULITO

Some of the experts have expressed surprise that this rose of the mid 1970s never became a best-seller. Its list of good qualities is most impressive — the blooms and trusses are large and the colour is dazzling. The bushes are attractive, the foliage is healthy and there is no shortage of flowers throughout the season. It is a good choice if you want a rich red Floribunda for the show-bench or a reliable red-flowering bush of average height for bedding.

Blooms: 35 petals
Crimson
Large
Slightly fragrant

Foliage: Dark green
Glossy

Health: Good disease resistance

Growth: Vigorous
Bushy

Awards:

Blooms: 35 petals
Orange yellow, shaded pink
Small, cupped
Slightly fragrant

Foliage: Dark green
Semi-glossy

Health: Prone to disease

Growth: Moderately vigorous
Branching

Awards:

CIRCUS

Circus was once a great favourite, but nowadays it does not appear in many rose catalogues or garden shops. Some of the vigour has gone, and it is prone to black spot. The attractive buds are yellow and look like small Hybrid Teas; as they mature the blooms become open-cupped and the petals are suffused with pink, buff, orange and red. The compact bushes are reasonably free-flowering and the trusses are usually large. The fragrance is described as spicy.

Blooms: 35 petals
Velvety orange scarlet
Small
Slightly fragrant

Foliage: Medium green
Glossy

Health: Good disease resistance

Growth: Moderately vigorous
Branching

Awards:

CITY OF BELFAST

City of Belfast is a compact bush with attractive glossy leaves, red when young and medium green when mature. It is often recommended for the small garden where not many roses can be grown, because its free-flowering habit produces a constant splash of colour throughout the season. Rain has little effect on the slightly frilled petals, and both mildew and black spot are rarely a problem. Die-back, however, can be troublesome (see page 98). It is a good rose for exhibiting and cutting.

Blooms: 20 petals
Rich salmon pink
Medium-sized
Slightly fragrant

Foliage: Dark green
Semi-glossy

Health: Average disease resistance

Growth: Vigorous
Upright

Awards:

CITY OF LEEDS

One of the most popular of all Floribundas, widely recommended where the gardener wants a massed planting of a single variety or simply an easy-to-grow variety for a beginner. *City of Leeds* proves that a rose does not have to be perfect to be popular. The scent is hardly noticeable, the foliage is small and the flowers spot after heavy rain. These drawbacks, however, are soon forgotten when you see the trusses of rich pink flowers covering the attractive bushes throughout the season.

Blooms: 18 petals
Orange yellow; copper reverse
Medium-sized
Slightly fragrant

Foliage: Dark green
Glossy

Health: Average disease resistance

Growth: Vigorous
Upright

Awards:

COPPER POT

The pale coppery shades of this variety were a novelty when it was first introduced in the late 1960s, and the display late in the season can be very attractive. With the advent of new varieties it is now a rarity in the catalogues and is not a good choice. The tall stems are generally lanky and unattractive, and the flower trusses perched on top are sometimes quite small. Fragrance is virtually absent and you would do much better to choose *Iced Ginger*, which is a richer copper colour.

Blooms: 35 petals
Golden yellow, flushed scarlet
Large
Slightly fragrant

Foliage: Medium green
Glossy

Health: Good disease resistance

Growth: Very vigorous
Upright

Awards:

DAME OF SARK

The reasons for choosing any particular rose can be many and varied. If your main object is to find a Floribunda which will appear striking and colourful from a distance, then there is no better choice than *Dame of Sark*. The large flowers may not be things of beauty when examined at close range but at long range the effect of glowing orange is spectacular. Choose this rose for low hedging or a large bed — health and rain resistance are good and it is reasonably free-flowering.

FLORIBUNDA ROSES

DEAREST

For many years *Dearest* was the top-selling pink Floribunda, but its popularity has now begun to wane. Its virtues are still there — beautiful pink blooms which are camellia-like and filled with spicy fragrance, trusses which are large and bushes which are clothed with dark and shiny foliage. As always, a good choice for bedding, cutting or exhibiting, but there are faults. This variety does not like wet weather and the foliage is susceptible to both rust and black spot.

Blooms:	30 petals Salmon pink Large Fragrant
Foliage:	Dark green Glossy
Health:	Prone to disease
Growth:	Vigorous Branching
Awards:	

ELIZABETH OF GLAMIS
Other Name: IRISH BEAUTY

It is hard to be disloyal to one of the great roses of our time and one which has been grown in countless gardens since its introduction in 1964, but it has problems these days. It is now only a sound choice for reasonably good soil — it is definitely unsuitable for cold soils or clays. When well-grown, the high-centred buds open into lovely flat blooms borne in large fragrant clusters. You must remember to spray to keep disease at bay, and die-back can be a problem.

Blooms:	35 petals Orange salmon Medium-sized Fragrant
Foliage:	Dark green Semi-glossy
Health:	Prone to disease
Growth:	Moderately vigorous Upright
Awards:	

ENGLISH MISS

An appropriate name for an English-bred rose which has petals of delicate blush pink. The classical pink Floribunda *Dearest* is one of its parents, but this new rose is much healthier and is less susceptible to rain. The buds open to form camellia-like flowers which possess a strong, sweet scent. The bush is densely clothed with shiny, leathery leaves which have a purplish tinge. *English Miss* is free-flowering and there is a quick repeat between flushes. A good choice for bedding or cutting.

Blooms:	35 petals Silver pink, edged deeper pink Medium-sized Very fragrant
Foliage:	Dark green Glossy
Health:	Good disease resistance
Growth:	Very vigorous Bushy
Awards:	

ESCAPADE

Some Floribundas are difficult to identify, even for an expert, but anyone can tell *Escapade* at a glance. The reason is its unique colouring — a white-centred ring of lilac petals surrounding a group of yellow stamens. The large flat blooms have a distinct musk-like perfume, and the bush is almost always in flower throughout the season. There is an abundance of foliage, healthy and shiny, and *Escapade* is a good choice for cutting and for garden display in the larger bed or rose border.

Blooms:	12 petals Rosy lilac; white eye Large Fragrant
Foliage:	Light green Glossy
Health:	Good disease resistance
Growth:	Vigorous Bushy
Awards:	

ESTHER OFARIM

Floribunda—
H.T. type

The bright and unusual colour of the blooms plus the dwarf growth habit make *Esther Ofarim* an excellent choice for the small front garden. The trusses are large and the fully double blooms are pointed in their early stages. The compact bush will be free-flowering provided that the soil is reasonably good and regularly fed with rose fertilizer. It is highly recommended for cutting — the blooms last for a long time in water and the red and yellow blends will add colour to any flower arrangement.

Blooms:	30 petals Orange vermilion; yellow at base Medium-sized Slightly fragrant
Foliage:	Medium green Matt
Health:	Average disease resistance
Growth:	Moderately vigorous Bushy
Awards:	

ht in feet

EUROPEANA

The red Floribunda which is easy to recognize. The foliage is distinct and outstandingly attractive — deep reddish purple when young and glistening bronzy green when mature. The huge trusses of deep red flowers bow down under their own weight, especially in rainy weather. A real eye-catcher, but you must know how to treat it. Plant *Europeana* in groups, with no more than 1¾ ft between the plants, so that the trusses will be supported. Spray regularly against mildew, especially in southern counties.

Blooms: 40 petals
Deep crimson
Medium-sized, rosette-shaped
Slightly fragrant

Foliage: Bronze-tinted
Glossy

Health: Prone to disease

Growth: Vigorous
Branching

Awards:

EVELYN FISON
Other Name: IRISH WONDER

One of the older bright red Floribundas but regarded by some experts as still the best. It has an excellent reputation for reliability, and neither bright sun nor heavy rain seems to damage the blooms. The trusses are large and well-spaced, and it is extremely prolific. *Evelyn Fison* is hard to fault as a bedding rose — perhaps the amount of foliage is sometimes inadequate and the reputation for outstanding disease resistance is a little overrated.

Blooms: 30 petals
Vivid scarlet
Medium-sized
Slightly fragrant

Foliage: Dark green
Glossy

Health: Average disease resistance

Growth: Vigorous
Branching

Awards:

EYE PAINT

This McGredy-bred rose is one of the most unusual of all Floribundas, and you will need to know something about its growth and flowering habit before planting it in the rose garden. The small flowers are borne in great profusion, looking quite unlike the rose blooms which appear on 'modern' roses. The bush is extremely vigorous, soon reaching 4 ft or more, and it is best grown as a hedge or in the shrub border, where its bright flowers from June to September make a welcome addition.

Blooms: 7 petals
Scarlet; white eye
Small
No fragrance

Foliage: Medium green
Semi-glossy

Health: Average disease resistance

Growth: Very vigorous
Bushy

Awards:

FRAGRANT DELIGHT

If you like Floribundas, strong fragrance and copper-coloured blooms, then *Fragrant Delight* is undoubtedly the rose for you. This offspring of *Chanelle* and *Whisky Mac* was introduced in the late 1970s, and the fine shape of the young blooms, together with the small size of the trusses has led at least one grower to include it in the Hybrid Tea section of his catalogue. The young leaves are bronzy green, turning mid-green and remaining very shiny as they mature.

Blooms: 20 petals
Coppery salmon; yellow at base
Large
Very fragrant

Foliage: Medium green
Glossy

Health: Good disease resistance

Growth: Very vigorous
Upright

Awards:

FRENSHAM

For many years after the war, *Frensham* was the most popular red Floribunda. Now it is available from only a few growers, because the new reds offer disease resistance and fuller blooms. *Frensham's* problem is that it has become susceptible to mildew, but if you are prepared to spray then this old favourite will provide large and spreading bushes for hedging or borders. Glossy foliage is abundant, the freedom and continuity of flowering are remarkable and the velvety red trusses are large.

Blooms: 15 petals
Deep crimson
Medium-sized
No fragrance

Foliage: Medium green
Glossy

Health: Prone to disease

Growth: Very vigorous
Branching

Awards:

GLENFIDDICH

Glenfiddich is one of the most popular of the newer Floribundas and is grown all over Britain, but it is truly a flower of Scotland. Raised by Cocker of Aberdeen, it was named after the Scotch Whisky which is reminiscent of its colour, and it is in Scotland and the northern counties where it is most successful. The well-formed flowers appear singly or in groups and there is good continuity throughout the season. In the south *Glenfiddich* is less reliable and the flowers are paler.

Blooms:	25 petals Golden amber Medium-sized Slightly fragrant
Foliage:	Dark green Glossy
Health:	Good disease resistance
Growth:	Vigorous Upright
Awards:	

GOLDEN SLIPPERS

An American variety which won top honours in its native country but has not caught the public fancy in Britain. Its supporters speak very highly of its excellence in a small bed — pointed orange buds appearing freely throughout the season, opening into attractive bi-coloured blooms on dwarf bushes. But it also has its critics, who have been disappointed in its spreading and rather slight growth plus its unreliability in sunny summers and infertile soil. Good disease resistance, but watch for black spot.

Blooms:	20 petals Rich orange; golden yellow reverse Medium-sized Fragrant
Foliage:	Medium green Glossy
Health:	Good disease resistance
Growth:	Moderately vigorous Branching
Awards:	

HONEYMOON
Other Name: HONIGMOND

Appropriately named, as it sometimes fails to live up to the promise of the first flush. It does not repeat as quickly as it should, and there can be a disappointing gap between flushes. The trusses are small and the perfume is slight. The colour fades rather quickly in hot weather, and *Honeymoon* should be seen in the northern counties in order to appreciate its virtues to the full. Vigorous growth, abundant shiny foliage and lovely flat blooms filled with petals.

Blooms:	40 petals Canary yellow Medium-sized, rosette-shaped Slightly fragrant
Foliage:	Light green Glossy
Health:	Good disease resistance
Growth:	Vigorous Upright
Awards:	

ICEBERG
Other Name: SCHNEEWITTCHEN

The finest and most popular white Floribunda of our time. The pink-tinged buds open to flat white blooms, the quantity and continuity being quite outstanding. *Iceberg* is seen everywhere, but unfortunately it is often denied the chance to show how beautiful it can be. It needs space where it can be grown, lightly pruned, as a tall specimen bush — then the blooms cover the whole plant and the chance of disease is reduced. It is also a good choice for a hedge or standard.

Blooms:	25 petals White Medium-sized Slightly fragrant
Foliage:	Medium green Glossy
Health:	Average disease resistance
Growth:	Vigorous Branching
Awards:	

ICED GINGER

Floribunda—H.T. type

There is a bewildering array of Floribundas from which you can choose, but if you are a keen flower arranger then *Iced Ginger* should be at the top of your list. Beautiful blooms, Hybrid Tea in shape with ivory, pink, yellow and copper all blended together, plus an ability to last in water which is unmatched by any other Floribunda. The blooms are large and disease resistance is above average, but there are drawbacks — the tall bush can look distinctly leggy and it is not always free-flowering.

Blooms:	45 petals Ivory tinted coppery pink; pink reverse Large Fragrant
Foliage:	Light green Semi-glossy
Health:	Good disease resistance
Growth:	Vigorous Upright
Awards:	

ight in feet

Blooms: 25 petals
Orange red
Medium-sized
Slightly fragrant

Foliage: Dark green
Semi-glossy

Health: Average disease resistance

Growth: Vigorous
Branching

Awards:

IRISH MIST

Floribunda – H.T. type

There seemed to be a great future for *Irish Mist* when it was awarded its Certificate of Merit in 1967. The blooms are an attractive pale vermilion and the shape is as fine as the average Hybrid Tea rose. It comes into bloom early in the season and the continuity is above average. Rain has little effect and the leaves, though small, are generally abundant. Yet it has never been popular and now appears in only a few catalogues. Its problem is that it fares badly in cold and exposed sites.

Blooms: 30 petals
Pink, edged deep pink
Medium-sized
No fragrance

Foliage: Medium green
Glossy

Health: Average disease resistance

Growth: Vigorous
Branching

Awards:

KERRYMAN

Floribunda – H.T. type

A hardy, reliable Floribunda with medium- to large-sized shapely blooms which are of the Hybrid Tea type. *Kerryman* has very few special points — its disease resistance is only average, the growth habit is spreading and not compact, and there is no noticeable perfume. It suffers in heavy rain and the clusters can be quite small, but there *is* one special point — the colouring of the blooms. The outer petals deepen with age, giving a most unusual effect.

Blooms: 35 petals
Canary yellow
Medium-sized
Slightly fragrant

Foliage: Light green
Matt

Health: Average disease resistance

Growth: Vigorous
Bushy

Awards:

KIM

Kim is one of the very few yellow Floribundas which are low-growing, full-flowered and really reliable. Unlike *Baby Bio*, the colour does not remain pure, tinges of pink appearing as the blooms age. Its growth habit is unusually compact, and has been described as cushion-like. Disease resistance is reasonable, but spraying may be necessary. Flowers are borne singly or in neatly-shaped trusses. A good choice for a small bed or the front of the border.

Blooms: 20 petals
Orange scarlet
Medium-sized
Slightly fragrant

Foliage: Dark green
Glossy

Health: Average disease resistance

Growth: Vigorous
Upright

Awards:

KORONA

An example of a rose which is in its declining years. Once it was the most popular vermilion Floribunda, now it is offered by very few growers. It still retains many of its good points — the trusses are large and are borne freely, although the colour fades in hot weather. The resistance to rain is excellent and established bushes are hardy. However, it now does badly in some areas for no apparent reason, and much of its reliable constitution seems to have gone.

Blooms: 35 petals
Bright yellow
Large
Fragrant

Foliage: Medium green
Glossy

Health: Good disease resistance

Growth: Moderately vigorous
Bushy

Awards: BB

KORRESIA
Other Names: FRIESIA, SUNSPRITE

No rose could have got off to a less promising start — unknown parentage and no awards in Britain. Yet within a few years it has become a star of the rose world — the first serious challenger to *Allgold* for its crown as the top yellow Floribunda. *Korresia* scores over its rival by having flowers which are larger, more fragrant and fully double. Continuity is very good, the trusses of unfading blooms appearing over a long period.

FLORIBUNDA ROSES

Height in fee

LILLI MARLENE

A good bedding rose, justifiably popular for more than 20 years. The bush is well-clothed with abundant foliage and the flowers are plentiful. The black buds open into velvety dark red blooms which shrug off the effects of rain or hot sun. It has a good reputation for reliability and hardiness, which makes it a suitable Floribunda for beginners. Each individual open bloom is not particularly beautiful, but the overall effect of red blooms surrounded by coppery foliage is excellent.

Blooms:	25 petals Deep crimson Medium-sized Slightly fragrant
Foliage:	Bronze-tinted Semi-glossy
Health:	Average disease resistance
Growth:	Vigorous Bushy
Awards:	

LIVING FIRE

A Cinderella of a rose, which is eye-catching and rated highly without any major faults, yet it is not listed by the majority of British growers. It is remarkably resistant to disease and is considered good enough to appear in the RNRS Analysis of reliable varieties. Whatever the reason for its lack of availability, it certainly isn't the fault of the rose. The large blooms are borne singly or in small clusters, excellent for providing maximum brightness in beds where there is no fear of a clash with pastel shades.

Blooms:	35 petals Orange, shaded scarlet Large Slightly fragrant
Foliage:	Dark green Glossy
Health:	Good disease resistance
Growth:	Vigorous Upright
Awards:	

MANX QUEEN
Other Name: ISLE OF MAN

A fine golden orange variety which has steadily declined in popularity. Nothing has gone wrong, it is still as remarkably disease-resistant as ever, but *Southampton* is considered brighter and it is this latter variety which has replaced it in the catalogues. *Manx Queen* is a free-flowering Floribunda, bearing its blooms in large open trusses. The leaves are leathery and abundant and the bush is rather taller than average.

Blooms:	20 petals Gold and pink, tipped orange Medium-sized Fragrant
Foliage:	Dark green Semi-glossy
Health:	Good disease resistance
Growth:	Vigorous Bushy
Awards:	

MARGARET MERRIL

Floribunda— H.T. type

Other Name: HARKULY

At last, a rose to challenge *Iceberg* for the white Floribunda crown. It does not have the height nor the abundance of flowers associated with *Iceberg*, but it beats its famous rival in two important ways — flower form and scent. The pearly flowers are high-centred beauties borne in small trusses, and the fragrance is considered by some to be the sweetest of any modern rose. The blooms do not stand up to rain like *Iceberg*, but health is generally better.

Blooms:	28 petals Pearly white Medium-sized Very fragrant
Foliage:	Dark green Glossy
Health:	Good disease resistance
Growth:	Very vigorous Bushy
Awards:	

MARLENA

A popular and reliable dwarf Floribunda, sometimes described as the ideal edging rose. Its bushy and compact growth habit and the profusion of its rich red flowers make it an excellent choice for ground cover or the front of the bed or border. The blooms are devoid of perfume — always unfortunate but perhaps less of a drawback for a dwarf than for a tall bush with nose-high blooms. It does have the essential feature of a good ground cover rose — lots of attractive foliage.

Blooms:	18 petals Crimson scarlet Medium-sized No fragrance
Foliage:	Bronze-tinted Glossy
Health:	Good disease resistance
Growth:	Vigorous Branching
Awards:	

Blooms:	15 petals Yellow, changing to pink and red Medium-sized Slightly fragrant
Foliage:	Dark green Glossy
Health:	Average disease resistance
Growth:	Vigorous Branching
Awards:	

MASQUERADE

There is a handful of roses which everybody can name, and *Masquerade* is one of them. This was the first of the multi-coloured varieties, and after 30 years it is still a popular choice for hedging or wherever a larger than average bush is required. The yellow buds quickly turn to salmon pink as they open and eventually to deep red, with each large truss bearing a medley of these colours. Flowering is profuse, but you must dead-head regularly or it will cease.

Blooms:	23 petals Vermilion; white eye; silver reverse Medium-sized Slightly fragrant
Foliage:	Dark green Glossy
Health:	Good disease resistance
Growth:	Vigorous Upright
Awards:	

MATANGI

One of the group of roses bred by McGredy which is described as "hand painted" (see page 5). Well-shaped buds open wide to reveal the unusual red and white coloration, the flowers being borne singly or in small trusses. A definite improvement on its parent *Picasso*, as its blooms appear in great profusion throughout the season and its foliage is glossy. An excellent bedding rose, healthy and rain-resistant, but unsuitable for cutting as it will not last in water.

Blooms:	22 petals Scarlet red Large No fragrance
Foliage:	Dark green Glossy
Health:	Average disease resistance
Growth:	Vigorous Upright
Awards:	

Floribunda—H.T. type

MEGIDDO

The sole claim to fame for this English-bred rose is the dazzling effect of its flowers in bright sunlight. Luminous red with a deeper reverse, the blooms are large and nicely formed. Borne in well-spaced trusses, the effect of a group of bushes can be quite spectacular when well grown. Continuity of flowering is good, but there are no other special virtues. Disease resistance is only average, there is no noticeable perfume and the blooms are only moderately full.

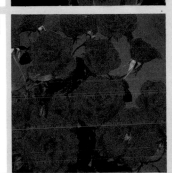

Blooms:	23 petals Salmon vermilion Medium-sized Slightly fragrant
Foliage:	Medium green Glossy
Health:	Average disease resistance
Growth:	Vigorous Upright
Awards:	

MEMENTO
Other Name: DICBAR

A welcome addition to the light red range, *Memento* provides a compact bush of average height which is densely clothed with glossy leaves. The number of flowers is quite remarkable, and the trusses continue to appear throughout the season. The clusters are large, bearing flat medium-sized flowers which have only a trace of perfume. Resistance to rain is outstanding, and disease resistance is reasonable. A good choice for bedding and cutting.

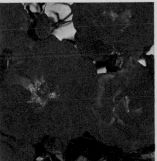

Blooms:	40 petals Orange scarlet Medium-sized No fragrance
Foliage:	Medium green Semi-glossy
Health:	Good disease resistance
Growth:	Moderately vigorous Bushy
Awards:	

METEOR
Other Name: GERTRUD WESTPHAL

Meteor was introduced more than 20 years ago, and with its full blooms and neat growth habit it became the first dwarf Floribunda to appear in the best-seller lists. Many other dwarf Floribundas have been launched since then, but *Meteor* remains one of the best. Free-flowering, extremely long flowering season, abundant foliage and good resistance to disease are its main virtues. The secret of success is to feed regularly with a good rose fertilizer.

FLORIBUNDA ROSES

Height in

MOLLY McGREDY

Floribunda—
H.T. type

If bi-colours with a distinct colour contrast appeal to you and if you like Hybrid Tea-type blooms on a Floribunda, then *Molly McGredy* is just the rose for you. The pointed flowers are borne in small or medium-sized clusters, and the colour of the blooms does not fade in strong sunlight. This bedding and exhibition variety is free-flowering and can be very effective in the garden, but be warned that some people find the colour combination distinctly unattractive.

Blooms: 35 petals
Cherry red; silver reverse
Medium-sized
No fragrance

Foliage: Dark green
Glossy

Health: Good disease resistance

Growth: Vigorous
Branching

Awards:

MOON MAIDEN

The buff-shaded yellow tones of *Moon Maiden* mix well with other roses, and the very full blooms may reach up to 4 in. across. The bush is usually rather open with a spreading growth habit, and small trusses appear in large numbers until the frosts arrive. *Moon Maiden* has won no major British awards and it has never been really popular. The perfume, despite the claims in some catalogues, is faint and the delicate colouring has neither the brilliance nor the novelty which popular taste often demands.

Blooms: 50 petals
Creamy yellow
Medium-sized
Slightly fragrant

Foliage: Dark green
Semi-glossy

Health: Good disease resistance

Growth: Vigorous
Branching

Awards:

NEWS

Perhaps "wine red" could have been a more flattering description of the unique colouring of *News*, rather than its official listing as "beetroot purple". The red buds open into large flat flowers, revealing showy golden stamens, and the petals of the mature blooms turn deep purple with age. The flowering season is an extremely long one and *News* is an attractive bedding Floribunda, especially when planted close to a cream or golden variety. Keep watch for rust and black spot.

Blooms: 18 petals
Beetroot purple
Large
Slightly fragrant

Foliage: Medium green
Matt

Health: Average disease resistance

Growth: Vigorous
Bushy

Awards:

OLD MASTER

A McGredy rose which belongs to the "hand painted" group (see page 5). The flowers are large and the bush is vigorous and healthy, but *Old Master* has failed to achieve the popular acclaim which has been accorded to some other successors to *Picasso*, the original "hand painted" variety. The foliage of *Old Master* is dark and glossy, but the effect of the red and white blends in the blooms of *Old Master* are usually less striking than the colours found in its more popular relatives.

Blooms: 18 petals
Carmine; white eye; silver reverse
Large
Slightly fragrant

Foliage: Dark green
Glossy

Health: Good disease resistance

Growth: Vigorous
Bushy

Awards:

ORANGE SENSATION

If carroty vermilion appeals to you, then choose *Orange Sensation* or *Orangeade*. There are many reasons why your choice should be *Orange Sensation* — the colour is vivid, the petals are more numerous and the perfume is strong and sweet. The spreading growth habit means that wide spacing between plants is acceptable, and the trusses are sometimes extremely large. The drawbacks are duller foliage and a rather later start to the flowering season — like *Orangeade* both black spot and mildew can be problems.

Blooms: 24 petals
Light vermilion; gold at base
Medium-sized
Fragrant

Foliage: Light green
Matt

Health: Prone to disease

Growth: Vigorous
Branching

Awards:

FLORIBUNDA ROSES

Blooms:	10 petals Light vermilion Medium-sized Slightly fragrant
Foliage:	Dark green Semi-glossy
Health:	Prone to disease
Growth:	Vigorous Branching
Awards:	RNRS RHS

ORANGEADE

Like *Orange Sensation*, this light vermilion rose was introduced over 20 years ago and is still popular for bedding where a splash of bright colour is required. The trusses are large and are borne very freely, the open blooms darkening with age. One of the secrets of success is to dead-head regularly, or flowering may cease quite quickly. Rain resistance is excellent, but the susceptibility of *Orangeade* to black spot, mildew and rust is a problem.

Blooms:	35 petals Deep rose pink Large Slightly fragrant
Foliage:	Dark green Semi-glossy
Health:	Prone to disease
Growth:	Moderately vigorous Branching
Awards:	RNRS RHS

PADDY McGREDY

Floribunda—H.T. type

A low-growing Floribunda with a difference — each individual flower is as large and as well-formed as an average Hybrid Tea. Flower shape is not the only virtue of *Paddy McGredy* — a well-fed and healthy bush will bear enough blooms in the first flush to cover nearly all of the foliage. Unfortunately there is usually a delay before the next flush, and this variety does have its share of faults. Rain resistance is not good, the colour fades in hot sun and there is little resistance to the common diseases.

Blooms:	10 petals Geranium red Medium-sized Slightly fragrant
Foliage:	Dark green Glossy
Health:	Good disease resistance
Growth:	Vigorous Branching
Awards:	RNRS RHS H

PAPRIKA

A thoroughly reliable and attractive red Floribunda. Its list of virtues is most impressive — beautiful healthy foliage, excellent freedom of flowering, rain-resistant blooms and large trusses. Yet despite its virtues and high awards you will have to search for a supplier because it has failed to capture public interest. The reason is probably the shortage of petals — flat blooms with just a few petals, a single colour and little or no fragrance find it difficult to reach the best-seller list.

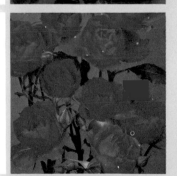

Blooms:	22 petals Salmon pink Medium-sized Fragrant
Foliage:	Medium green Semi-glossy
Health:	Good disease resistance
Growth:	Vigorous Branching
Awards:	RNRS

PERNILLE POULSEN

The first flush of flowers on *Pernille Poulsen* is a welcome sight. It appears a week or two before other Floribundas start to bloom, and the number of pink, sweet-smelling flowers is remarkable. Unfortunately there is often a delay before the second flush appears. The flowers are borne in large clusters and the petals fade with age. Disease resistance is good, but the popularity of this useful bedding rose has continued to decline.

Blooms:	25 petals Deep pink, blotched red; silver reverse Medium-sized No fragrance
Foliage:	Medium green Matt
Health:	Average disease resistance
Growth:	Vigorous Bushy
Awards:	RNRS B

PICASSO

The first of the "hand painted" roses — pink on a white background with irregular splashes of cherry red. The shades and intensity vary with the time of the year and the age of the bloom. The stems are slender and light pruning is recommended. The flowers are produced over a long season, but many people feel the newer roses of the *Picasso* type are a better choice. These recent ones have glossier foliage, more flowers and the blooms, as in *Priscilla Burton*, may be larger and more attractively coloured.

Height in

PINEAPPLE POLL

Pretty *Pineapple Poll*, low-growing but very showy, is listed by only a few growers. Its lack of popularity may be surprising from its photograph — full of petals and as colourful as anyone could ask for. The compact and bushy growth habit makes it a good choice for the front of the border, and the buds and young flowers are suitable for cutting. The spicy scent is strong for a Floribunda, but there are drawbacks — growth is not robust and black spot can be a menace.

Blooms:	30 petals Orange yellow, flushed red Medium-sized Fragrant
Foliage:	Medium green Glossy
Health:	Prone to disease
Growth:	Moderately vigorous Bushy
Awards:	

PINK PARFAIT

Floribunda—H.T. type

Pinks and creams blend in variable amounts in this delightful American-bred Floribunda. A great favourite found in many catalogues, there seems to be little agreement on the height you can expect it to grow. However, all the books agree that it is an excellent choice for the bed or border, or grown lightly pruned as a specimen bush. Flowering is extremely prolific and it is one of the best of all Floribundas for cutting. The shapely blooms resist rain, and the stems are slender and almost thornless.

Blooms:	22 petals Pink; cream at base Medium-sized No fragrance
Foliage:	Medium green Semi-glossy
Health:	Good disease resistance
Growth:	Vigorous Branching
Awards:	

PRISCILLA BURTON
Other Name: MACRAT

One of the first "hand painted" roses (see page 5) to receive top honours in Britain, *Priscilla Burton* is generally regarded as a great step forward compared to *Picasso,* the original "hand painted" variety. The buds are attractive, and the blooms are large and beautifully coloured. The foliage is dark, shiny and healthy, although spraying against black spot is advisable. Continuity of flowers is very good, but rain resistance is inferior to *Picasso*.

Blooms:	15 petals Deep carmine; white eye Large Slightly fragrant
Foliage:	Dark green Glossy
Health:	Good disease resistance
Growth:	Vigorous Upright
Awards:	

QUEEN ELIZABETH

Floribunda—H.T. type

An American-bred rose named in the 1950s after Britain's young monarch, *Queen Elizabeth* has become one of the world's great roses. It will grow almost anywhere, but your garden might not be the right place. It is definitely not suitable for a small bed, as it grows 5 ft or more. Plant it as a specimen shrub or as a hedge; best of all put it at the back of the border with lower-growing roses in front to screen the bare stems. Fine foliage, lovely blooms, excellent keeping qualities in water — an outstanding rose.

Blooms:	35 petals Light pink Large Slightly fragrant
Foliage:	Dark green Glossy
Health:	Good disease resistance
Growth:	Very vigorous Upright
Awards:	

REDGOLD

Floribunda—H.T. type

The name of this Floribunda aptly describes the young flowers — red on the petal edges and gold on the inside. The colours fade and merge with age and the mature blooms are an overall pale orange. *Redgold* is a reliable variety which has attractive red-tinted young foliage as well as gay flowers, making it a useful rose for bedding. It is also a good exhibition variety as the flowers are exceptionally long-lasting. Flowering is generally prolific and the blooms have good rain resistance.

Blooms:	25 petals Golden yellow, edged cherry red Medium-sized Slightly fragrant
Foliage:	Medium green Semi-glossy
Health:	Average disease resistance
Growth:	Vigorous Upright
Awards:	

FLORIBUNDA ROSES

Blooms:	22 petals Scarlet crimson Large Slightly fragrant
Foliage:	Dark green Semi-glossy
Health:	Good disease resistance
Growth:	Vigorous Upright
Awards:	

ROB ROY

It has been claimed that *Rob Roy* has the finest red colour to be found in any rose. The blooms appear freely, and continuity is good. Both cold and wet weather are tolerated, yet this Scottish-bred rose has never become really popular. Perhaps the bush is a little too tall and vigorous — it is better suited to be planted as a hedge or in the border than in an average-sized bed. Perhaps the wide spacing of blooms in the truss is a drawback — whatever the reason for the lack of universal appeal, it is still a fine rose.

Blooms:	35 petals Rosy red Large, rosette-shaped Fragrant
Foliage:	Bronze-tinted Matt
Health:	Prone to disease
Growth:	Vigorous Branching
Awards:	

ROSEMARY ROSE

A post-war rose with an old-fashioned look. The trusses are large and the blooms have been described as camellia-like or zinnia-like. The medium-sized bush has a rather spreading growth habit, with leaves which are remarkably different. They are bronze red, similar in shade to the foliage of a copper beech. A lovely Floribunda if you like red foliage and 19th century flowers, but *Rosemary Rose* is not usually recommended these days because it is so prone to infection by mildew, black spot and rust.

Blooms:	10 petals Bright scarlet Large No fragrance
Foliage:	Dark green Semi-glossy
Health:	Good disease resistance
Growth:	Vigorous Branching
Awards:	

SARABANDE
Other Name: MEIHAND

A dazzling red rose for the front of the border or along the driveway. Lower than average height, each compact bush bears an abundance of foliage which is almost covered by a succession of blooms from June to November. The trusses are large and the rain resistance is good, but *Sarabande* has never been really popular. It is unfairly damned by its shortage of petals, although the flowers are large with an attractive central cushion of yellow anthers.

Blooms:	25 petals Pale scarlet Medium-sized No fragrance
Foliage:	Dark green Semi-glossy
Health:	Good disease resistance
Growth:	Vigorous Bushy
Awards:	

SATCHMO

An excellent bedding rose in the bright red colour range. It has no unique features; it is just a thoroughly reliable Floribunda free from any serious fault. The blooms do not fade in hot sun nor do they suffer badly in heavy rain. Freedom of flowering is very good and the compact bushes have an attractive shape. It was judged to be the best Floribunda of the year at The Hague in 1970, but *Satchmo* has never received a fraction of the acclaim given to its illustrious parent *Evelyn Fison*.

Blooms:	25 petals Orange scarlet Medium-sized, globular Slightly fragrant
Foliage:	Dark green Semi-glossy
Health:	Good disease resistance
Growth:	Vigorous Upright
Awards:	

SCARLET QUEEN ELIZABETH

A tall red-flowering Floribunda which is used for hedging or as a specimen shrub. It is available from most nurserymen, but its popularity is no doubt due to its famous name rather than its beauty. Unlike the blooms of its pink parent, the flowers of *Scarlet Queen Elizabeth* are loose and open, and appear later in the season than most other Floribundas. Flowering is not particularly free and the blooms are often hidden by the foliage. Not a great rose, but health and weather resistance are good.

FLORIBUNDA ROSES

SCENTED AIR

As you would expect from its name, fragrance is the outstanding quality of this pink Floribunda. The perfume is rich and fruity, and the flowers are large and usually plentiful. At first the blooms are shapely but they quickly become open and loose. The foliage is a notable feature — large glossy leaves which are much healthier than the average Floribunda. A good and reliable bedding rose for the larger bed, but its colour and flower form are nothing special.

Blooms:	20 petals Deep salmon pink Large Very fragrant
Foliage:	Dark green Glossy
Health:	Good disease resistance
Growth:	Vigorous Upright
Awards:	

SCHERZO
Other Name: MEIPUMA

A good rose for the bi-colour enthusiast — bright red and white with a sweet scent as a bonus. The growth habit is rather open and spreading, with a large number of flowers appearing throughout the season. The trusses are usually large, and the young flowers have an excellent form. At this stage they are suitable for the show-bench, but this H.T. shape is soon lost as the blooms mature. This rose of the mid 1970s has a high reputation for reliability.

Blooms:	35 petals Scarlet; silver reverse Medium-sized Fragrant
Foliage:	Medium green Semi-glossy
Health:	Good disease resistance
Growth:	Vigorous Bushy
Awards:	

SEA PEARL

Floribunda — H.T. type

Other Name: FLOWER GIRL

The young flowers of *Sea Pearl* have the classic shape and beauty of a well-formed H.T. bloom. These flowers lose their pointed shape as they mature and their colour is variable. The blends of pink, peach and yellow can be most attractive, especially in autumn, and flowers are generally plentiful. But there are faults — there is a short pause between flushes and flowers can be spotted by heavy rain. Plant as an eye-catching group of 2 or 3, not as a massed bed.

Blooms:	25 petals Pink; yellow reverse Large Slightly fragrant
Foliage:	Medium green Glossy
Health:	Good disease resistance
Growth:	Vigorous Upright
Awards:	

SOUTHAMPTON

Introduced in 1971, *Southampton* has become one of the leading Floribundas. It combines the marmalade colour beloved by flower arrangers with the robust good health desired by all gardeners. The slightly ruffled blooms are borne singly at the start of the season, but more usually they occur in medium-sized trusses. Growth is taller than average, so use *Southampton* for the large bed, border or hedge. Although the form of the bush is distinctly upright the effect is not gaunt as side shoots are plentiful.

Blooms:	25 petals Apricot orange, flushed scarlet Large Slightly fragrant
Foliage:	Dark green Semi-glossy
Health:	Good disease resistance
Growth:	Very vigorous Upright
Awards:	

STARGAZER

A dwarf rose, covered with bright single flowers — not an age-old wild variety but a Harkness hybrid introduced in 1977. It certainly looks quite different to the usual Floribunda, and it is quite at home in a tub on the terrace or at the front of the shrub border. Not popular — you wouldn't expect a single rose to be in the best-seller list — but worth growing if you like roses with a difference. Remember to dead-head regularly, and keep well-fed with a rose fertilizer.

Blooms:	5 petals Orange scarlet; golden eye Medium-sized Slightly fragrant
Foliage:	Medium green Matt
Health:	Good disease resistance
Growth:	Vigorous Bushy
Awards:	

SUNSILK

Floribunda—
H.T. type

A Hybrid Tea, according to some experts. A Floribunda, according to others, including the man who raised it. *Sunsilk* is indeed a borderline variety, with large blooms which have a distinct H.T. shape when young and are often borne singly. Classification, however, is not the gardener's worry and *Sunsilk* is a fine bedding and cutting rose. The colour can fade in hot sun, but in autumn the number and quality of the flowers are excellent. Not a good choice where rust is a problem.

Blooms: 35 petals
Lemon yellow
Large
Slightly fragrant

Foliage: Medium green
Semi-glossy

Health: Average disease resistance

Growth: Vigorous
Upright

Awards: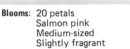

TIP TOP

Dwarf Floribundas have an important place in the garden — they can fill a small bed or edge a border or pathway. When a pink variety is required, the usual choice is *Tip Top*. It blooms over a long season, and the continuity is excellent. The large trusses seem to appear in profusion whatever the weather and the fragrance, although not strong, is sweet and "old-fashioned". Disease is the only problem — susceptibility to mildew is average but black spot can be a menace.

Blooms: 20 petals
Salmon pink
Medium-sized
Slightly fragrant

Foliage: Medium green
Matt

Health: Prone to disease

Growth: Vigorous
Bushy

Awards:

TOPSI

Another dwarf Floribunda for planting in a tub or at the front of the bed, and it is one to choose if you want a really brilliant display. It won the British supreme award in 1972 — its foliage is large and attractive, the period of flowering and the rapid repeat between flushes are outstanding and rain resistance is good. The glowing orange red of the petals does not fade, and only its health stops it being an ideal dwarf Floribunda. It is prone to black spot, and die-back can be a problem.

Blooms: 12 petals
Bright vermilion
Medium-sized
No fragrance

Foliage: Medium green
Semi-glossy

Health: Prone to disease

Growth: Vigorous
Bushy

Awards:

TRUMPETER
Other Name: MACTRU

One of the newer bright red Floribundas, low-growing and compact. Introduced in 1978, *Trumpeter* has already earned a high reputation as a front-of-the-border bedding rose which has almost unequalled disease resistance amongst roses in this group. There are plenty of flowers, and the trusses appear almost continually. Another advantage is the large number of flowers in each truss, but this is a fault in rainy weather as the heads may bow down when wet.

Blooms: 35 petals
Bright vermilion
Medium-sized
Slightly fragrant

Foliage: Dark green
Glossy

Health: Good disease resistance

Growth: Vigorous
Bushy

Awards:

VIOLET CARSON

Floribunda—
H.T. type

Violet Carson is often described as a rose of refinement. The delicate and unusual colouring could never have the universal appeal of a vibrant red or a glowing yellow, but it is a good choice where pastel shades are required. The vigorous spreading bush has attractive foliage, dark and coppery, with beautiful buds of H.T. form which open slowly into fully double blooms. The scent is pleasant, although it is faint, and some fading takes place in sunny weather. A reliable rose for bedding.

Blooms: 35 petals
Peach pink; paler reverse
Medium-sized
Slightly fragrant

Foliage: Bronze-tinted
Semi-glossy

Health: Good disease resistance

Growth: Vigorous
Branching

Awards:

FLORIBUNDA ROSES

WARRIOR

There are many fine dwarf Floribundas these days, but even in such distinguished company this new red variety has attracted considerable attention. The colour is bright and unfading, and the flowering season is exceptionally long. The leaves are rather pale and not particularly attractive, but the growth habit is bushy and compact, making *Warrior* a good subject for the front of the border. No health problems have arisen, and it performed well in the British Association of Rose Breeders' trials.

Blooms:	30 petals Scarlet Medium-sized Slightly fragrant
Foliage:	Light green Semi-glossy
Health:	Good disease resistance
Growth:	Vigorous Branching
Awards:	

WOBURN ABBEY

A popular and long-established orange Floribunda, taller than average and pleasantly perfumed. The colour and not the beauty of the blooms is the reason for the popularity of *Woburn Abbey*, as the flowers are rather untidy and appear crowded in the trusses. Lack of good flower shape is not the major drawback—disease is a more important problem. Mildew, black spot and rust can all be serious, and regular spraying is needed if you grow this variety.

Blooms:	25 petals Coppery orange, shaded gold Medium-sized Fragrant
Foliage:	Dark green Semi-glossy
Health:	Prone to disease
Growth:	Vigorous Branching
Awards:	

YELLOW QUEEN ELIZABETH

Floribunda—H.T. type

The idea of having the much-loved *Queen Elizabeth* with rich yellow flowers instead of the standard pink is appealing. Unfortunately this sport of *Queen Elizabeth* does not live up to the promise — the flowers are a dull yellow, without the substance of its illustrious parent. Some of the vigour is missing, and it is not as tall-growing. Many of the good points remain — health, attractive foliage and long-lasting as a cut flower. A useful hedging variety.

Blooms:	30 petals Pale straw yellow Large Slightly fragrant
Foliage:	Dark green Glossy
Health:	Good disease resistance
Growth:	Vigorous Upright
Awards:	

YESTERDAY

Other Name: TAPIS D'ORIENT

A clever name — *Yesterday* is a modern Floribunda with a distinctly Victorian appearance. In some catalogues you will find it in the Shrub section rather than with the Floribundas. The spreading bush has long graceful shoots, and the flower trusses are borne throughout the season. Each truss bears dozens of sweet-smelling small blooms which are excellent as cut flowers. Grow it as a low hedge or lightly prune and treat as a specimen Shrub.

Blooms:	13 petals Mauve pink; silver eye Small Fragrant
Foliage:	Medium green Glossy
Health:	Good disease resistance
Growth:	Moderately vigorous Bushy
Awards:	

ZAMBRA

In 1961 this low-growing bedding rose received Gold Medals on the Continent and a Certificate of Merit in Britain. Its colouring was unique among Floribundas, and *Zambra* is still admired when seen in full flower. But it is not an ideal garden plant — it is particularly prone to black spot and should be avoided in gardens where this disease is a problem. The flowers are smaller than average and soon open flat. The trusses may be medium-sized or large, and the freedom of flowering is good.

Blooms:	15 petals Orange; buttercup yellow reverse Medium-sized Slightly fragrant
Foliage:	Medium green Glossy
Health:	Prone to disease
Growth:	Moderately vigorous Branching
Awards:	

MINIATURE ROSES

Miniature Roses are at last becoming popular in Britain, but this slowly-awakening interest for these scaled-down versions of "normal" roses does not begin to match the enthusiasm in the U.S. The rose has for many years been Britain's favourite flower, and it is therefore surprising that we should have lagged behind. Some people believe that the price is to blame — a tiny bush does not seem good value when it costs the same as a Floribunda. Others feel that we don't need Miniatures in the same way — we set out to fill our gardens whereas the Americans have apartments to decorate.

It can't be that simple. A major factor may be the way we raise our plants — in the U.S. they are propagated from cuttings and so grow on their own roots. Such plants are rather slow-growing and can be somewhat tender, but they do remain truly miniature all their lives. In Britain we generally raise our Miniatures as grafted plants on rootstocks — these plants are hardier, more drought-resistant and quicker-growing. Unfortunately, they also tend to be too vigorous and the fairy-like form may be lost. An 18 in. "Miniature" can be disappointing.

Another disappointment has been their failure as reliable house plants. So many people have bought them, put them on the sideboard and expected them to bloom quite

merrily from June to November like their outdoor counterparts. Miniature Roses may not be as easy to grow indoors as some people expect, but they are not as difficult as some experts claim — just follow the rules on page 118.

Miniature Roses most certainly do have a place in our gardening scene. Buy plants in pots — they do not like root disturbance. The best time for planting outdoors is spring or early summer and they will reward you each year by coming into leaf in March, opening their first flowers in May and continuing to bloom until the first frosts arrive.

There is an impressive list of uses. Edging beds and planting in rockeries can both be recommended, but perhaps the most successful use is planting in a raised bed devoted entirely to Miniatures.

The plants you buy will probably be grafted on to a rootstock — you will be able to see the join at the base. If you want to grow Miniatures as pot plants, take cuttings as described on page 115 — the success rate is high and the resulting plants will remain compact and dwarf.

Maintenance is straight-forward, but not quite as easy as some books suggest. Pruning (page 92) is no problem, but you must keep a careful watch for pests and diseases. The major nuisances are mildew, black spot, die-back and greenfly. Don't forget to water in dry weather — they don't have the root system of their big sisters. Feeding is necessary — use a liquid fertilizer on a little-and-often basis for Miniatures in pots.

The history of Miniatures is as fascinating as the plants themselves. They were popular pot plants in Victorian times — *Pompon de Paris* was a well-known variety. Then they went out of fashion and disappeared at the end of the 19th century, apparently lost for ever. In 1918 Major Roulet saw a tiny rose growing in a pot in Switzerland — this survivor became *R. roulettii* and the modern Miniature story began — hybridists have given us the wide choice available today.

And the story goes on. A new race has appeared — the Micro-Roses which grow only 4 in. tall. There are also new colours and new shapes —— and a new interest in these fascinating plants.

ANGELA RIPPON
Other Name: OCARU

A new star, bred in Holland and introduced in 1978. It has been acclaimed by some experts — growth is compact and bushy, reaching about 12 in. in height. The double blooms are pale carmine pink, freely borne amongst the healthy foliage. The blooms are quite fragrant.

BABY DARLING

A variety from the United States, where it is rated as 'excellent' by the American Rose Society. The pointed buds open into double flowers which are a blend of orange and pink. There is no fragrance, and the blooms are borne amongst the dark glossy foliage. Growth is bushy and the height is about 12 in.

BABY FAURAX

Really a Dwarf Polyantha (see page 78) but this tiny bush is usually listed as a Miniature in the catalogues. The 12 in. bush is not particularly attractive, but the clusters of very small and fragrant blooms are eye-catching. These flowers are pale violet — as close to a blue rose as you'll find.

BABY GOLD STAR

An unpredictable rose, growing to 1½ ft when grafted on a stock or reaching less than 1 ft when grown on its own roots. The leaves may stay healthy or be covered in black spot — the stems may be numerous or very sparse. Even the slightly fragrant blooms are changeable — fading from golden yellow to cream.

BABY MASQUERADE

One of the top three Miniatures in many ways — in popularity, ease of cultivation, number of blooms and length of flowering season. It is rather tall and bushy, reaching 15 in. or more. The double and slightly fragrant blooms change from yellow to pink and finally to rosy red. Dead-head regularly.

CINDERELLA

Tiny flowers crowded with petals, white with touches of pink. A most attractive plant, with abundant shiny foliage and blooms which look like miniature Hybrid Teas. The thornless stems are upright, with the slightly scented flowers being borne in clusters. *Cinderella* needs rather shady conditions.

COLIBRI
Other Name: MEIDANOVER

A free-flowering variety, very bushy and about 10 in. tall. The double blooms are brightly coloured — orange yellow with an edging of vermilion. There is some confusion over naming — the original *Colibri* was introduced in 1958, since then *Colibri 79* has been introduced.

CORALIN

Coralin is one of the many introductions from Pedro Dot, the Spanish hybridist. The orange red flowers are large for a Miniature Rose — many-petalled and attractive but devoid of fragrance. The well-branched bush is abundantly clothed with small bronze-tinted leaves. This variety grows 12—15 in.

DARLING FLAME
Other Name: MINUETTO

Introduced in 1971, this variety has become one of the most popular Miniature Roses in Europe. It has all the requirements for success — beautiful double flowers, rich orange vermilion with a golden reverse, borne in profusion on a healthy bushy plant which reaches 12 in.

EASTER MORNING

Large ivory white flowers set amongst small shiny leaves. The blooms have 60 petals or more, yet resistance to rain as well as to disease is excellent. This American-bred variety is not a profuse bloomer, but it is highly recommended for edging the front of the border. It reaches a height of about 12 in.

ELEANOR

The flowers are small, even for a Miniature Rose. The coral pink blooms, slightly scented and bearing 20—30 petals, darken with age. The small bush has an upright growth habit with medium green leaves, healthy and glossy, and a height of 10—12 in. One of the many Miniatures bred by Moore in the U.S.

GOLDEN ANGEL

A Miniature of the mid 1970s — sweetly fragrant, bright in bloom and spreading in growth habit. Each flower has a Hybrid Tea shape — deep yellow and very full with more than 60 petals. These blooms are long-lasting as cut flowers. *Golden Angel* grows to about 15 in. and is a good choice for edging.

JOSEPHINE WHEATCROFT
Other Name: ROSINA

A lovely bright yellow Miniature, with blooms which are perfectly shaped when young. The fragrance is slight and there are not many petals, but this variety has been a favourite for many years. The trusses appear freely, bearing up to 10 blooms. Height is about 15 in.

JUDY FISCHER

An excellent choice for edging, planting in a rockery or growing indoors as a pot plant. This free-flowering bushy variety reaches 8—10 in., the small double flowers arising from pointed buds. The colour is rose pink, non-fading in strong sunlight. Lack of scent is its only fault.

LAVENDER LACE

A popular Miniature in the United States, but not often seen in Britain. The lavender or mauve flowers are very full, with 55 petals or more, and they are fragrant. The flower trusses are borne freely over a long period — the best of the pale purple Miniatures, although *Lavender Lace* is susceptible to black spot.

LITTLE BUCKAROO

A rather tall-growing variety (15—18 in.), well-suited to the front of the border. It has a spreading growth habit, with shiny bronze-tinted leaves. The blooms are bright red with a white centre, small in size and pleasantly scented. There are about 25 petals. Disease resistance is good.

LITTLE FLIRT

A bi-coloured Miniature Rose, with small *Piccadilly*-like blooms. The petals are orange red with a yellow reverse, and 40—50 are packed into each small fragrant bloom. The bush bears abundant foliage, light green and glossy, and the height is above average — about 15 in. A popular rose for 20 years.

MAGIC CARROUSEL

A striking and unusual Miniature, excellent for indoor decoration and the show-bench. The shapely flowers have white petals, and each petal has a clearly defined red edge. The fragrance is slight and the growth is above average, reaching about 15 in. *Magic Carrousel* is a hardy and reliable variety.

MR BLUEBIRD

Mr Bluebird has its friends, and occasionally you can see why — dark green foliage studded with pale lavender flowers. In most cases it is frankly disappointing — spindly growth, poor colouring and shyness in flowering. If you like pale violet or lavender Miniatures, choose *Lavender Lace* or *Baby Faurax*.

NEW PENNY

Aptly named, with shining leaves and coppery pink flowers. A most attractive Miniature —— ideal for growing as a pot plant. The red buds are freely produced, opening into semi-double blooms which fade with age. There is no fragrance. The plant is well-branched and vigorous, but rarely exceeds 10 in.

PERLA DE ALCANADA
Other Name: BABY CRIMSON

A Spanish name, for this is one of the Miniatures bred by Pedro Dot. The 12 in. bush bears dark glossy foliage and clusters of rosy red blooms. These semi-double flowers open flat, revealing white markings at the base of the petals. A tough and free-flowering variety.

PERLA DE MONTSERRAT

One of the smaller Miniatures — grown since the end of the war but still highly recommended by some experts. It is free-flowering, the clusters of small semi-double blooms appearing regularly over a long period. The petals are clear pink, paling at the edges to pearly pink. Very compact, reaching 9 in.

POUR TOI
Other Name: PARA TI

A favourite Miniature, highly rated for the beauty of its flowers and the attractive nature of the bush. The foliage is glossy and the growth habit short (7–9 in.) and very bushy. The flowers appear profusely, white with a greenish yellow tinge at the base of the petals.

SCARLET GEM

Scarlet Gem has the reputation for being the brightest red Miniature so far. It is a popular pot plant, producing a mass of very full flowers throughout the season. The blooms keep their colour in bright sunlight and the attractive foliage is dark and glossy. Proneness to mildew is its major fault.

STARINA
Other Name: MEIGABI

Starina remains the queen of the Miniature Roses —— well-formed bright vermilion flowers with a golden reverse covering the plant from May until November. It is renowned for its vigour, and can be grown as a pot plant, dwarf bush for bedding or as a miniature standard.

SWEET FAIRY

Apple-blossom pink blooms with a sweet fragrance are the trade mark of this veteran variety. Each small bloom has 60 or more tiny pointed petals, and these flowers are borne amid the small dark leaves. *Sweet Fairy* is a low-growing Miniature, rarely exceeding 8 in. in height. Hardy and reliable.

YELLOW DOLL

A fine soft yellow variety, popular on the show-bench and as a pot plant. The attractive buds are borne singly or in clusters, opening into fragrant blooms crowded with 50 or more narrow petals. The dwarf bush has a spreading growth habit and reaches about 10 in. Keep watch for black spot.

CLIMBERS & RAMBLERS

About a century ago, the standard horticultural text book described climbing roses as the most precious flowers that have ever adorned the garden. No longer true, perhaps, but they are still regarded as indispensable for some purposes. Their main use is, of course, to cover part of the house — occasionally helping to bring the garden indoors by framing a window. Other uses include covering arches, poles, fences, pergolas and old trees.

There is much more to succeeding with this group than simply picking a pretty picture from a catalogue and then planting the specimen. It is an area where there are pitfalls for the unwary and where you can't afford to make a mistake. A wall, fence or pergola which suddenly loses its floral cover can look extremely bare. To ensure an abundance of leaves *and* flowers you must learn to choose wisely and then care for the plants in the proper way.

There are two basic types of climbing rose — Ramblers and Climbers. Ramblers have been around since Victorian times, their long pliable stems bearing huge trusses of small flowers. Growth is very vigorous and they can be a mass of colour in summer, but there is only one flush of flowers. Ramblers are no longer a popular choice — their mildew-prone leaves need regular spraying and pruning can be a tiresome chore. Blooms are borne on new wood, so that each year the old wood should be cut out. If you want to cover a wall or screen, it is usually better to choose a Climber, but Ramblers do have a few special uses. They make splendid weeping standards, and can also be left to trail along the soil as ground cover or to clamber up dead trees as born-again foliage and flowers.

Climbers have much stiffer stems, larger flowers and smaller trusses than Ramblers. Flowers are borne on the framework of mature wood which is more or less permanent, so pruning and maintenance is much easier. As you will see from the A–Z guide (pages 52–60) there are several types — the extremely tough and disease-resistant Kordesii Climbers, which like the Climbing Bourbon and Climbing China Roses are repeat flowering, and the Large-flowered Climbers — the most important group of all.

Of course it is a temptation to buy a Climbing Hybrid Tea — the idea of covering a wall with well-known beautiful blooms is appealing. Unfortunately, the climbing form has usually lost much of the repeat flowering nature of the bush form, and there may be little blossom after the first or second flush.

Don't guess with climbing roses — choose carefully, plant properly and don't expect too much in the first year. Train the stems to stimulate flowering (see page 89) and prune as directed.

KEY TO THE ROSE GUIDES

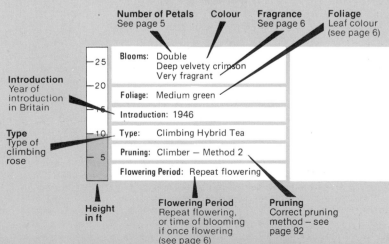

Number of Petals See page 5

Colour

Fragrance See page 6

Foliage Leaf colour (see page 6)

Introduction Year of introduction in Britain

Type Type of climbing rose

Blooms: Double
Deep velvety crimson
Very fragrant

Foliage: Medium green

Introduction: 1946

Type: Climbing Hybrid Tea

Pruning: Climber — Method 2

Flowering Period: Repeat flowering

Height in ft

Flowering Period Repeat flowering, or time of blooming if once flowering (see page 6)

Pruning Correct pruning method – see page 92

Height in

ALBERIC BARBIER

A great old favourite, seen in gardens everywhere. It has a well-deserved reputation for flourishing under poor conditions and in difficult situations when there is little direct sunlight. It blooms profusely in late June or July, the small yellow buds opening into flat creamy white flowers. The foliage is dark and glossy, lasting through most of the winter. Grow it on a pillar rather than on a wall.

Blooms:	Double Cream Fragrant
Foliage:	Dark green
Introduction:	1900
Type:	Rambler
Pruning:	Rambler — Method 2
Flowering Period:	Midsummer

25 —
20 —
15 —
10 —
5 —

ALBERTINE

One of the great names in Rambler Roses — vigorous branching growth which stretches over walls or up old trees and then bursts into bloom in June. The coppery buds open into medium-sized flowers which scent the air, and when not in flower the reddish young foliage keeps the plant attractive. There are difficulties — mildew can be a serious problem and the blooms are often ruined by heavy rain.

Blooms:	Double Pale pink Very fragrant
Foliage:	Dark green
Introduction:	1921
Type:	Rambler
Pruning:	Rambler — Method 2
Flowering Period:	Early summer

25 —
20 —
15 —
10 —
5 —

ALOHA

If you want a pink climber like *Albertine* with more beauty in the flowers but with much less vigour in the stems, then choose *Aloha*. It is recommended for pillars or walls where slow and restricted growth is required — its only fault is that occasionally it remains bushy and fails to climb at all. The foliage is attractive and healthy, the flowers are very full and sweetly scented. The Hybrid Tea-type blooms are resistant to rain.

Blooms:	Double Rose pink Fragrant
Foliage:	Medium green
Introduction:	1949
Type:	Large-flowered Climber
Pruning:	Climber — Method 2
Flowering Period:	Repeat flowering

25 —
20 —
15 —
10 —
5 —

ALTISSIMO

A short climber, sturdy and healthy, with eye-catching blooms. They first appear in June, and the plant stays in flower until autumn. There is no sudden flush of a myriad small flowers — instead there are large blooms here and there on the stems and each one is a thing of beauty. The petals are a rich red and at the centre of each flower is a boss of golden stamens. It is suitable for walls, posts and fences.

Blooms:	Single Blood red Slightly fragrant
Foliage:	Dark green
Introduction:	1967
Type:	Large-flowered Climber
Pruning:	Climber — Method 2
Flowering Period:	Repeat flowering

25 —
20 —
15 —
10 —
5 —

AMERICAN PILLAR

Before the war everyone agreed that *American Pillar* was an excellent choice as a climbing rose, but now the experts are divided. A few feel that its remarkable profusion of flower trusses in late June or July still earn it a place in the garden, but most feel that more modern varieties, such as *Dortmund*, should be used in its place. The faults are serious — there is no resistance to mildew and a good deal of pruning is required.

Blooms:	Single Deep pink; white eye No fragrance
Foliage:	Dark green
Introduction:	1902
Type:	Rambler
Pruning:	Rambler — Method 1
Flowering Period:	Midsummer

25 —
20 —
15 —
10 —
5 —

BANTRY BAY

Bantry Bay can be grown against a wall, as it has good resistance against mildew, but it is usually recommended for clothing a pillar or fence. Don't expect a rampant grower which will quickly cover large areas — its growth habit has been described as "restrained". The shapely buds open into flat pink blooms, which are well-spaced in the truss. These fairly large flowers are borne in profusion throughout the season.

Blooms:	Semi-double Pale rose pink Slightly fragrant
Foliage:	Medium green
Introduction:	1967
Type:	Large-flowered Climber
Pruning:	Climber — Method 2
Flowering Period:	Repeat flowering

25 —
20 —
15 —
10 —
5 —

ht in feet

Blooms:	Double Primrose yellow Slightly fragrant
Foliage:	Dark green
Introduction:	1963
Type:	Large-flowered Climber
Pruning:	Climber — Method 1
Flowering Period:	Repeat flowering

CASINO

The catalogue description will make you want to rush out and buy one — deep yellow buds, Hybrid Tea in shape, opening to produce lovely full flowers which are soft yellow in colour and pleasantly scented. But there is a strong word of caution — *Casino* can be delicate so don't choose it if you live in the colder part of the country or if the planting site is exposed to cold winds.

Blooms:	Double Shell pink Slightly fragrant
Foliage:	Dark green
Introduction:	1894
Type:	Climbing China Rose
Pruning:	Climber — Method 2
Flowering Period:	Repeat flowering

CECILE BRUNNER, CLIMBING

Cécile Brunner is a dainty bush, just 2½ ft x 2½ ft. The climbing sport is a giant, capable of reaching 20 ft x 20 ft. Although technically described as repeat flowering, there is an impressive flush of small pink flowers in June but only sporadic flowering later in the season. The young blooms are beautifully shaped, but there is usually much more leaf than flower in summer. It is a good choice for growing up trees.

Blooms:	Double Pink, shaded apricot Very fragrant
Foliage:	Dark green
Introduction:	1973
Type:	Large-flowered Climber
Pruning:	Climber — Method 2
Flowering Period:	Repeat flowering

COMPASSION

According to many experts, *Compassion* is one of the best of the newer climbing roses. The flowers are beautifully shaped with forty petals, and the apricot pink colouring is unusual in this group. The scent is outstanding and the profusion of flowers is excellent. It produces new shoots freely from the base but it will not cover the side of the house — see it at its best on a pillar or against a white wall.

Blooms:	Double Scarlet Fragrant
Foliage:	Bronze-tinted
Introduction:	1964
Type:	Large-flowered Climber
Pruning:	Climber — Method 2
Flowering Period:	Repeat flowering

COPENHAGEN

Large-flowered Climbers with showy red flowers are not plentiful, so gardeners who want a variety in this colour range and size often choose the Danish-bred *Copenhagen*. They are not disappointed in the flowers — there is a pleasant fragrance and the trusses appear freely. The leaves are healthy and attractive, but there is a problem. As the plant ages the lower leaves often fall, so the stems appear leggy.

Blooms:	Double Deep velvety crimson Very fragrant
Foliage:	Medium green
Introduction:	1946
Type:	Climbing Hybrid Tea
Pruning:	Climber — Method 2
Flowering Period:	Repeat flowering

CRIMSON GLORY, CLIMBING

Once the bush form of *Crimson Glory* was Britain's favourite red rose, but now it has been replaced by many newer reds without its faults. The faults are to be found in the climbing form — flowers which purple with age and leaves which are susceptible to mildew. But *Climbing Crimson Glory* has virtues which are still unmatched — velvety, dark red flowers borne in such profusion that the whole garden is scented.

Blooms:	Double Crimson Slightly fragrant
Foliage:	Light green
Introduction:	1951
Type:	Rambler
Pruning:	Rambler — Method 1
Flowering Period:	Late summer

CRIMSON SHOWER

An excellent choice for people who like Rambler Roses but don't like mildew. It is free-flowering, the small rosette-shaped blooms appearing in large clusters when other Ramblers have passed their flowering season. From late July until early September the red flowers will clothe trellises, arches or pillars. *Crimson Shower* makes an excellent weeping standard. The fragrance is very faint.

Height in f

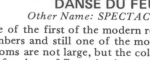

DANSE DU FEU
Other Name: SPECTACULAR

One of the first of the modern repeat flowering climbers and still one of the most popular. The blooms are not large, but the colour is vivid and the freedom of flowering is outstanding. Trusses appear until well into the autumn and this variety is well-known for its ability to bloom in its first season. Its major fault is also well known — the flowers turn purple with age.

Blooms:	Double Orange scarlet No fragrance
Foliage:	Bronze-tinted
Introduction:	1954
Type:	Large-flowered Climber
Pruning:	Climber — Method 2
Flowering Period:	Repeat flowering

DOROTHY PERKINS

Eighty years after its introduction you will still find the most famous name amongst Rambler Roses in some catalogues. Grow it for sentimental reasons, but it is no longer a good choice for garden display. It is extremely prone to mildew, making it unsuitable for growing against a wall. The small flowers appear in large clusters in late July, and the best use for *Dorothy Perkins* is to screen an open fence or arch.

Blooms:	Double Rose pink No fragrance
Foliage:	Medium green
Introduction:	1901
Type:	Rambler
Pruning:	Rambler — Method 1
Flowering Period:	Late summer

DORTMUND

A healthy and hardy rose, which is excellent for covering a pillar or it can be kept pruned as a large specimen bush. The big flowers have five petals, white-centred with a boss of yellow stamens. The trusses appear throughout the summer and autumn, but dead flowers should be removed or the flowering season will be shortened. The foliage is glossy and abundant, but the flowers have no noticeable scent.

Blooms:	Single Red; white eye No fragrance
Foliage:	Dark green
Introduction:	1955
Type:	Kordesii Climber
Pruning:	Climber — Method 2
Flowering Period:	Repeat flowering

DUBLIN BAY

You will find this McGredy-bred rose in most catalogues, where you can read about its virtues — rich red and beautifully formed flowers borne profusely on healthy stems which are clothed with abundant glossy foliage. Unfortunately it has a drawback — at first its growth habit is inclined to be bush-like, and on some occasions it remains as an upright bush instead of a vigorous Large-flowered Climber.

Blooms:	Double Deep red Slightly fragrant
Foliage:	Dark green
Introduction:	1976
Type:	Large-flowered Climber
Pruning:	Climber — Method 2
Flowering Period:	Repeat flowering

EMILY GRAY

An old favourite, with two outstanding reasons for keeping its place in the catalogues. The flowers, with their unique chamois-leather colouring and the foliage, red at first and then dark and glossy when mature. These leaves are almost evergreen — a great advantage when it is used to clothe a wall or screen. *Emily Gray* is a reasonably healthy rose, but it is not free-flowering. The secret is to prune very lightly.

Blooms:	Double Buff yellow Fragrant
Foliage:	Dark green
Introduction:	1918
Type:	Rambler
Pruning:	Rambler — Method 3
Flowering Period:	Midsummer

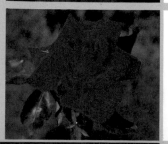

ENA HARKNESS, CLIMBING

The drooping nature of the blooms, a disadvantage in the bush form of *Ena Harkness*, becomes a positive virtue in the climbing form. All the advantages of this old but much-loved Hybrid Tea are there — beauty of colour, form and fragrance. It flowers freely in summer but the autumn display may be disappointing. Plant it against a south-facing wall and enjoy the blooms in May.

Blooms:	Double Crimson scarlet Very fragrant
Foliage:	Medium green
Introduction:	1954
Type:	Climbing Hybrid Tea
Pruning:	Climber — Method 1
Flowering Period:	Repeat flowering

Blooms:	Double Deep red Very fragrant
Foliage:	Dark green
Introduction:	1931
Type:	Climbing Hybrid Tea
Pruning:	Climber — Method 1
Flowering Period:	Repeat flowering

ETOILE DE HOLLANDE, CLIMBING

The bush form of *Etoile de Hollande* was the Queen of the Reds between the wars, and its climbing sport still remains popular. In fact, it is often recommended as the best of all climbing red roses for clothing the wall of a house. There the hanging flowers, velvety red and richly fragrant, can be enjoyed to the full. The summer flush of flowers is impressive, but the quantity of autumn flowering is unpredictable.

Blooms:	Double Rosy crimson; white centre No fragrance
Foliage:	Medium green
Introduction:	1909
Type:	Rambler
Pruning:	Rambler — Method 1
Flowering Period:	Midsummer

EXCELSA
Other Name: RED DOROTHY PERKINS

The red Rambler of yesteryear — its place has now been taken by the much healthier *Crimson Shower*. But *Excelsa* still keeps its place in many catalogues as it makes an excellent weeping standard. When grown in this way or on an arch or pillar it is festooned with small globular flowers, white-centred with crimson petals, during July. It is a rampant grower.

Blooms:	Double Ivory, flecked red Slightly fragrant
Foliage:	Dark green
Introduction:	1827
Type:	Rambler
Pruning:	Rambler — Method 3
Flowering Period:	Midsummer

FELICITE ET PERPETUE

An antique Rambler — age-old specimens still cover cottage walls and new plants can still be bought from rose growers. The vigour remains — it can reach the roof of a two-storey house and the glossy leaves stay on the stems nearly all winter long. In July the rosette-shaped blooms appear, many-petalled but capable of standing up to rainy weather. The secret of success is to prune very lightly.

Blooms:	Double Pale pink Fragrant
Foliage:	Bronze-tinted
Introduction:	1906
Type:	Rambler
Pruning:	Rambler — Method 1
Flowering Period:	Early summer

FRANCOIS JURANVILLE

This old Rambler remains an excellent choice to cover a large structure such as a pergola or large screen. It is a very vigorous grower, reaching 20 ft or more. The flowers are large for a Rambler Rose, and have a heavy old-world fragrance. They appear in late June, at first deep salmon pink but soon fading to pale pink. The long flexible stems have few thorns and the leaves are small and shiny.

Blooms:	Double Pink Slightly fragrant
Foliage:	Medium green
Introduction:	1966
Type:	Large-flowered Climber
Pruning:	Climber — Method 2
Flowering Period:	Repeat flowering

GALWAY BAY

This offspring of *Queen Elizabeth* has the properties you would expect in a modern pillar rose — restrained growth reaching about 8 ft high and leaves with good disease resistance. Although there is nothing special about the growth habit of *Galway Bay*, the flowers are noteworthy. They are large, well-formed and borne in remarkable profusion. The small clusters appear regularly during the summer and autumn.

Blooms:	Double Buff yellow Fragrant
Foliage:	Medium green
Introduction:	1853
Type:	Noisette Climber
Pruning:	Climber — Method 2
Flowering Period:	Repeat flowering

GLOIRE DE DIJON

Victorian rose experts wrote about the great beauty of this old climbing rose, and you can see why if you look at a mature and vigorous plant in June. The flowers are large, strikingly coloured and sweetly scented. Having started early in the season, flowering continues until the autumn. Recommended for walls, but watch out for mildew. Many modern stocks have deteriorated, so buy from a reputable supplier.

CLIMBERS & RAMBLERS

Height in feet

GOLDEN SHOWERS

By far the most popular yellow climbing rose — you can buy it anywhere. There are several reasons for its universal appeal — resistance to rain, bright flowers and foliage, and above all the prolonged flowering season from June until the frosts arrive. It is excellent for a small garden as it is easily kept in check. It has faults — the blooms soon become loose and growth at first is bushy rather than climbing.

Blooms:	Double Golden yellow Fragrant
Foliage:	Dark green
Introduction:	1956
Type:	Large-flowered Climber
Pruning:	Climber — Method 2
Flowering Period:	Repeat flowering

GUINEE

You will love or hate this blackest of all garden roses. Velvety deep red, the blooms may look dull on a cloudy day but can glow in full sunshine. These flowers are large, opening flat and emitting a strong perfume. Very free-flowering in June, but the later flushes are disappointing. Foliage is leathery and plentiful, but you must watch for mildew. A good variety for walls and screens.

Blooms:	Double Very dark red, shaded black Very fragrant
Foliage:	Medium green
Introduction:	1938
Type:	Large-flowered Climber
Pruning:	Climber — Method 2
Flowering Period:	Repeat flowering

HAMBURGER PHOENIX

An attractive rose with an unattractive name. The foliage is healthy and glossy, the flowers are large and unfading. The first blooms open in June — dead-head regularly to ensure continuity until autumn. Hardiness is a feature of the Kordesii Hybrids, so *Hamburger Phoenix* is a good choice for a north- or east-facing wall, even in northern counties. The fragrance is unfortunately very faint.

Blooms:	Semi-double Dark red Slightly fragrant
Foliage:	Medium green
Introduction:	1954
Type:	Kordesii Climber
Pruning:	Climber — Method 2
Flowering Period:	Repeat flowering

HANDEL

Handel is a star of the climbing rose world. The secret of its appeal lies in the unique colouring of its blooms, for it has no other unusual feature. The flowers are nicely shaped, but are rather short of petals. The stems are relatively thornless and the leaves are glossy, but mildew and black spot can be problems. The flowers are borne singly or in clusters over a long period, and are not spoilt by rain.

Blooms:	Double Cream, edged rosy pink Slightly fragrant
Foliage:	Bronze-tinted
Introduction:	1965
Type:	Large-flowered Climber
Pruning:	Climber — Method 2
Flowering Period:	Repeat flowering

ICEBERG, CLIMBING

This sport of the most successful white Floribunda of our time has not become really popular. Surprising, perhaps, because it has many admirers and is regarded as one of the most reliable climbing sports of recent years. It will clothe a wall with abundant glossy foliage studded with large trusses of flat white blooms, and this display continues until the autumn. Spraying against mildew may be necessary.

Blooms:	Double White Slightly fragrant
Foliage:	Medium green
Introduction:	1968
Type:	Climbing Floribunda
Pruning:	Climber — Method 2
Flowering Period:	Repeat flowering

LEVERKUSEN

As you would expect from a Kordesii Climber, the leaves are healthy and the flowers appear freely. Even on an exposed site or in one of the colder areas of the country *Leverkusen* can be relied upon to provide an attractive display on a pillar or wall. Large clusters of blooms appear in June and further flushes follow — the autumn show is outstanding for a rose in this German-bred group.

Blooms:	Semi-double Pale yellow Slightly fragrant
Foliage:	Medium green
Introduction:	1954
Type:	Kordesii Climber
Pruning:	Climber — Method 2
Flowering Period:	Repeat flowering

Blooms:	Semi-double Bronze yellow Fragrant
Foliage:	Medium green
Introduction:	1953
Type:	Large-flowered Climber
Pruning:	Climber — Method 2
Flowering Period:	Early summer

MAIGOLD

Maigold has many virtues, and it is not surprising to find it in the best-seller lists of climbing roses. It comes to flower in May, when roses are so welcome. It also blooms early in the life of the plant — a problem with many climbers. The foliage is healthy and attractive, and the fragrance is strong. There are drawbacks — the stems are thorny, the blooms are unshapely and flowering after the first flush is unlikely.

Blooms:	Semi-double Yellow, then pink and red Slightly fragrant
Foliage:	Dark green
Introduction:	1958
Type:	Climbing Floribunda
Pruning:	Climber — Method 2
Flowering Period:	Repeat flowering

MASQUERADE, CLIMBING

The visual effect of large trusses bearing yellow, pink and deep red flowers is even more spectacular on the climbing sport of *Masquerade* than on the more familiar bush form. This variety is suitable for a fence or pillar, and has a good reputation for reliability. There is a profuse flush in June, but if you fail to remove the dead flowers before the hips form then there will be few flowers later in the season.

Blooms:	Semi-double Pink; apricot at base Fragrant
Foliage:	Dark green
Introduction:	1954
Type:	Large-flowered Climber
Pruning:	Climber — Method 2
Flowering Period:	Repeat flowering

MEG

A Large-flowered Climber to grow for its beautiful blooms — 5 in. across, apricot and pink with a large boss of red stamens. The many-flowered clusters appear in June, but even with regular dead-heading the later flushes are disappointing. *Meg* is a good choice for a pergola, pillar or fence, but you must remember to tie it in regularly as the stems are wide-spreading and rigid. The leaves are large and glossy.

Blooms:	Single Primrose yellow Fragrant
Foliage:	Medium green
Introduction:	1918
Type:	Large-flowered Climber
Pruning:	Climber — Method 1
Flowering Period:	Repeat flowering

MERMAID

The giant of the climbing rose world – a plant to cover the wall of a large house. It should, however, be a west- or south-facing wall as *Mermaid* can be killed by frost. This lack of hardiness is not the only fault of *Mermaid* — the stems are brittle and thorny, and a new plant will take a couple of years to establish. But in full flower it is supreme — the very large blooms are eye-catching and fragrant.

Blooms:	Double White, flushed pink Very fragrant
Foliage:	Light green
Introduction:	1879
Type:	Noisette Climber
Pruning:	Climber — Method 2
Flowering Period:	Repeat flowering

MME ALFRED CARRIERE

In Victorian times a wide range of Noisette Climbers were used to clothe cottages and castles; today very few remain in the catalogues. *Mme Alfred Carrière* is one, because its ability to clothe a north-facing wall of a house has not been matched by many modern varieties. It grows quickly, and the large, fragrant blooms open regularly during summer and autumn. A century old, but as vigorous as ever.

Blooms:	Double Pink, shaded crimson Very fragrant
Foliage:	Medium green
Introduction:	1927
Type:	Large-flowered Climber
Pruning:	Climber — Method 1
Flowering Period:	Early summer

MME GREGOIRE STAECHELIN
Other Name: *SPANISH BEAUTY*

A sight to behold — a full-grown specimen of *Mme Grégoire Staechelin* in full flower. The H.T.-type blooms are large, with frilled pink petals and a scent which is heavy and sweet. These blooms smother the abundant foliage of this very vigorous variety in June, but the flowering season lasts for only a few weeks after which the large hips begin to develop.

CLIMBERS & RAMBLERS

Height i

MORNING JEWEL

The pink of the large blooms has been described in many ways — "rich", "glowing" and so on. With a backcloth of shiny leaves this Scottish-bred variety gives an eye-catching display during the summer months. The autumn show can be disappointing. New shoots appear readily from the base — a useful Large-flowered Climber for fences or pillars. Not very popular — perhaps the continuity of flowering is not good enough.

Blooms:	Semi-double Pink Slightly fragrant
Foliage:	Medium green
Introduction:	1969
Type:	Large-flowered Climber
Pruning:	Climber — Method 2
Flowering Period:	Repeat flowering

25
20
15
10
5

MRS SAM McGREDY, CLIMBING

As stated on page 22, the climbing form is the way to enjoy once again the former glory of *Mrs Sam McGredy*. Here is the old vigour, and here are the bronze buds, the copper red blooms and the purple young foliage. The blooms are borne in large numbers and the flowering period lasts well into the autumn. Really colourful and reliable on a wall, the only drawback with this variety is its susceptibility to black spot.

Blooms:	Double Coppery orange, flushed red Fragrant
Foliage:	Bronze-tinted
Introduction:	1937
Type:	Climbing Hybrid Tea
Pruning:	Climber — Method 2
Flowering Period:	Repeat flowering

25
20
15
10
5

NEW DAWN

Dr W. van Fleet was once a popular Rambler, but it has now been replaced by its sport *New Dawn*. There are two distinct advantages with the newer variety — the growth is much less rampant and the flower clusters continue to appear throughout the summer. The blooms are small, but they are present in great numbers above the shiny leaves. A multipurpose rose — use as a hedge, specimen shrub or climber.

Blooms:	Semi-double Shell pink Fragrant
Foliage:	Medium green
Introduction:	1930
Type:	Rambler
Pruning:	Rambler — Method 2
Flowering Period:	Repeat flowering

25
20
15
10
5

PARKDIREKTOR RIGGERS

This variety has the profusion of flowers and the hardiness associated with Kordesii Climbers, but it does not have the family resistance to disease — both mildew and black spot can be problems. The large clusters of glowing crimson blooms are borne with remarkable freedom, and this has led to the popularity of this climbing rose. Once the flowers are dead remove them to ensure continuous flowering.

Blooms:	Semi-double Blood red Slightly fragrant
Foliage:	Dark green
Introduction:	1957
Type:	Kordesii Climber
Pruning:	Climber — Method 1
Flowering Period:	Repeat flowering

25
20
15
10
5

PAUL'S SCARLET CLIMBER

The top climbing red rose for many years, *Paul's Scarlet* is sadly past its prime. There are newer red varieties which don't dull with age, and there are varieties which have much better resistance to disease. Still, it remains an eye-catching rose in June, with masses of cupped red flowers which last for a month or more and then they are gone — there is no repeat flowering. It is less vigorous than the average old-fashioned Rambler.

Blooms:	Semi-double Scarlet, shaded crimson Slightly fragrant
Foliage:	Medium green
Introduction:	1916
Type:	Rambler
Pruning:	Rambler — Method 2
Flowering Period:	Early summer

25
20
15
10
5

PINK PERPETUE

A best-selling variety, due to its free-flowering nature and the ability to produce an autumn display of flower trusses which rivals the summer show. *Pink Perpétue* does not grow very tall, but it is vigorous and wide-spreading which makes it a good choice for covering a fence or wall. The blooms are not large, but they have plenty of petals and an attractive globular shape. Rust can be a serious problem.

Blooms:	Double Rose pink; carmine reverse Slightly fragrant
Foliage:	Dark green
Introduction:	1965
Type:	Large-flowered Climber
Pruning:	Climber — Method 2
Flowering Period:	Repeat flowering

25
20
15
10
5

Blooms:	Double Deep pink; white centre Slightly fragrant
Foliage:	Light green
Introduction:	1960
Type:	Kordesii Climber
Pruning:	Climber — Method 2
Flowering Period:	Repeat flowering

RITTER VON BARMSTEDE

An excellent pillar rose, vigorous and healthy, but lacking the popular appeal of some other Kordesii Climbers such as *Dortmund*. The clusters are very large with thirty flowers or more, and they appear in profusion from mid June onwards, but the individual blooms are small. Flower size is the problem, but each one is attractive — velvety petals opening to reveal a white centre and boss of yellow stamens.

Blooms:	Single Creamy white Fragrant
Foliage:	Medium green
Introduction:	1954
Type:	Rambler
Pruning:	Rambler — Method 3
Flowering Period:	Midsummer

RCSA FILIPES KIFTSGATE

A rambling giant of a rose, tall and wide-spreading, used for covering sheds or for growing up old trees. In July there is a cascade of bloom — enormous clusters of small fragrant flowers. These blooms are followed by bright red hips in the autumn. Treat it as an enormous bush — don't try to keep it in bounds in a small garden by pruning and don't try to flatten it against the side of the house.

Blooms:	Double Deep rose pink Fragrant
Foliage:	Dark green
Introduction:	1968
Type:	Large-flowered Climber
Pruning:	Climber — Method 2
Flowering Period:	Repeat flowering

ROSY MANTLE

A well-bred rose — it has the reliable climbing habit of *New Dawn* and some of the floral beauty of its other parent, *Prima Ballerina*. The large and shapely blooms are borne in small clusters throughout the season, and the display is especially good in autumn. The glossy leaves are rarely troubled by disease, but the wiry stems need regular attention to ensure that they are trained properly.

Blooms:	Double Deep yellow Slightly fragrant
Foliage:	Medium green
Introduction:	1957
Type:	Large-flowered Climber
Pruning:	Climber — Method 2
Flowering Period:	Repeat flowering

ROYAL GOLD

A variety which sounds irresistible in the catalogue — fragrant golden blooms, high-centred like a Hybrid Tea and 4 in. in diameter. But *Royal Gold* in the garden is not as desirable as its catalogue description — it does not flower freely and vigour is distinctly lacking if the soil is not fertile. The major problem is lack of hardiness — this is a rose for a south or west wall on a sheltered site.

Blooms:	Double Apricot orange Fragrant
Foliage:	Dark green
Introduction:	1964
Type:	Large-flowered Climber
Pruning:	Climber — Method 2
Flowering Period:	Repeat flowering

SCHOOLGIRL

It is not surprising that *Schoolgirl* should have become so popular. Good orange climbing roses are extremely rare, and the blooms of this McGredy-bred rose are large and fragrant. The leaves are glossy and abundant, and the flowers appear throughout the summer and autumn. Its main fault is the loss of the lower leaves, so that the stems appear leggy. Another drawback is the failure to produce a mass of flowers.

Blooms:	Double Salmon pink, shaded gold Very fragrant
Foliage:	Medium green
Introduction:	1931
Type:	Climbing Hybrid Tea
Pruning:	Climber — Method 1
Flowering Period:	Repeat flowering

SHOT SILK, CLIMBING

A darling of the pre-war rose world which can still be enjoyed in its climbing form. The beauty of the flowers is still there — full of pink, orange and yellow. The fragrance is heavy and sweet, and the foliage is glossy and coppery when young. The blooms are not spoilt by rain, and the first flowers appear early in the season. Unfortunately the display after the first flush is disappointing.

Height in

SWAN LAKE

One of the best white climbers you can buy — the flowers are large and shapely, and the foliage is abundant. The blooms are not spoilt by wet weather — an unusual advantage for a white rose. The flowers, bearing fifty petals or more, are borne freely throughout the season, but the foliage is prone to attack by mildew and black spot so spraying is necessary. A good choice for an arch or pillar.

Blooms:	Double White, tinged pink Slightly fragrant
Foliage:	Medium green
Introduction:	1968
Type:	Large-flowered Climber
Pruning:	Climber — Method 2
Flowering Period:	Repeat flowering

25 20 15 10 5

SYMPATHIE

As you would expect from a climbing rose bred by Kordes, *Sympathie* is a tough variety which will grow quite happily on a north wall. It is vigorous and disease resistant, and the attractive blooms appear in profusion from early summer to early autumn. These flowers are velvety and fragrant, and their shape is high-centred like a Hybrid Tea. *Sympathie* is not in any of the best-seller lists, even though it has no serious faults.

Blooms:	Double Bright red Fragrant
Foliage:	Medium green
Introduction:	1964
Type:	Large-flowered Climber
Pruning:	Climber — Method 2
Flowering Period:	Repeat flowering

25 20 15 10 5

THE GARLAND

You will still find this 19th century climbing rose in some catalogues, and it has never lost its appeal to lovers of old-fashioned roses. The blooms are small, opening pale pink but soon fading to white. The clusters which appear in June bear many blooms, so the overall effect is eye-catching. Use *The Garland* to climb up an old tree or clamber over a tall fence, or keep it pruned as a large bush.

Blooms:	Semi-double Blush pink Fragrant
Foliage:	Medium green
Introduction:	1835
Type:	Rambler
Pruning:	Rambler — Method 2
Flowering Period:	Early summer

25 20 15 10 5

VEILCHENBLAU
Other Name: *VOILET BLUE*

A black and white photograph of *Veilchenblau* in bloom reveals a very ordinary rose — small, semi-double and cupped flowers. In the garden, grown against a wall shaded from the noon-day sun, it is a most unusual variety — one of the closest yet to the elusive "blue" rose. The mature bloom is perhaps more grey than blue, but it is worth growing if you like unusual roses.

Blooms:	Semi-double Violet, fading to slate grey Fragrant
Foliage:	Light green
Introduction:	1909
Type:	Rambler
Pruning:	Rambler — Method 2
Flowering Period:	Midsummer

25 20 15 10 5

WHITE COCKADE

Like *Swan Lake*, this Scottish-bred variety is one of the best modern white climbers available. The blooms are beautifully formed with a pleasant fragrance, and there is a prolonged flowering period. It is a short-growing climber — obviously not a rose to cover the side of the house. Use it to clothe a low pillar or fence, or grow it as a tall bush. Disease resistance is good, and the glossy foliage is attractive.

Blooms:	Double White Slightly fragrant
Foliage:	Medium green
Introduction:	1969
Type:	Large-flowered Climber
Pruning:	Climber — Method 2
Flowering Period:	Repeat flowering

25 20 15 10 5

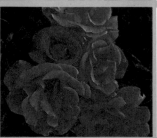

ZEPHIRINE DROUHIN
Other Name: *THORNLESS ROSE*

Zephirine Drouhin deserves its place in the Rose Hall of Fame — after more than 100 years it still appears in nearly all the catalogues, and the praise from the experts is as loud as ever. Grow it as a climber, or keep it pruned as a tall bush or hedge. Dead-head regularly, and there will be a succession of blooms from June onwards. Spray regularly with a fungicide.

Blooms:	Semi-double Carmine pink Very fragrant
Foliage:	Light green
Introduction:	1868
Type:	Climbing Bourbon Rose
Pruning:	Climber — Method 2
Flowering Period:	Repeat flowering

25 20 15 10 5

SHRUB ROSES

A recent survey revealed that for every 25 Hybrid Teas and Floribundas purchased in Britain, only one Shrub Rose is bought. The reason is, of course, the faults which everybody knows — Shrub Roses only bloom once, they are far too large for an average garden and they are far too old-fashioned for a modern garden.

Not one of these allegations is true. Consider the first misconception — lack of repeat flowering. Some Shrubs, such as the Species Roses, the Gallicas and the Centifolias do produce only one spectacular showing, but other Shrub Roses are repeat flowering, and many examples are listed on pages 62-72. Even the once flowering varieties should not be decried. The flowering period often lasts for many weeks and the timing, as with *Canary Bird* in May, may not be achievable with a Floribunda or Hybrid Tea. Furthermore, the sight of some of the once flowering varieties in full bloom in June or July exceeds the display value of most of the shrubs we grow.

The second incorrect idea about Shrub Roses concerns their size. Some indeed are giants, like *William Lobb*, *Nevada* and *Frühlingsmorgen*, but there are others which could look up to an average Floribunda — dainty Shrubs such as *Cécile Brunner* and *The Fairy*.

Finally, the question of the old-fashioned look. Of course there are cottage-type roses — pink, overblown and full of fragrance, and that's their charm. But every flower form is available, from *Fred Loads* with its 5-petalled blooms to *Fountain* with its high-centred, H.T.-type flowers.

Shrub Roses are underestimated, under-utilized and misunderstood. One of the problems is that they are not a clear-cut group — quite frankly they are a rag-bag of varieties which do not belong in any of the other neatly-defined classes. Included are the Species Roses (wild varieties and their near relatives) and the Old-Fashioned Roses (varieties dating back to the pre-Hybrid Tea era). Finally there are the Modern Shrub Roses, which usually have a flowering habit rather similar to a Floribunda or Hybrid Tea but grow too tall for use in formal beds.

Somewhere in this class is a variety for nearly every garden. Many Shrubs will thrive in soil and conditions which would not support a Hybrid Tea, and both pruning and upkeep are simple. But, as stated at the beginning, for every 25 Hybrid Teas and Floribundas purchased, only one Shrub Rose is bought.

KEY TO THE ROSE GUIDES

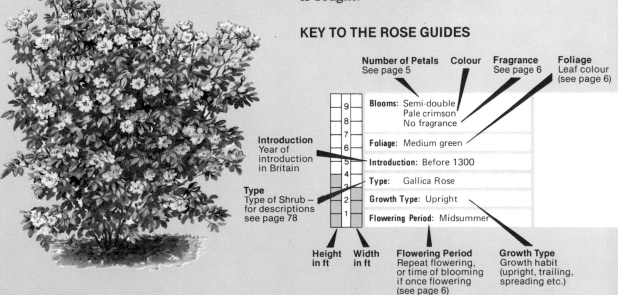

Number of Petals See page 5

Colour

Fragrance See page 6

Foliage Leaf colour (see page 6)

Introduction Year of introduction in Britain

Type Type of Shrub — for descriptions see page 78

Blooms: Semi-double
Pale crimson
No fragrance

Foliage: Medium green

Introduction: Before 1300

Type: Gallica Rose

Growth Type: Upright

Flowering Period: Midsummer

Height in ft

Width in ft

Flowering Period Repeat flowering, or time of blooming if once flowering (see page 6)

Growth Type Growth habit (upright, trailing, spreading etc.)

Height W
in feet in

ANGELINA

A rounded bush which is quite small for a Shrub Rose. *Angelina* is suitable for planting at the front of the shrub border or as a hedge, but despite its good points and compact size it has not become popular. The blooms are borne in trusses, appearing regularly until early autumn. There are not many petals, but the slightly cupped blooms with their prominent stamens are most attractive. Growth is vigorous and healthy.

Blooms:	Semi-double Deep pink; white eye Slightly fragrant
Foliage:	Light green
Introduction:	1975
Type:	Modern Shrub Rose
Growth Type:	Bushy
Flowering Period:	Repeat flowering

AUSTRIAN COPPER
Other Name: R. FOETIDA BICOLOR

The brightest of the Species Roses — a superb sight in full bloom. Unfortunately the flowering season lasts for only a couple of weeks and for the rest of the summer the bush is rather dull and highly susceptible to black spot. The smell is neither strong nor pleasant. Some (but not all) experts believe it to be the original parent of all orange H.T.s.

Blooms:	Single Coppery orange; yellow reverse No fragrance
Foliage:	Medium green
Introduction:	Before 1590
Type:	Species Rose
Growth Type:	Arching
Flowering Period:	Midsummer

BALLERINA

Masses of tiny flowers are borne in hydrangea-like heads which appear all summer long. The bush bears an abundance of small glossy leaves, and this healthy variety is suitable for the herbaceous border and rose bed. It can also be planted as a hedge or grown as a standard. There is a pleasant musk-like perfume and for lovers of *Ballerina* there is now a similar red variety *(Marjorie Fair)* available.

Blooms:	Single Pale pink; white eye Slightly fragrant
Foliage:	Light green
Introduction:	1937
Type:	Modern Shrub Rose
Growth Type:	Bushy
Flowering Period:	Repeat flowering

BLANC DOUBLE DE COUBERT

This old French-bred Shrub remains popular. Its flowers are large and sweet-smelling, first appearing in June and continuing into the autumn. The great virtue is outstanding disease resistance, making spraying unnecessary. There are drawbacks — the papery petals are easily damaged by rain, the foliage is too sparse and the stem bases are too bare to make it either a reliable hedge or an attractive bush.

Blooms:	Semi-double Pure white Very fragrant
Foliage:	Medium green
Introduction:	1892
Type:	Rugosa Shrub
Growth Type:	Bushy
Flowering Period:	Repeat flowering

BLOOMFIELD ABUNDANCE

A large Shrub — definitely not for the small garden. Despite the size of its almost thornless stems, the flowers are no bigger than a thimble. Each one looks like a miniature Hybrid Tea rose when in bud, and highly recommended for those who like to wear roses in their buttonholes. Flowering begins in June and continues until the end of the summer. The flowers at the end of the season are borne in huge clusters.

Blooms:	Double Shell pink Fragrant
Foliage:	Dark green
Introduction:	1920
Type:	China Rose
Growth Type:	Open
Flowering Period:	Repeat flowering

BOULE DE NEIGE

The English translation of the name of this French-bred Bourbon Rose is Snowball — and how appropriate it is. The red-tinged buds, borne in small clusters, open into white, ball-like blooms about 2½ in. across. The petals are silky, the fragrance is strong — undoubtedly one of the best Bourbons you can buy. The main problem is balling (see page 96) in wet weather — black spot can also be a problem.

Blooms:	Double Ivory Very fragrant
Foliage:	Dark green
Introduction:	1867
Type:	Bourbon Rose
Growth Type:	Upright
Flowering Period:	Repeat flowering

BUFF BEAUTY

Blooms:	Double Pale apricot Fragrant
Foliage:	Purple-tinted
Introduction:	1939
Type:	Hybrid Musk
Growth Type:	Arching
Flowering Period:	Repeat flowering

The flowers are borne in large clusters, buff yellow at first then fading to a warm ivory. They are shapely in bud, but soon become confused and formless as they mature. *Buff Beauty* is a good choice for a hedge or for cutting — the perfume is pleasant and the foliage is attractive. The spreading branches will need spraying against mildew — if kept healthy, the autumn display is outstanding.

CANARY BIRD
Other Name: R. XANTHINA SPONTANEA

Blooms:	Single Canary yellow Fragrant
Foliage:	Grey green
Introduction:	After 1907
Type:	Species Rose
Growth Type:	Arching
Flowering Period:	Late spring

The popular choice as the rose to herald in the flowering season. In May the dainty yellow blooms appear in profusion along the arching stems. The period of flowering lasts for about a month. The ferny foliage makes an attractive bush when flowering is over. *Canary Bird* makes a good hedge — grow it as a standard where space is limited. Die-back occasionally occurs.

CECILE BRUNNER
Other Name: SWEETHEART ROSE

Blooms:	Double Shell pink Slightly fragrant
Foliage:	Dark green
Introduction:	1881
Type:	China Rose
Growth Type:	Open
Flowering Period:	Repeat flowering

A hundred years old, and still a favourite in many gardens. You will still find it in some catalogues, for nothing has replaced the charm of the small bush bearing tiny pink flowers which are perfectly formed at the bud stage. Excellent for cutting or as a buttonhole rose — the clusters are large but the foliage is sparse. Flowering is from June until October.

CELESTIAL
Other Names: CELESTE, MINDEN ROSE

Blooms:	Double Blush pink Fragrant
Foliage:	Grey green
Introduction:	About 1780
Type:	Alba Rose
Growth Type:	Upright
Flowering Period:	Midsummer

Like all the Albas, *Celestial* is robust, hardy and trouble-free. It is free-flowering, the richly scented pink blooms appearing at the end of June to provide a midsummer display. The blooms have about 25 petals, opening to reveal the stamens within — a favourite old-fashioned variety which is excellent for hedging or as a tall specimen bush.

CHAPEAU DE NAPOLEON
Other Name: R. CENTIFOLIA CRISTATA

Blooms:	Double Rose pink Fragrant
Foliage:	Medium green
Introduction:	1827
Type:	Centifolia Rose
Growth Type:	Open
Flowering Period:	Midsummer

A true Centifolia Rose — full, globular blooms with a pleasant old-fashioned perfume. The buds are unique — a winged extension on the buds giving the appearance of "Napoleon's hat". The bush is hardy and spreading, the flowers appearing in June or July in drooping clusters. The stems may need support and protection from mildew.

CHINATOWN
Other Name: VILLE DE CHINE

Blooms:	Double Yellow, edged pink Fragrant
Foliage:	Medium green
Introduction:	1963
Type:	Modern Shrub Rose
Growth Type:	Bushy
Flowering Period:	Repeat flowering

A popular large bush rose — you will find it in the Floribunda or Shrub section of the catalogue. The fragrant flowers will withstand rainy weather and the bush is healthy and tolerant of exposed situations. The flowers are borne in large trusses and appear freely throughout the season — a good choice for hedging or the back of the border.

SHRUB ROSES

		Height in feet

COMMON MOSS ROSE
Other Name: R. CENTIFOLIA MUSCOSA

The original and perhaps the best of the Moss Roses. The large, globular blooms open flat when mature, appearing in June or July. Both the buds and stems bear green "moss" and this variety has a distinct old-fashioned look. It is suitable for the smaller garden, where it can be used as a hedge or as a specimen bush. Keep watch for mildew.

Blooms:	Double Rose pink Fragrant
Foliage:	Medium green
Introduction:	About 1700
Type:	Moss Rose
Growth Type:	Open
Flowering Period:	Midsummer

COMPLICATA
Other Name: R. GALLICA COMPLICATA

The outstanding feature of this age-old variety is the size of the blooms which appear in June — 4 or 5 in. across, double and with a pleasing if not strong perfume. The stems bearing these blooms are long and lax, and this variety is best grown next to an old tree so that it can clamber upwards without artificial support. Easily rooted from cuttings.

Blooms:	Single Pink; white eye Slightly fragrant
Foliage:	Light green
Introduction:	Unknown
Type:	Gallica Rose
Growth Type:	Arching
Flowering Period:	Midsummer

CORNELIA

Grow *Cornelia* as a hedge — if you have lots of space you can grow it as a specimen bush. It is recognised by the unusually dark appearance of its stems and leaves plus its small and fragrant pink flowers, which first appear in June. These blooms are resistant to rain, and the best floral display occurs in autumn. The large trusses and free-flowering habit makes *Cornelia* a popular Shrub Rose.

Blooms:	Double Apricot pink Very fragrant
Foliage:	Dark green
Introduction:	1925
Type:	Hybrid Musk
Growth Type:	Spreading
Flowering Period:	Repeat flowering

DOROTHY WHEATCROFT

A rather gaunt Shrub (a Floribunda in some catalogues) which should be planted at the back of the border. Its glory is the profusion of large heads of bright red flowers on long stems, so large that they often bow down under their own weight, so some support may be necessary. Rain resistance is good, but spraying is essential if you live in a black spot area. Fragrance is unfortunately very slight.

Blooms:	Semi-double Orange red, flushed scarlet Slightly fragrant
Foliage:	Medium green
Introduction:	1960
Type:	Modern Shrub Rose
Growth Type:	Upright
Flowering Period:	Repeat flowering

FELICIA

A Hybrid Musk which is noted for its long flowering season — the first sweet-smelling blooms appear in June and flowering continues throughout the summer. The best display is in the autumn and flowers are still found on the wide-spreading bushes in November. The blooms are shapely, like a Hybrid Tea, and are borne in large trusses. Excellent for cutting, *Felicia* makes a good hedge or specimen bush.

Blooms:	Double Apricot pink Very fragrant
Foliage:	Medium green
Introduction:	1928
Type:	Hybrid Musk
Growth Type:	Spreading
Flowering Period:	Repeat flowering

F.J. GROOTENDORST
Other Name: NELKENROSE

In most ways this Shrub has very little to offer. There is neither fragrance nor hips, and the flowers are small and rather dull. The foliage is pale and small, although it is attractive in the autumn months. The unique feature of *F.J. Grootendorst* is the distinct frill at the edge of the petals, giving a carnation-like effect. Like all Rugosas, it is reliable under poor conditions.

Blooms:	Double Crimson No fragrance
Foliage:	Light green
Introduction:	1918
Type:	Rugosa Shrub
Growth Type:	Open
Flowering Period:	Repeat flowering

SHRUB ROSES

9	
8	
7	
6	
5	
4	
3	
2	
1	

Blooms: Double
Blood red
Fragrant

Foliage: Dark green

Introduction: 1972

Type: Modern Shrub Rose

Growth Type: Upright

Flowering Period: Repeat flowering

FOUNTAIN

The blooms of this upright Shrub helped to gain it the supreme British awards in 1971. Large, velvety, blood red — the H.T.-type flowers are borne singly or in small trusses throughout the season. The bush is abundantly clothed with dark foliage which is reddish when young. It has a good reputation for reliability and resistance to disease, but the tall shoots occasionally snap in autumn storms.

Blooms: Single
Shell pink
Very fragrant

Foliage: Dark green

Introduction: 1914

Type: Rugosa Shrub

Growth Type: Bushy

Flowering Period: Repeat flowering

FRAU DAGMAR HARTOPP

Frau Dagmar Hartopp lacks the height of many of the Rugosas, but it is considered by many experts to be one of the best. It has all the good properties of the group — freedom from disease, continuous flowering, blooms which are attractive and strongly scented and finally hips which are red and large. The bush will grow almost anywhere and is ideal as a low-growing hedge. Leaves turn an attractive yellow in the autumn.

Blooms: Double
White
No fragrance

Foliage: Medium green

Introduction: 1901

Type: Hybrid Perpetual

Growth Type: Upright

Flowering Period: Repeat flowering

FRAU KARL DRUSCHKI
Other Name: SNOW QUEEN

Frau Karl Druschki first appeared 80 years ago, but it is still going strong and is widely offered for sale. Its everlasting appeal is at first surprising — there is no scent and no resistance to mildew. But its virtues can be seen in a large garden — a stately bush covered with masses of pure white blooms opening from red-splashed buds. Prune lightly; peg down long shoots.

Blooms: Single
Orange vermilion
Fragrant

Foliage: Light green

Introduction: 1967

Type: Modern Shrub Rose

Growth Type: Upright

Flowering Period: Repeat flowering

FRED LOADS

This variety has become really popular, even though it has only five petals. The reason is that it makes up for its shortage of petals with bright colouring and huge trusses which can exceed 18 in. across. The flowers are large and unfading, and the bush is well-clothed with leaves. Healthy and vigorous, *Fred Loads* is an excellent choice, although it can look rather top heavy in full flower.

Blooms: Double
Salmon pink
Fragrant

Foliage: Dark green

Introduction: 1940

Type: Modern Shrub Rose

Growth Type: Arching

Flowering Period: Midsummer

FRITZ NOBIS

A handsome Shrub, bearing masses of flowers for about three weeks in June and attractive dark red hips in autumn. The buds are beautifully formed, opening into flat blooms with a pleasant clove-like smell. The leathery leaves are healthy, and this Kordes-bred Shrub is regarded as one of the best summer flowering Modern Shrub Roses. Give it room to grow, as it has a somewhat sprawling growth habit.

Blooms: Semi-double
Creamy yellow
Fragrant

Foliage: Light green

Introduction: 1937

Type: Species Rose

Growth Type: Arching

Flowering Period: Early summer

FRÜHLINGSGOLD
Other Name: SPRING GOLD

Kordes bred a number of splendid hybrids from *R. spinosissima*, the Scotch Briar. *Frühlingsgold* is perhaps the finest — a mature bush in full flower in May is one of the great sights of the rose world. The arching branches are festooned with saucer-sized flowers, and the air is filled with fragrance. The flowering period lasts for only a fortnight, and ample space is essential.

SHRUB ROSES

Height in feet

FRÜHLINGSMORGEN
Other Name: SPRING MORNING

Another Kordes hybrid, smaller and bushier that its yellow sister described on the previous page. The small-leaved Shrub is not particularly attractive, but the flowers are — large, scented and colourful. The pale centre of each pink-edged petal highlights the maroon stamens. The second flush of flowers in September are smaller and not as prolific as the early summer flush.

Blooms: Single
Deep pink; yellow centre
Fragrant

Foliage: Grey green

Introduction: 1942

Type: Species Rose

Growth Type: Open

Flowering Period: June & September

GOLDEN WINGS

A popular and highly praised variety, perhaps the best of all the large-flowered yellow Shrubs. From June onwards the blooms appear in regular flushes provided the old flowers are dead-headed. The flowers are large and sweet-smelling — light primrose with prominent buff yellow stamens. These blooms are not damaged by rain, but they do fade slightly with age. Disease resistance is good — an excellent choice.

Blooms: Single
Pale yellow
Fragrant

Foliage: Light green

Introduction: 1956

Type: Modern Shrub Rose

Growth Type: Bushy

Flowering Period: Repeat flowering

HEIDELBERG

You will not find *Heidelberg* in many catalogues, but it fares much better in the Royal National Rose Society's Analysis than many of its more popular rivals. The large flowers are bright red and are borne in trusses, first appearing in June and continuing to appear throughout the season. The display is especially good in autumn. Recommended for hedging or as a specimen bush — keep watch for black spot.

Blooms: Double
Bright crimson
Slightly fragrant

Foliage: Dark green

Introduction: 1959

Type: Modern Shrub Rose

Growth Type: Open

Flowering Period: Repeat flowering

JOSEPH'S COAT

Seen at its best in June or July, this offspring of *Circus* bears medium-sized blooms in large trusses. The petals change from yellow to orange and finally to cherry red as they age. This bright but gaudy variety can be trained as a climber, reaching 10 ft high, or it can be grown as a hedge or 6 ft specimen shrub. It can also be kept pruned as a 4 ft bush for the small garden, but it is happiest when grown as a shrub.

Blooms: Semi-double
Yellow, edged red
Slightly fragrant

Foliage: Dark green

Introduction: 1964

Type: Modern Shrub Rose

Growth Type: Open

Flowering Period: Repeat flowering

KASSEL

A large lax-growing Shrub best known for its huge heads of dusky red flowers. These appear in profusion throughout the summer months and the autumn display is excellent. *Kassel* is a good choice if you like large red flowers on a healthy bush, but you must give it the space it requires. In a few catalogues it is described as a Climber; it can be trained as a pillar rose (see page 89).

Blooms: Semi-double
Scarlet
Slightly fragrant

Foliage: Dark green

Introduction: 1957

Type: Modern Shrub Rose

Growth Type: Open

Flowering Period: Repeat flowering

KÖNIGIN VON DÄNEMARCK
Other Name: QUEEN OF DENMARK

An attractive offspring of *Maiden's Blush* — perhaps the best Alba Rose for the smaller garden. There is the robust good health and leaden green foliage you would expect, but the growth habit is more spindly than the usual Alba and the flowers change from scarlet pink to pale pink as they open — most unusual for an old rose. The fragrance is superb.

Blooms: Double
Pale pink
Very fragrant

Foliage: Grey green

Introduction: 1826

Type: Alba Rose

Growth Type: Open

Flowering Period: Midsummer

SHRUB ROSES

Blooms: Single
Copper; yellow centre
Very fragrant

Foliage: Dark green

Introduction: 1894

Type: Species Rose

Growth Type: Open

Flowering Period: Early summer

LADY PENZANCE

R. rubiginosa (the Sweet Briar of Eglantine) is a wild English rose with a most unusual property — the foliage emits an apple-like odour after rain. The best hybrid for the ordinary garden is *Lady Penzance* which blooms in early June. The flowers are small and the flowering period lasts for only a week or two — this variety is grown for its fragrant foliage and not for its blooms.

Blooms: Double
Lilac pink
Fragrant

Foliage: Light green

Introduction: 1959

Type: Modern Shrub Rose

Growth Type: Open

Flowering Period: Repeat flowering

LAVENDER LASSIE

Despite its name, the flowers of this Floribunda-type Shrub are usually pink rather than lavender. The blooms appear in large trusses at the top of the upright canes — staking is necessary. The rosette-shaped blooms have sixty or more small petals, and the fragrance is occasionally (but not always) strong. Both disease and rain resistance are very good, and *Lavender Lassie* is quite popular as a specimen bush.

Blooms: Double
Blush pink
Fragrant

Foliage: Grey green

Introduction: Before 1500

Type: Alba Rose

Growth Type: Bushy

Flowering Period: Midsummer

MAIDEN'S BLUSH
Other Name: CUISSE DE NYMPHE EMUE

Maiden's Blush is living rose history — the rose in the old paintings and the rose in the cottage gardens of 200 years ago. The warm pink blooms fade to ivory with age, and the old-fashioned fragrance is a delight. It is hardy, long-living and free from disease. The drooping dull leaves have the characteristic grey-green colour of the Alba roses.

Blooms: Semi-double
Pink, shaded deep pink
Slightly fragrant

Foliage: Medium green

Introduction: 1959

Type: Modern Shrub Rose

Growth Type: Arching

Flowering Period: June & September

MARGUERITE HILLING
Other Name: PINK NEVADA

A sport of the popular Shrub *Nevada*. It is identical to its parent in many ways — the same growth habit, foliage and size. It is however, more free-flowering and the blooms are pale pink overlaid with a deeper shade of pink. The whole base can be covered by the first flush of blooms in June. The leaves are small and dull, and black spot can be a problem.

Blooms: Single
Pink; white centre
Fragrant

Foliage: Medium green

Introduction: 1919

Type: Rugosa Shrub

Growth Type: Trailing

Flowering Period: Midsummer

MAX GRAF

The first and still one of the best ground cover roses. The prostrate stems spread over the soil surface, rooting as they go, and quickly produce a dense green mat. The single pink flowers appear freely over a long period in June and July, but there is no repeat flowering. The flowers, borne in clusters, have an apple-like fragrance. The stems are thorny, which makes weeding a problem.

Blooms: Double
White
Fragrant

Foliage: Medium green

Introduction: 1832

Type: Damask Rose

Growth Type: Open

Flowering Period: Midsummer

MME HARDY

A lovely white old-fashioned rose — full of petals and fragrance. *Mme Hardy* is a Damask Rose, with the dull foliage and lax stems which characterize the group. The blooms are borne in large clusters during June or July. Considered by some to be the most beautiful white Shrub blooms, they are certainly not the hardiest. Both rain and strong winds damage them and stems may need support against bad weather.

SHRUB ROSES

Height in feet · W in

MME ISAAC PEREIRE

Pity the poor novice who seeks advice from the experts about this Bourbon Rose. For most of them this old-fashioned variety is a joy — huge flowers with a fragrance which is probably unmatched by any other Shrub. To others it is an ugly plant with unattractive foliage and with flowers which are sometimes misshapen... and both sides are telling the truth. The stems need support — it can be grown as a pillar rose.

Blooms: Double
Deep carmine pink
Very fragrant

Foliage: Medium green

Introduction: 1881

Type: Bourbon Rose

Growth Type: Open

Flowering Period: Repeat flowering

MME PIERRE OGER

Another Bourbon Rose, with blooms which lack the size and intense fragrance of *Mme Isaac Pereire* but with a much greater beauty. The creamy pink petals are delicate and pearly, forming bowl-shaped flowers which bow down the lax stems. Support is essential — grow it on a tripod or pillar. In hot weather the blooms lose their creaminess and turn rose pink. Keep watch for mildew and black spot.

Blooms: Double
Cream, shaded pink
Fragrant

Foliage: Light green

Introduction: 1878

Type: Bourbon Rose

Growth Type: Upright

Flowering Period: Repeat flowering

MOONLIGHT

Moonlight is the Hybrid Musk which is best known for its attractive leaves — glossy and red-tinted. The flower trusses are extremely large, especially in the autumn, and the blooms are small, creamy and rather loose. Surprisingly, it is not popular although it is attractive, pleasantly fragrant and can be used in several ways — as a specimen bush, as a pillar rose or for scrambling up a small tree.

Blooms: Semi-double
Ivory
Fragrant

Foliage: Dark green

Introduction: 1913

Type: Hybrid Musk

Growth Type: Open

Flowering Period: Repeat flowering

NEVADA

Nevada is one of the great sights of the rose world. In June the whole bush is covered with large creamy white blooms. When mature and well-grown both the small leaves and thornless red stems may be almost completely hidden. Space is essential — trying to keep the bush small by hard pruning leads to disappointing results. If black spot is a problem in your area, regular spraying will be necessary.

Blooms: Semi-double
Creamy white
Slightly fragrant

Foliage: Medium green

Introduction: 1927

Type: Modern Shrub Rose

Growth Type: Arching

Flowering Period: June & September

NOZOMI

Technically it is a Climbing Miniature, but you will find *Nozomi* amongst the Shrub Roses in the catalogues. This Japanese variety is becoming increasingly popular as a ground cover plant. Its trailing stems bear small glossy leaves, and in summer there are clusters of tiny pearly flowers. Not as good or as wide-spreading as *Max Graf*, but still very useful for edging. Stems may be pegged down to improve the cover.

Blooms: Single
Pearly pink
No fragrance

Foliage: Dark green

Introduction: 1968

Type: Modern Shrub Rose

Growth Type: Trailing

Flowering Period: Midsummer

NYMPHENBURG

A fine Shrub Rose, renowned for its prolific flowering habit and the large number of blooms in each cluster. It is perhaps best used as a hedge, in which the abundant foliage makes a dense screen. It is also suitable for use as a large specimen bush or it can be allowed to climb as a pillar rose. The blooms are large and sweet-scented — dead-head regularly to ensure continuity of flowering. Watch for black spot.

Blooms: Semi-double
Pink, shaded pale orange
Fragrant

Foliage: Medium green

Introduction: 1954

Type: Modern Shrub Rose

Growth Type: Arching

Flowering Period: Repeat flowering

Blooms:	Semi-double Rose pink Slightly fragrant
Foliage:	Bronze-tinted
Introduction:	1752
Type:	China Rose
Growth Type:	Bushy
Flowering Period:	Repeat flowering

OLD BLUSH
Other Name: MONTHLY ROSE

A truly historical rose — this old China was one of the forebears which gave the modern Hybrid Tea Rose its repeat flowering nature. *Old Blush* is an airy, graceful bush, bearing loose sprays of small scented blooms. The continuity of flowering is remarkable — from June until Christmas if the site is sheltered. Disease resistance is good. More than 200 years old, and still worth growing.

Blooms:	Semi-double Shell pink Fragrant
Foliage:	Bronze-tinted
Introduction:	1924
Type:	Hybrid Musk
Growth Type:	Spreading
Flowering Period:	Repeat flowering

PENELOPE

Several Hybrid Musks are described in this section, and *Penelope* is easily the most popular. It can be grown in almost every garden — left unpruned it will produce a large spreading Shrub; regularly pruned it can be grown as a 3 ft bush. It also makes an excellent hedge. Large clusters of pale flowers cover the bush in June — deadhead regularly to ensure that later blooms will appear in early autumn.

Blooms:	Double Apricot Fragrant
Foliage:	Dark green
Introduction:	1884
Type:	China Rose
Growth Type:	Open
Flowering Period:	Repeat flowering

PERLE D'OR
Other Name: YELLOW CECILE BRUNNER

A close relative of *Cécile Brunner*, hence its age-old alternative name. The tiny buds are pointed and classically shaped, opening into miniature flowers which are apricot at first but turn almost white with age. Excellent for cutting for indoor use — outdoors use it for bedding rather than as a specimen Shrub. Growth more robust than *Cécile Brunner*.

Blooms:	Double Rose pink No fragrance
Foliage:	Light green
Introduction:	1923
Type:	Rugosa Shrub
Growth Type:	Open
Flowering Period:	Repeat flowering

PINK GROOTENDORST

A sport of *F.J. Grootendorst*, with a little more to offer. The novelty of the frilled petals remains, but the colour is much more attractive. The blooms are highly recommended for display as a cut flower. As with its parent, the bush is not attractive but it is tough and hardy. A good choice for hedging in cold and windswept areas — the small clusters of small flowers appear throughout summer and autumn.

Blooms:	Semi-double Ivory Very fragrant
Foliage:	Dark green
Introduction:	1919
Type:	Hybrid Musk
Growth Type:	Spreading
Flowering Period:	Repeat flowering

PROSPERITY

The flower form is unusual for a Hybrid Musk — the many small petals of *Prosperity* form a rosette. The colour is cream at first, but fades to white. There is usually a profusion of flowers, borne in clusters, and this wide-spreading variety can be used to make a reliable hedge. *Prosperity* will bloom until late autumn, but you will have to spray against mildew. The fragrance is unsurpassed by any other Hybrid Musk.

Blooms:	Semi-double Pale crimson No fragrance
Foliage:	Medium green
Introduction:	Before 1300
Type:	Gallica Rose
Growth Type:	Upright
Flowering Period:	Midsummer

ROSA GALLICA OFFICINALIS
Other Name: APOTHECARY'S ROSE

One of the earliest roses still grown in our gardens, this original Red Rose of Lancashire is the ancestor of many of today's red H.T.s and Floribundas. In June or July clusters of pale red flowers appear, followed by small round hips. It is available from many rose suppliers, and it can be grown in an average-sized garden. You will have to spray to keep mildew under control.

SHRUB ROSES

Height
in feet

ROSA HUGONIS
Other Name: GOLDEN ROSE OF CHINA

A popular wild rose, rather like *Canary Bird* when not in flower. The stems are arching, the leaves are ferny and the bush has a graceful appearance. The flowers appear in May, and have the annoying habit of often remaining half closed. *R. hugonis* is subject to die-back, especially after a hard winter, and it is better to choose *Canary Bird* or *R. cantabrigiensis*.

Blooms: Single
Buttercup yellow
Slightly fragrant

Foliage: Grey green

Introduction: 1908

Type: Species Rose

Growth Type: Arching

Flowering Period: Late spring

ROSA MOYESII GERANIUM
Other Name: GERANIUM

The wild rose *R. moyesii*, grown for its beautiful red flowers and spectacular hips, is a gaunt giant of a shrub. It is better to grow the variety *Geranium* — smaller, more compact and with orange red, flagon-shaped hips which are even better than those on the wild variety. The bright red flowers appear among the small leaves in May or June — the 2 in. long hips appear later.

Blooms: Single
Scarlet
No fragrance

Foliage: Medium green

Introduction: 1938

Type: Species Rose

Growth Type: Arching

Flowering Period: Early summer

ROSA MUNDI
Other Name: R. GALLICA VERSICOLOR

By far the most popular of the Gallica Roses, *Rosa Mundi* is a novelty which is about 300 years old. The small flowers are distinctly striped and they appear on the twiggy, upright bushes for about a month in June or July. Like all Gallicas, this variety will succeed in poor soil but regular spraying against mildew will be necessary. The bushes sucker freely from the base.

Blooms: Semi-double
Pale pink, striped crimson
No fragrance

Foliage: Medium green

Introduction: 1650

Type: Gallica Rose

Growth Type: Upright

Flowering Period: Midsummer

ROSA RUBRIFOLIA
Other Name: R. FERRUGINEA

A wild rose of central Europe, grown in our gardens for the beauty of its foliage. These leaves have a purplish bloom and the stems are practically free from thorns — a favourite material for flower arrangers. The small flowers are insignificant and short-lived, but the clusters of dark red hips are highly decorative. If space is limited, keep in check by pruning.

Blooms: Single
Pink
No fragrance

Foliage: Grey green, tinged purple

Introduction: Unknown

Type: Species Rose

Growth Type: Arching

Flowering Period: Midsummer

ROSA RUGOSA ALBA

A typical Rugosa Rose — wrinkled disease-free leaves, fragrant blooms, attractive hips and an iron constitution. *R. rugosa alba* produces large flowers which appear throughout the summer and autumn months, and the orange red tomato-like hips are very large. It forms an attractive hedge, the dense foliage turning gold in the autumn. It can also be grown as a specimen bush, but it must never be hard pruned.

Blooms: Single
White
Fragrant

Foliage: Light green

Introduction: Unknown

Type: Rugosa Shrub

Growth Type: Bushy

Flowering Period: Repeat flowering

ROSA SERICEA PTERACANTHA
Other Name: R. OMEIENSIS PTERACANTHA

A tall impenetrable Shrub with a number of unusual features. The small white flowers which appear fleetingly in early June are four-petalled, and the leaves are ferny. The most unusual and decorative features are the thorns on young wood — large and triangular with 1 in. red bases. Another unusual feature is the need for regular pruning to ensure a supply of new wood.

Blooms: Single
White
No fragrance

Foliage: Light green

Introduction: 1890

Type: Species Rose

Growth Type: Bushy

Flowering Period: Early summer

	Blooms:	Single, Pink, Slightly fragrant
9 8 7 6 5 4 3 2 1	Foliage:	Medium green
	Introduction:	Before 1700
	Type:	Species Rose
	Growth Type:	Spreading
	Flowering Period:	Late summer

ROSA VIRGINIANA
Other Name: R. PLENA

As the name indicates, a wild American rose. It will provide season-long colour in the British garden — bright green and glossy foliage, pink flowers in late summer, golden leaves in the autumn and showy red hips throughout the winter. Growth is wide-spreading so provide plenty of space. Makes a good barrier — growth is impenetrable and the thorns are vicious.

	Blooms:	Single, Lilac pink, Fragrant
9 8 7 6 5 4 3 2 1	Foliage:	Medium green
	Introduction:	1904
	Type:	Species Rose
	Growth Type:	Arching
	Flowering Period:	Midsummer

ROSA WILLMOTTIAE

Most Shrubs are grown for their flowers, a few are grown for their hips, leaves or even thorns. *R. willmottiae* is grown for the beauty of the whole plant — a willowy bush with long plum-coloured stems covered with delicate ferny foliage. In summer a mass of pale purple flowers appear, and these are followed by hips, glistening red on the arching stems. For maximum effect, grow it next to a large-leaved shrub.

	Blooms:	Double, Wine red, Fragrant
9 8 7 6 5 4 3 2 1	Foliage:	Light green
	Introduction:	1902
	Type:	Rugosa Shrub
	Growth Type:	Bushy
	Flowering Period:	Repeat flowering

ROSERAIE DE L'HAŸ

One of the best of the Rugosas, and one of the best Shrub Roses for hedging. The plant is densely clothed with tough foliage which remains free from disease. It will grow in poor soil, salt-laden air and in exposed sites. Its toughness, however, is not reflected in its blooms — large, velvety and sweetly scented. Flowering is prolific; its only fault compared with other Rugosas is the lack of hips.

	Blooms:	Single, Magenta pink, Fragrant
9 8 7 6 5 4 3 2 1	Foliage:	Light green
	Introduction:	Before 1939
	Type:	Rugosa Shrub
	Growth Type:	Spreading
	Flowering Period:	Repeat flowering

SCABROSA
Other Name: R. RUGOSA SCABROSA

A rival to *Roseraie de L'Haÿ* as the best Rugosa Rose. Both are remarkably healthy, hardy and bear large fragrant flowers. *Scabrosa* scores by producing tomato red hips in the autumn. Flowering begins at the end of spring and continues well into the autumn. Excellent as a hedge or specimen bush — choose it if you do not have the room for its rival.

	Blooms:	Semi-double, White, Slightly fragrant
9 8 7 6 5 4 3 2 1	Foliage:	Light green
	Introduction:	1912
	Type:	Rugosa Shrub
	Growth Type:	Spreading
	Flowering Period:	Repeat flowering

SCHNEEZWERG

The smallest of the Rugosa Roses, and not the most attractive. The scent is weak, and the foliage is dull and uninteresting. The flowering season, however, is excellent — from late May until the end of autumn the white anemone-like blooms appear. In autumn new flowers open among the small scarlet hips, but the foliage does not take on the attractive autumn colouring of other Rugosas.

	Blooms:	Double, Pale pink, No fragrance
9 8 7 6 5 4 3 2 1	Foliage:	Medium green
	Introduction:	1932
	Type:	Polyantha Rose
	Growth Type:	Spreading
	Flowering Period:	Repeat flowering

THE FAIRY

The Fairy is one of the few remaining Polyanthas and it has its enthusiasts. They praise the profusion of blooms which appear in the heat of late summer plus the attraction of the glossy box-like foliage. The flowers are very small and rosette-shaped, but they are borne in large clusters throughout the late summer and autumn. There is a major drawback — flowering does not start until mid or late July.

SHRUB ROSES

Height in feet

THREEPENNY-BIT ROSE
Other Name: R. FARRERI PERSETOSA

The flowers are tiny — only a little larger than the pre-war threepenny-bit after which it is named. The ferny foliage with its miniature leaflets is in keeping with the flowers, but the bush itself is in complete contrast — it is a thorny mass of dense and tangled shoots. The blooms are borne in great profusion, in early June, and are followed by hips.

Blooms:	Single Pink Slightly fragrant
Foliage:	Medium green
Introduction:	1914
Type:	Species Rose
Growth Type:	Spreading
Flowering Period:	Early summer

UNCLE WALTER

Some catalogues call it a Hybrid Tea, but it is more generally classed as a Shrub Rose. It is a tall and untidy bush, but the flowers are neat and attractive — velvety, high-centred and full of petals. The colour does not fade nor turn blue with age, and the foliage has good resistance to disease. Too tall for bedding — use it as a specimen bush or hedge. *Uncle Walter* is highly recommended for cutting.

Blooms:	Double Crimson scarlet Slightly fragrant
Foliage:	Bronze-tinted
Introduction:	1963
Type:	Modern Shrub Rose
Growth Type:	Upright
Flowering Period:	Repeat flowering

WHITE BATH
Other Name: WHITE MOSS

A sport of the *Common Moss Rose*, with flowers which open pure white from pink-tinged buds. The fragrance is more intense than that of the parent, but the blooms are smaller. Both buds and stems are covered with green moss and the Shrub is suitable for use as a specimen bush or a low hedge. It may appear as *Shailer's White* or *R. centifolia muscosa alba* in the catalogues.

Blooms:	Double White Very fragrant
Foliage:	Medium green
Introduction:	1810
Type:	Moss Rose
Growth Type:	Open
Flowering Period:	Midsummer

WILLIAM LOBB
Other Name: OLD VELVET MOSS

A gaunt giant of a Moss Rose, used as a large specimen bush or as a pillar rose. There is a single flush of flowers, in late June or early July, with wide trusses of large blooms — at first fuchsia purple and finally slate grey in colour. The buds and flower stalks are mossy, but there is little moss on the stems and leaves. Choose *White Bath* if you want mossy stems.

Blooms:	Semi-double Purple magenta Fragrant
Foliage:	Dark green
Introduction:	1855
Type:	Moss Rose
Growth Type:	Open
Flowering Period:	Midsummer

YORK AND LANCASTER ROSE
Other Name: R. DAMASCENA VARIEGATA

The old *York and Lancaster Rose*, with its pink and white blooms on the same bush, may be of great interest to the historian but is of little interest to the ordinary gardener. Few flowers are produced and the Shrub is not vigorous. Sometimes there are pink and white petals on a single bloom, but if you want pink-and-white roses it is much better to choose *Rosa Mundi*.

Blooms:	Double Pink and white Fragrant
Foliage:	Light green
Introduction:	Before 1550
Type:	Damask Rose
Growth Type:	Bushy
Flowering Period:	Midsummer

YVONNE RABIER

Nearly all the old Polyantha Roses are now dead and forgotten, yet this 70 year old variety is still to be found in some catalogues. Keep it lightly pruned and grow it as a small specimen bush — in mild districts it is practically evergreen. The Polyantha trade-mark is there — small and open Rambler Rose-like blooms borne in large clusters. Disease resistance is only average, so spraying will be necessary.

Blooms:	Double White Fragrant
Foliage:	Medium green
Introduction:	1910
Type:	Polyantha Rose
Growth Type:	Bushy
Flowering Period:	Repeat flowering

CHAPTER 3
CHOOSING & BUYING ROSES

The secret of success for choosing the right roses is to start early. In summer, look through the selector guides (pages 74—78) and the A—Z sections (pages 7—72). Look through rose catalogues to find larger photographs of your chosen varieties, but never let a pretty picture be your sole guide. Try to see the roses growing in a display garden or nursery — only then will you know if the shape, colour and general form are right for you.

Shop early. If you are buying from a shop or garden centre, the widest selections should be available in autumn. This rule is even more important when shopping by mail order — the grower will substitute a similar variety if the one you have ordered is sold out. If you don't want this to happen, write 'No Substitutes' on your order.

Bargain Offers should be treated with great caution — you really do get what you pay for. Collections are different — they can be a good idea for a beginner but do check on the properties of each variety before buying. Most suppliers offer some form of guarantee system, but do make sure that failure isn't your own fault before claiming.

The type to buy

There are three types of planting material. The **bare-root** bush is lifted at the nursery during the dormant season (October-March) and sold over the counter or by post to the customer. In recent years an increasing number of these bare-root plants have been **prepackaged** for sale through shops, supermarkets and department stores as well as garden centres.

The correct type for some Climbers and Shrubs, most Miniatures and *all* roses during the growing season is the **container-grown** plant.

Bare-root

The traditional type for planting — dug up at the nursery or garden centre and taken home, or put on display with damp peat packed around the roots. Alternatively, the dormant roses are dug up and placed in wax-lined paper containers which are sent by post to the customer. The danger is drying out, see page 86 for instructions on how to deal with this problem.

Prepackaged

Prepackaged roses are bare-root plants with moist peat around the roots and the whole plant housed in a polythene bag and/or a box. There are advantages — reasonable price, ready availability from shops everywhere and coloured pictures plus instructions. But there can be problems — premature growth and shrivelled stems if kept too warm.

Container-grown

Container-grown roses can be bought to provide instant colour, but they are more expensive than bare-root plants and need extra care at planting time. Choose a specimen for its sturdiness and good health — not for the beauty of its few flowers. Make sure it has been grown in the container — not transferred into it from open ground.

What to look for

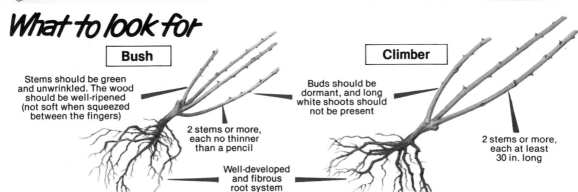

Bush

Stems should be green and unwrinkled. The wood should be well-ripened (not soft when squeezed between the fingers)

2 stems or more, each no thinner than a pencil

Well-developed and fibrous root system

Climber

Buds should be dormant, and long white shoots should not be present

2 stems or more, each at least 30 in. long

HYBRID TEA SELECTOR

Hybrid Teas are chosen for the reason given on page 8. Now you have chosen this group, it is necessary to pick the varieties which will suit your situation and personal preferences.

Using the keys on this page you will obtain a short list of roses, selected on the basis of three fundamental features—colour, height and fragrance. Next, look up each variety in the A—Z guide (pages 9—29) to discover its good and bad points. Note carefully that some roses are recommended for producing exhibition blooms and not for garden display—such varieties often produce only a few blooms and may be easily damaged by bad weather.

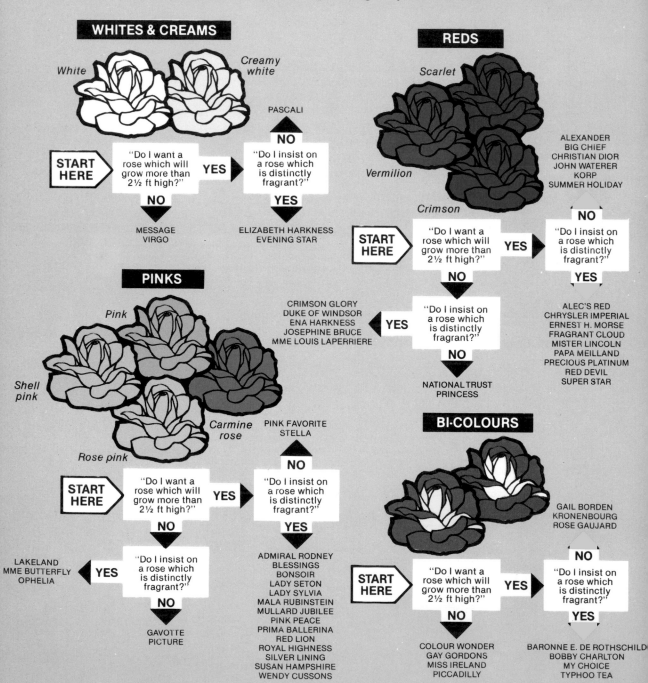

WHITES & CREAMS

White

Creamy white

PASCALI

START HERE → "Do I want a rose which will grow more than 2½ ft high?" **YES** → "Do I insist on a rose which is distinctly fragrant?" **NO**

NO → MESSAGE VIRGO

YES → ELIZABETH HARKNESS EVENING STAR

REDS

Scarlet

Vermilion

Crimson

ALEXANDER
BIG CHIEF
CHRISTIAN DIOR
JOHN WATERER
KORP
SUMMER HOLIDAY

START HERE → "Do I want a rose which will grow more than 2½ ft high?" **YES** → "Do I insist on a rose which is distinctly fragrant?" **NO**

NO → "Do I insist on a rose which is distinctly fragrant?"

YES → CRIMSON GLORY
DUKE OF WINDSOR
ENA HARKNESS
JOSEPHINE BRUCE
MME LOUIS LAPERRIERE

NO → NATIONAL TRUST PRINCESS

YES → ALEC'S RED
CHRYSLER IMPERIAL
ERNEST H. MORSE
FRAGRANT CLOUD
MISTER LINCOLN
PAPA MEILLAND
PRECIOUS PLATINUM
RED DEVIL
SUPER STAR

PINKS

Pink

Shell pink

Rose pink

Carmine rose

Pink favorite
STELLA

CRIMSON GLORY
DUKE OF WINDSOR
ENA HARKNESS
JOSEPHINE BRUCE
MME LOUIS LAPERRIERE

START HERE → "Do I want a rose which will grow more than 2½ ft high?" **YES** → "Do I insist on a rose which is distinctly fragrant?" **NO**

NO → "Do I insist on a rose which is distinctly fragrant?"

YES → LAKELAND
MME BUTTERFLY
OPHELIA

NO → GAVOTTE PICTURE

YES → ADMIRAL RODNEY
BLESSINGS
BONSOIR
LADY SETON
LADY SYLVIA
MALA RUBINSTEIN
MULLARD JUBILEE
PINK PEACE
PRIMA BALLERINA
RED LION
ROYAL HIGHNESS
SILVER LINING
SUSAN HAMPSHIRE
WENDY CUSSONS

BI-COLOURS

GAIL BORDEN
KRONENBOURG
ROSE GAUJARD

START HERE → "Do I want a rose which will grow more than 2½ ft high?" **YES** → "Do I insist on a rose which is distinctly fragrant?" **NO**

NO → COLOUR WONDER
GAY GORDONS
MISS IRELAND
PICCADILLY

YES → BARONNE E. DE ROTHSCHILD
BOBBY CHARLTON
MY CHOICE
TYPHOO TEA

YELLOWS

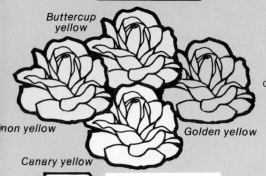

Buttercup yellow

mon yellow

Golden yellow

Canary yellow

BUCCANEER
CITY OF GLOUCESTER
FRED GIBSON
GOLD CROWN
GRANDPA DICKSON
SUMMER SUNSHINE
SUNBLEST

START HERE → "Do I want a rose which will grow more than 2½ ft high?" **YES** → "Do I insist on a rose which is distinctly fragrant?"

 NO

NO ↓

"Do I insist on a rose which is distinctly fragrant?" **YES** ← LLE BLONDE / G'S RANSOM

YES ↓ (from top question)

DIORAMA
DUTCH GOLD
GOLDEN TIMES
LOLITA
MISS HARP
SUTTER'S GOLD

NO ↓

YELLOW PAGES

LILACS

BLUE MOON

STRIPES

HARRY WHEATCROFT

ORANGES & BLENDS

Apricot

Blends

Salmon

Peach

Tangerine

APRICOT SILK
CHICAGO PEACE
DORIS TYSTERMAN
MISCHIEF
MOJAVE
PEACE
PEER GYNT
PERFECTA
SWEET PROMISE

START HERE → "Do I want a rose which will grow more than 2½ ft high?" **YES** → "Do I insist on a rose which is distinctly fragrant?"

NO ↓

ALPINE SUNSET
BETTINA
CHAMPION
DR A.J. VERHAGE
MRS SAM McGREDY
SHOT SILK
SILVER JUBILEE
TYPHOON
WHISKY MAC

YES ← "Do I insist on a rose which is distinctly fragrant?"

YES ↓

ADOLF HORSTMANN
DEKORAT
DOUBLE DELIGHT
HELEN TRAUBEL
TENERIFE
TROIKA

NO ↓

BEAUTE
CHESHIRE LIFE
JUST JOEY
MICHELE MEILLAND

FLORIBUNDA SELECTOR

Floribundas are chosen in preference to Hybrid Teas where a large splash of garden colour is required, especially where the setting is informal.

The varieties you choose must be right for your garden and right for your personal taste. Use the keys on this page to obtain a short list, and then look up each variety in the A—Z guide (pages 31—46) for its good and bad points. Check the average height—Floribundas range from 1½ ft dwarfs to 5 ft giants, and catalogues are sometimes a little vague about the meaning of 'short' and 'tall'.

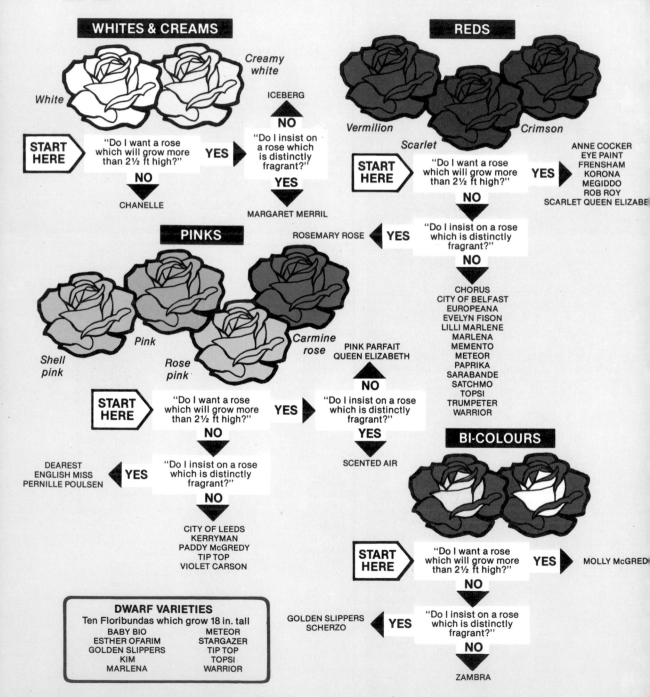

WHITES & CREAMS

White   *Creamy white*

ICEBERG

START HERE → "Do I want a rose which will grow more than 2½ ft high?" → **YES** → "Do I insist on a rose which is distinctly fragrant?"

NO ↓   **NO** ↑

CHANELLE   **YES** ↓

MARGARET MERRIL

REDS

Vermilion   *Scarlet*   *Crimson*

START HERE → "Do I want a rose which will grow more than 2½ ft high?" → **YES** →

ANNE COCKER
EYE PAINT
FRENSHAM
KORONA
MEGIDDO
ROB ROY
SCARLET QUEEN ELIZABETH

NO ↓

ROSEMARY ROSE ← **YES** ← "Do I insist on a rose which is distinctly fragrant?"

NO ↓

CHORUS
CITY OF BELFAST
EUROPEANA
EVELYN FISON
LILLI MARLENE
MARLENA
MEMENTO
METEOR
PAPRIKA
SARABANDE
SATCHMO
TOPSI
TRUMPETER
WARRIOR

PINKS

Shell pink   *Pink*   *Rose pink*   *Carmine rose*

PINK PARFAIT
QUEEN ELIZABETH

START HERE → "Do I want a rose which will grow more than 2½ ft high?" → **YES** → "Do I insist on a rose which is distinctly fragrant?"

NO ↓   **NO** ↑

DEAREST
ENGLISH MISS
PERNILLE POULSEN ← **YES** ← "Do I insist on a rose which is distinctly fragrant?"

NO ↓   **YES** ↓

SCENTED AIR

CITY OF LEEDS
KERRYMAN
PADDY McGREDY
TIP TOP
VIOLET CARSON

BI-COLOURS

START HERE → "Do I want a rose which will grow more than 2½ ft high?" → **YES** → MOLLY McGREDY

NO ↓

GOLDEN SLIPPERS
SCHERZO ← **YES** ← "Do I insist on a rose which is distinctly fragrant?"

NO ↓

ZAMBRA

DWARF VARIETIES
Ten Floribundas which grow 18 in. tall

BABY BIO
ESTHER OFARIM
GOLDEN SLIPPERS
KIM
MARLENA
METEOR
STARGAZER
TIP TOP
TOPSI
WARRIOR

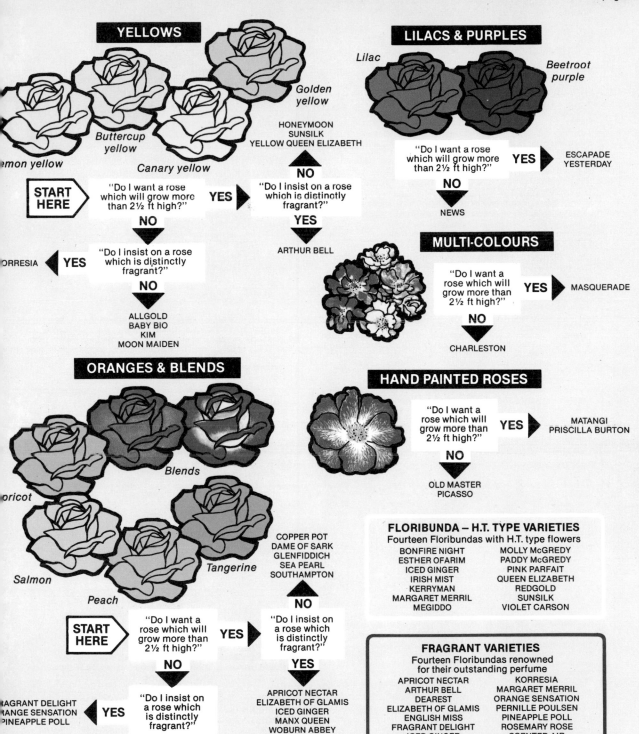

YELLOWS

Lemon yellow
Buttercup yellow
Canary yellow
Golden yellow

HONEYMOON
SUNSILK
YELLOW QUEEN ELIZABETH

START HERE → "Do I want a rose which will grow more than 2½ ft high?" — **YES** → "Do I insist on a rose which is distinctly fragrant?"

NO ↓ (from first question)

NO ↓ (from fragrant question) → HONEYMOON / SUNSILK / YELLOW QUEEN ELIZABETH

YES ↓ → ARTHUR BELL

"Do I insist on a rose which is distinctly fragrant?" — **YES** → KORRESIA

NO ↓
ALLGOLD
BABY BIO
KIM
MOON MAIDEN

LILACS & PURPLES

Lilac
Beetroot purple

"Do I want a rose which will grow more than 2½ ft high?" — **YES** → ESCAPADE / YESTERDAY

NO ↓
NEWS

MULTI-COLOURS

"Do I want a rose which will grow more than 2½ ft high?" — **YES** → MASQUERADE

NO ↓
CHARLESTON

ORANGES & BLENDS

Apricot
Blends
Salmon
Peach
Tangerine

COPPER POT
DAME OF SARK
GLENFIDDICH
SEA PEARL
SOUTHAMPTON

START HERE → "Do I want a rose which will grow more than 2½ ft high?" — **YES** → "Do I insist on a rose which is distinctly fragrant?"

NO ↓ → **NO** ↓ → COPPER POT / DAME OF SARK / GLENFIDDICH / SEA PEARL / SOUTHAMPTON

YES ↓ →
APRICOT NECTAR
ELIZABETH OF GLAMIS
ICED GINGER
MANX QUEEN
WOBURN ABBEY

"Do I insist on a rose which is distinctly fragrant?" — **YES** → FRAGRANT DELIGHT / ORANGE SENSATION / PINEAPPLE POLL

NO ↓
ANNA WHEATCROFT
BONFIRE NIGHT
CIRCUS
IRISH MIST
LIVING FIRE
ORANGEADE
REDGOLD
STARGAZER

HAND PAINTED ROSES

"Do I want a rose which will grow more than 2½ ft high?" — **YES** → MATANGI / PRISCILLA BURTON

NO ↓
OLD MASTER
PICASSO

FLORIBUNDA – H.T. TYPE VARIETIES
Fourteen Floribundas with H.T. type flowers

BONFIRE NIGHT	MOLLY McGREDY
ESTHER OFARIM	PADDY McGREDY
ICED GINGER	PINK PARFAIT
IRISH MIST	QUEEN ELIZABETH
KERRYMAN	REDGOLD
MARGARET MERRIL	SUNSILK
MEGIDDO	VIOLET CARSON

FRAGRANT VARIETIES
Fourteen Floribundas renowned for their outstanding perfume

APRICOT NECTAR	KORRESIA
ARTHUR BELL	MARGARET MERRIL
DEAREST	ORANGE SENSATION
ELIZABETH OF GLAMIS	PERNILLE POULSEN
ENGLISH MISS	PINEAPPLE POLL
FRAGRANT DELIGHT	ROSEMARY ROSE
ICED GINGER	SCENTED AIR

EASY-TO-GROW VARIETIES
Fifteen Floribundas for beginners, poor soils and industrial areas

ALLGOLD	ICEBERG	PINK PARFAIT
ANNE COCKER	LILLI MARLENE	QUEEN ELIZABETH
ARTHUR BELL	LIVING FIRE	ROB ROY
CITY OF LEEDS	MATANGI	SCENTED AIR
EVELYN FISON	PERNILLE POULSEN	SOUTHAMPTON

SHRUB ROSE SELECTOR

Shrub Roses suffer by being in the shadow of their universally popular relatives — the Floribunda and Hybrid Tea. Regard them as extremely useful shrubs — alternatives to Lilac and Rhododendron rather than rivals to *Piccadilly* and *Super Star*. There are many groups of Shrub Roses as shown below. Representatives of each one appear in the A—Z guide (pages 62—72).

SPECIES ROSES

All wild roses are included in this group, together with their close relatives. Many are known by their Latin names (e.g. *Rosa rubrifolia*) but some have Common names (e.g. *Canary Bird*). Most Species Roses bloom only once a year, but this flowering period may be earlier than for any bush rose.

The origin of most Species Roses is lost in history, but some are modern. The Kordes hybrids (*Frühlingsgold* and *Frühlingsmorgen*) are 20th century improvements of the Scotch Briar. The Penzance Briars (*Lady Penzance*) are 19th century improvements of the Sweet Briar.

OLD-FASHIONED ROSES

Most Shrub Roses belong here. In general these are the garden roses of yesteryear — dating back to the era when there were no Hybrid Teas or Floribundas. There are two exceptions — both the Hybrid Musks and Rugosa Shrubs are 20th century creations.

RUGOSA SHRUB

Rosa rugosa alba and the modern hybrids are hardy shrubs which will thrive in soils and conditions where hardly any other rose would survive. The leaves are uniquely wrinkled and remarkably disease-free. The repeat flowering stems are dense and thorny, making this group an excellent choice for hedging. The flowers are fragrant, and the hips are usually large.

ALBA ROSE

You can easily recognize an Alba Rose by its soft and drooping grey-green leaves. The vigorous bush resists both pests and diseases, and some rigorous pruning may be necessary to keep it in check. The flowers appear in a single flush in midsummer — pink or white with a rich scent. Alba Roses withstand partial shade better than most other roses.

DAMASK ROSE

The perfume of the white or pink flowers is the glory of the Damask Rose. It has never been really popular — the arching, weak stems bear dull foliage, and the weak flower stalks allow the blooms to droop. The flowers are borne mainly in clusters, and appear as a single flush in midsummer. Damask Roses are very hardy, but need good soil and proper cultivation.

POLYANTHA ROSE

A group of low-growing Shrub Roses, rarely reaching more than 3 ft. The bushes are extremely hardy, and produce large clusters of small blooms more or less continually throughout the summer and autumn. A few Polyanthas remain in the catalogues, but this group has been almost completely replaced by their much showier offspring — the Floribundas.

CENTIFOLIA ROSE

This is the Cabbage Rose, so-called from its double, globular flowers. With its cottage garden colours and heavy fragrance, the Centifolia Rose is the epitome of old-fashioned roses. Unfortunately, this group has none of the robustness of the Rugosas or the Albas — the stems are lax and need support, and the bushes require regular spraying and feeding.

MOSS ROSE

About 300 years ago an unknown Centifolia Rose produced a sport — the Moss Rose. All Moss Roses are rather similar to the parent type but bear distinctive green or brown "moss" (sticky hairs) all over the sepals and flower stalks. The sweet-smelling blooms have an old-fashioned look, appearing once a year in midsummer.

GALLICA ROSE

The first garden rose of all, which has collected many common names on the way — French Rose, Apothecary's Rose and Rose of Provins. The hybrids grown today are usually compact, with rough leaves and semi-double or double blooms. *Rosa Mundi* is the one you are most likely to see, and like other Gallicas it is practically thornless, midsummer flowering, successful in poor soils and prone to mildew.

CHINA ROSE

The importance of China Roses in the development of modern varieties has been described elsewhere (see page 110). *Old Blush*, one of the original imports from China in the 18th century, is still available and so is the Victorian favourite, *Cécile Brunner*. The hybrids you can buy are slender open shrubs, bearing large clusters of small flowers throughout the summer. Plant in a sunny, protected site.

BOURBON ROSE

In about 1818 a cross occurred between *Autumn Damask* and a China Rose, and the Bourbon group of roses was born. The fragrant globular flowers, large and many-petalled, became the most popular roses in Victorian gardens, for they had the advantage of blooming in autumn as well as June. Eventually they lost their crown to the Hybrid Perpetuals, and today you will find very few varieties in the catalogues.

HYBRID PERPETUAL

At the end of the 19th century the Hybrid Perpetual became the most popular garden rose in Britain. A few of the thousands of varieties are still available, but of course the Floribundas and Hybrid Teas have taken over. The H.P. lost its crown because it is *not* perpetual — there is a summer flush followed by an autumn one. The bush tends to be too vigorous for average gardens and the blooms are cupped, not high-centred.

HYBRID MUSK

Reverend Pemberton introduced and named this group at the beginning of the 20th century. The scent is similar to that of the old Musk Rose, but there is no close relationship. They are suitable for the average-sized garden, provided that their sprawling habit is kept in check. An abundance of trusses appears in June and July, and the autumn show is particularly impressive.

MODERN SHRUB ROSES

A widely diverse group of roses with little in common apart from their 20th century origin. Most, but not all, are repeat flowering and the shape of the blooms is usually modern rather than old-fashioned.

CHAPTER 4
USING ROSES

As everybody knows, roses are for growing in beds and borders, growing up walls and growing over arches and screens. But on this page you will find many more uses for the Queen of Flowers. On the appropriate page you will find a list of rules for each of these uses, but do remember that it is *your* garden to use in any way you like . . . with one proviso. Make sure that the variety or varieties you choose are suitable for the use you have in mind.

PLANTING IN BEDS page 80

PLANTING IN BORDERS page 81

PLANTING AS SPECIMENS page 82

COVERING SCREENS page 84

GROWING UNDER GLASS page 83

COVERING TREES page 84

PLANTING AS SPECIMENS page 82

PLANTING IN ROCKERIES page 81

COVERING WALLS page 84

USING AS CUT FLOWERS page 117

USING AS HOUSE PLANTS page 118

GROWING IN TUBS page 83

PLANTING AS GROUND COVER page 82

PLANTING AS HEDGES page 82

USING IN BUTTONHOLES page 119

USING IN THE KITCHEN page 119

EXHIBITING page 112

MAKING PERFUME page 118

Planting in Beds

A bed is a planted area which is designed to be viewed from all sides.

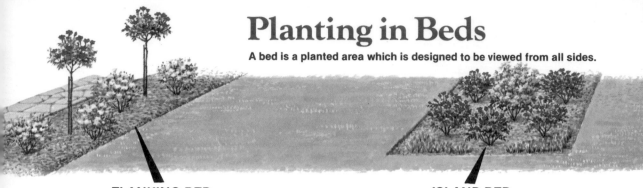

FLANKING BED

Many gardens have one or more beds which divide the lawn from a path or driveway. These can be turned into attractive flanking beds by using a single line of roses.

Standards and weeping standards are the most important types for this purpose, and the bed must be wide enough to support them.

Underplanting is essential here. Where roses are used, choose compact varieties which will not compete with the standards. Dwarf Floribundas are ideal for this purpose.

Colour

According to some purists, you should only plant one variety per bed. In most gardens this is not practical and would lead to a distinctly dull appearance. It is important to avoid the other extreme — a large bed filled with single plants of many varieties, giving a patchwork quilt effect.

The best plan is to use 3–5 bushes of each variety. You can obtain all sorts of advice from the experts about which colours harmonize and which do not, but the grouping of colour is a matter of taste and you should not worry too much about colour clashes. Reds, however, can be a problem as some shades clash horribly. It is advisable to separate groups of red roses by planting white, cream or pale yellow varieties as dividers between them.

Underplanting

Some rose experts believe that no other plants should be grown in a rose bed. Their reason is usually based on the old tradition that the glory of roses is spoilt by "inferior" flowers, but there are also sound practical reasons for not underplanting. Mulching is made difficult or impossible, reserves of water and nutrients are depleted and walking between the bushes for maintenance work may become a tricky operation.

If you select the right plants, the drawbacks of underplanting become insignificant and the advantages are important — a colourful display when the roses are leafless or flowerless. The plants chosen must be low-growing and shallow-rooting, and when grown as an edging there is no inconvenience.

Spring bulbs are useful — Crocus, Snowdrop, etc., but avoid bulbs which have to be lifted regularly and avoid the larger bulbs with foliage which looks unsightly after flowering. Other favourites for underplanting are Primula Wanda, Auricula, Primrose, Candytuft, Ageratum, Viola, Aubretia, Alpine Phlox and Arabis.

ISLAND BED

Rose beds first began to appear about 100 years ago, and now they are a basic feature of the British garden. Gravel or crazy-paving is sometimes used to surround them, but grass is the traditional and still the best pathway between beds. Avoid lots of tiny beds — large and few is the general rule.

Beds are usually formal, with the roses planted in a strictly geometric pattern. Hybrid Teas or Floribundas can be used, but it is advisable not to mix the two types. Use Hybrid Teas if the bed is close to the house and where each bloom is to be admired. Choose Floribundas where a large splash of continuous colour is the prime need.

Keep things in proportion — small bushes in small beds. An appearance of flatness is a danger, especially in medium-sized or large beds. This can be avoided by planting a standard or a tall-growing variety in the centre.

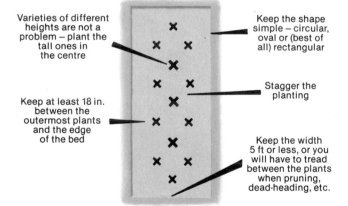

Varieties of different heights are not a problem – plant the tall ones in the centre

Keep the shape simple – circular, oval or (best of all) rectangular

Stagger the planting

Keep at least 18 in. between the outermost plants and the edge of the bed

Keep the width 5 ft or less, or you will have to tread between the plants when pruning, dead-heading, etc.

The Ideal Bedding Rose

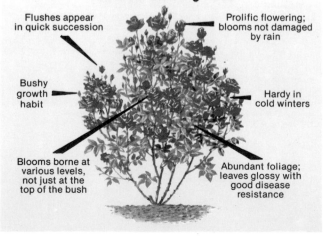

Flushes appear in quick succession

Prolific flowering; blooms not damaged by rain

Bushy growth habit

Hardy in cold winters

Blooms borne at various levels, not just at the top of the bush

Abundant foliage; leaves glossy with good disease resistance

Planting in Borders

A border is a planted area which is designed to be viewed from one, two or three sides but not the back.

In the formal border, the rules on page 80 for the formal rose bed apply apart from the fact that the tallest-growing varieties are planted at the back of the border and the shortest at the front. A mass of colour is all-important and so Floribundas are more widely used than Hybrid Teas.

It is much more usual for a rose border to be informal, with the plants grouped and spaced according to their height and width. Here you can choose from the whole of the rose kingdom. In a large border you can use Climbers and Ramblers as well as tall Shrubs to make up the back row — in a smaller garden pillar roses and more modest Shrubs will be used.

Exploit the wide range of roses to the full — as a rough guide fill about half the space with Floribundas and a few Hybrid Teas, planting the rest of the border with roses of other types. Plant *Canary Bird* for flowers in the spring, and *Rosa rugosa* hybrids for red hips in the winter.

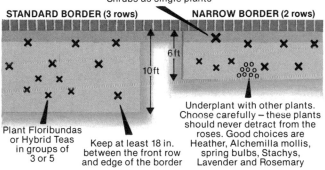

Grow Climbers and large Shrubs as single plants

STANDARD BORDER (3 rows)

NARROW BORDER (2 rows)

6 ft

10 ft

Plant Floribundas or Hybrid Teas in groups of 3 or 5

Keep at least 18 in. between the front row and edge of the border

Underplant with other plants. Choose carefully — these plants should never detract from the roses. Good choices are Heather, Alchemilla mollis, spring bulbs, Stachys, Lavender and Rosemary

Planting in Rockeries

Some years ago it would have been unthinkable to grow roses in the rockery, but the wide range of Miniatures now available has changed all that. The taller-growing varieties, such as *Baby Masquerade*, can add height when set amongst low clumps of alpines, in the same way that dwarf Conifers are used. The smaller varieties, such as *Sweet Fairy*, can be used to form 6 in. mounds of green leaves and double blooms.

Whatever variety is used, Miniature Roses bring the blessing of midsummer flowers to an area of the garden where spring colour is abundant but summer colour is scarce. Careful maintenance is essential. The root run may be restricted, so watering will be necessary in dry weather. Spray against mildew and black spot, and keep the plants properly shaped by pruning with scissors. Do not plant Miniatures amongst rampant growers.

The Mixed Shrub Border

A visit to some of the great gardens of Britain will reveal the full extent of the beauty of a rose border. More modest examples can be seen in large private gardens throughout the country, but the simple truth is that for most people there is only room for one shrub border, and that is made up of Forsythia, Hydrangea, Ribes, Lilac and the rest.

It is surprising that so many of these shrub borders do not contain one Shrub Rose — even though it could provide colour and fragrance in midsummer when so many shrubberies are short of flowers.

For the rose lover a border of roses interspersed with approximately the same number of shrubs is an excellent idea. The roses are helped in three ways:

- Grey-leaved shrubs such as Lavender provide an excellent background for the pinks and purples of old-fashioned roses when in bloom.
- Evergreens such as Conifers provide a leafy skeleton for the border when roses are not in leaf.
- Winter- and early spring-flowering shrubs such as Forsythia and Viburnum tinus provide a floral display when roses are not in bloom.

The Mixed Herbaceous Border

For many people there are rose beds and herbaceous borders, and never the twain shall meet. In recent years the clear-cut barriers have started to break down, and many writers now sing the praises of Floribundas amongst the perennials.

The benefit to the border is obvious — an abundance of flowers throughout the summer to liven up the large blank spaces which sometimes occur.

The roses also benefit — bare stem bases can be successfully hidden and there is surrounding colour before the rose season begins. Careful selection is obviously important. First of all, get the height right — tall varieties such as *Queen Elizabeth* or *Alexander* are for the back of the border, the 1½–3ft Floribundas for the middle region, and the Miniatures for the front of the border where they make a welcome change from low-growing perennials.

Colour should also be carefully watched. Brilliant reds can be too eye-catching — the pinks and creams are especially suitable. Finally, make sure the bushes are given ample space — overcrowding can lead to mildew.

Planting as Hedges

A hedge is a continuous line of bushes in which the individuality of each plant is lost. Unlike a plant-covered fence (see page 84) a hedge requires little or no support.

The text books are right — roses can make a splendid hedge for both large and small gardens. Rose lovers sometimes scorn the all-too-familiar privet and yew, but before digging up your present hedge it would be wise to study the drawbacks of roses used in this way. Firstly, a rose hedge loses its leaves in winter. Next, it is informal and uneven in shape, and must not be chopped into a neat, squared-off outline with shears. Finally, it will not succeed in dense shade.

In the right situation, however, no other living screen will provide such an abundant and continuous display of flowers. Maintenance is simple — just dead-heading in summer and pruning in winter. Pick your variety with care — remember that many shrubs grow more than 5ft wide. A hedging variety should be hardy, repeat flowering, abundantly supplied with foliage and it should be healthy — nobody wants to spray a hedge every fortnight! Rugosa Shrubs (see page 78) are the best of all boundary hedges. The prickly stems are animal- and child-proof, the handsome foliage is mildew-free and many varieties bear attractive hips in winter. *Scabrosa* takes pride of place, closely followed by *Roseraie de l'Haÿ*. The Hybrid Musks are another popular group with *Penelope* as the favourite. With this group some support may be necessary, and long summer shoots may have to be cut back. The tall-growing Floribunda *Queen Elizabeth* has become a familiar hedge, but it can be disappointing. The secret is to prune the stems to different lengths. In this way leaves and flowers will be borne at varying heights instead of just at the top.

TALL HEDGE (5ft and over)
Shrub Roses or tall Floribundas
Plant 3ft apart (Exception: Queen Elizabeth — 2ft apart)

Recommended Varieties:

CANARY BIRD	FELICIA	QUEEN ELIZABETH
CELESTIAL	NYMPHENBURG	ROSA RUGOSA ALBA
CHINATOWN	PENELOPE	ROSERAIE DE L'HAŸ
CORNELIA	PINK GROOTENDORST	SCABROSA

MEDIUM HEDGE (2½ – 5ft)
Floribundas, Hybrid Teas or compact Shrub Roses
Plant 1½ft apart   Single row planting is possible, but 2 staggered rows are better

Rows 1½ft apart

Recommended Varieties:

ALEXANDER	FRAU DAGMAR HARTOPP	PEACE
ANGELINA	ICEBERG	PINK PARFAIT
BALLERINA	MARGARET MERRIL	SILVER JUBILEE
EYE PAINT	MASQUERADE	SOUTHAMPTON

SMALL HEDGE (under 2½ft)
Dwarf Floribundas or Miniature Roses

Planting as Specimens

A specimen rose is one which is grown to be admired on its own as distinct from being grouped with other plants.

The faults of a rose in a bed or border are partly hidden by its neighbours. Bare stems can be hidden by low-growing plants in the foreground, and lop-sided growth is often compensated for by the stems of nearby plants.

A specimen rose stands on its own. When well-grown it is a thing of unmatched beauty — when badly grown it can be an eyesore. So for all specimen roses careful selection and proper maintenance are especially important.

The basic rule is to keep the plant in balance with its surroundings. An average-sized Hybrid Tea could look insignificant set as a solitary specimen in a large lawn, in the same way that a giant cascading shrub has no place in the centre of a tiny front garden. A favourite specimen is the standard rose, grown in a circular bed in the lawn. Weeping, full, half and miniature versions are available (see page 4). In addition, many shrubs make excellent specimen roses where space is adequate. The catalogues sing the praises of *Nevada*, but there are also *Fred Loads*, *Frühlingsgold*, *Joseph's Coat* and *Moonlight*.

For the smaller garden, the choice is made from Floribundas and Hybrid Teas. Of course, there are *Iceberg*, *Masquerade*, *Peace*, and *Queen Elizabeth* as a walk along any suburban road will reveal, but there are many others to choose from, such as *Arthur Bell*, *Mala Rubinstein* and *National Trust*.

Planting as Ground Cover

A ground cover rose is a low-growing and spreading plant which forms a dense leafy mat.

Roses as ground cover plants may seem a modern idea, but some wild roses grow this way in their natural habitat. The uses of these prostrate roses in the garden are quite numerous — such as hiding unsightly mounds and manhole covers, edging rose beds and covering steep banks.

Never regard ground cover roses as weed eliminators — planting in couch grass-infested soil will leave you with the hopeless task of trying to pull out grass from a tangled thorny mass of rose stems. Before planting always remove the roots of perennial weeds from the soil.

The best variety to choose will depend on the job you want it to do. If there is a large stretch of land to cover, use a Rambler Rose. It is strange that the tall growing older varieties can be used in this way, but without their usual support. *Albéric Barbier*, *Crimson Shower*, *Dorothy Perkins* and *François Juranville* will happily grow along the ground.

Such vigorous Ramblers have no place in the average-sized garden where a small patch or narrow strip of ground is to be covered. Use *Max Graf*, which will quickly produce a 5ft mat of green leaves and pink flowers, or if you want a more limited spread choose the Japanese rose *Nozomi* with its tiny leaves and small pearly flowers.

Growing under Glass

The appearance of the first blooms of the year are eagerly awaited by every rose lover. By growing roses in pots in an unheated greenhouse these first flowers can be obtained in mid April. If the greenhouse is heated, the plants will bloom in March. There are extra benefits — the flowers are perfect, free from wind and rain damage, and delicate varieties such as *Baccara* can be grown.

Planting takes place in October or November. Use a bare-root plant and a 10 in. clay or plastic pot. A clay pot should be soaked in water before use. If a plastic pot is chosen, put a few large pebbles in the bottom to increase stability.

Use John Innes or a peat-based compost. Keep the crown level with the top of the pot and use the end of a blunt stick to firm the compost around the roots. Leave a 2 in. space between the top of the compost and the rim. Finally, water the compost thoroughly.

Stand the pot outdoors on a firm surface (concrete, gravel, ash etc.), not in contact with the soil. The site should be unshaded but protected from strong winds and look after it during the spring and summer as if it was an ordinary tub rose (see below). Water in dry weather, spray when necessary and cut off dead flowers. There are one or two differences — remove nearly all flower buds so that only a few blooms appear and feed by spraying the leaves with a foliar feed such as Fillip.

In November or December cut the stems back to 6 in. and move the pots into the greenhouse. Add 1 oz of Toprose Fertilizer to the surface of the compost in each pot.

Avoid the various pitfalls which are likely during this forcing stage. Water properly — soak the pot thoroughly and then allow the compost to become partly dry before rewatering. On mild sunny days during spring ventilate the greenhouse adequately to avoid mildew. Paint the glass with Coolglass if the weather remains sunny.

From April onwards, use a liquid feed such as Bio Plant Food on a little-but-often basis. Once flowering is over, move the pots outdoors again until November, and then begin the sequence all over again. Repot every three years.

Recommended Varieties:

ALLGOLD	MME BUTTERFLY
BACCARA	MY CHOICE
BLESSINGS	NATIONAL TRUST
CIRCUS	PASCALI
CRIMSON GLORY	PEER GYNT
DR A. J. VERHAGE	PERFECTA
ENA HARKNESS	PICCADILLY
ERNEST H. MORSE	PINK FAVORITE
FRAGRANT CLOUD	PRINCESS
GAVOTTE	RED DEVIL
GRANDPA DICKSON	RED LION
JOSEPHINE BRUCE	STELLA
KORP	SUPER STAR
LADY SYLVIA	SUTTER'S GOLD
MICHELE MEILLAND	WENDY CUSSONS

The Quick Method

The traditional method outlined above results in a gap of 18 months between planting and the appearance of the first greenhouse blooms. A quicker but less satisfactory method is to use a container-grown rose instead of a bare-root plant. Pot up the specimen in an 8 in. pot in October, carefully avoiding root disturbance. Bring the pot indoors in December, and treat according to the general rules. After flowering, stand the pot outdoors and at the end of the summer transplant into a 10 in. pot.

Growing in Tubs

Growing roses in tubs on the terrace is a welcome addition to the plants in the beds and borders of the garden, but for balconies and in some town gardens it is the *only* way to grow roses.

The first step is to choose the right container. Some experts believe that wooden casks make the only truly satisfactory type, but you can choose from a large range of materials — plastic, fibreglass, stone, metal and so on. Much more important than material is size — a good root run is essential which means a depth of 9 in. for Miniatures and 15 in. for average-sized Floribundas and Hybrid Teas.

The tub should be stood on blocks to allow free drainage, and a 1–2 in. layer of rubble or crocks placed over the drainage holes. Use a soil-based compost or, if weight is a problem, a peat-based compost.

There is a wide selection of roses to choose from, but reject all varieties which do not have good disease resistance and avoid all Hybrid Teas and Floribundas which are described as tall and upright. As a general rule the most satisfactory tub roses are the dwarf Flori-bundas listed on page 76. Standards can be grown, provided firm staking is used.

Edging with spring flowering plants such as primroses and miniature bulbs or with trailing plants such as Lobelia is a matter of personal taste. The cultural rules, however, must be followed. Place the tub in a sunny spot away from overhanging trees. Water during dry weather but never keep the compost permanently wet. Feed twice a year with Toprose Fertilizer — 2 oz per container when the leaves are beginning to unfold, and 1 oz in June or July.

Covering Screens

There are Climber and Rambler varieties, but no rose has a natural climbing habit of growth. They neither twist around supports nor send out tendrils like a vine, so you will need both a sturdy support and some way of attaching the stems to the support.

Fence

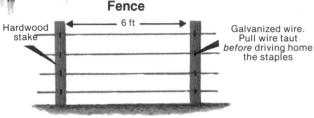

Hardwood stake

6 ft

Galvanized wire. Pull wire taut *before* driving home the staples

Trellis

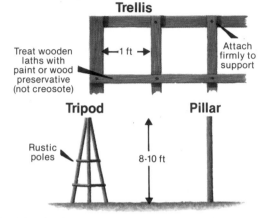

Treat wooden laths with paint or wood preservative (not creosote)

1 ft

Attach firmly to support

Tripod

Rustic poles

Pillar

8-10 ft

- The basal shoots of climbing roses must be trained as described on page 89. Use plastic-covered wire ties to attach the stems to the support — do not wind the young stems around the straining wires of a fence. Do not twist the wire ties too tightly around the main stems — leave room for the canes to increase in diameter.

- Ensure that all fence posts and pillars are well-anchored. Strong winds can cause havoc when the roses are in full leaf if the underground part of the support is too shallow or rotten.

- Ramblers can be grown on open screens, arches, pergolas, etc. where a large area is to be covered. Try to avoid tangling the stems when training. Before choosing a Rambler, read about the drawbacks on page 51.

Recommended Varieties:

Pillars & Fences

ALOHA	GOLDEN SHOWERS	PARKDIREKTOR RIGGERS
ALTISSIMO	HAMBURGER PHOENIX	PINK PERPETUE
BANTRY BAY	HANDEL	ROSY MANTLE
COMPASSION	ICEBERG, CLIMBING	SCHOOLGIRL
COPENHAGEN	LEVERKUSEN	SHOT SILK, CLIMBING
DANSE DU FEU	MAIGOLD	SWAN LAKE
DORTMUND	MASQUERADE, CLIMBING	SYMPATHIE
DUBLIN BAY	MEG	WHITE COCKADE
GALWAY BAY	NEW DAWN	ZEPHIRINE DROUHIN

Arches & Pergolas

Ramblers are once flowering, prone to mildew and difficult to prune. For some gardeners, however, the thin pliable stems still make them first choice for arches and pergolas.

ALBERIC BARBIER	EXCELSA
ALBERTINE	FRANÇOIS JURANVILLE
CRIMSON SHOWER	PAUL'S SCARLET CLIMBER
EMILY GRAY	VEILCHENBLAU

Covering Walls

There were roses growing on the walls of British houses before the birth of Hybrid Teas and Floribundas, and they remain an important feature. But they can be more trouble than they are worth if you don't choose wisely and provide a proper support.

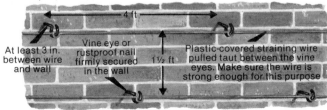

At least 3 in. between wire and wall

Vine eye or rustproof nail firmly secured in the wall

4 ft

1½ ft

Plastic-covered straining wire pulled taut between the vine eyes. Make sure the wire is strong enough for this purpose

Recommended Varieties:

Never choose a variety which is particularly prone to mildew, which rules out most Ramblers.

North & East Walls

DANSE DU FEU
FELICITE ET PERPETUE
GUINEE
HAMBURGER PHOENIX
LEVERKUSEN
MAIGOLD
MME ALFRED CARRIERE
SYMPATHIE

South & West Walls

The N&E varieties plus –
CASINO
ENA HARKNESS, CLIMBING
ETOILE DE HOLLANDE, CLIMBING
MERMAID
MRS SAM McGREDY, CLIMBING
ROYAL GOLD
SHOT SILK, CLIMBING

Covering Trees

A dead tree is an eyesore in the garden, and if it is weak or rotten it should be felled. If it is sturdy, however, it can be used as a support for a climbing rose in the same way that some living trees can be employed. In this role the vigorous Rambler is supreme — this is no job for the compact modern Climber. Plant the rose on the side of the tree from which the prevailing wind blows, and provide some means of attachment to the trunk. The climbing rose will be self-supporting once its canes become entwined among the branches.

Recommended Varieties:

CECILE BRUNNER, CLIMBING
FRANCOIS JURANVILLE
ROSA FILIPES KIFTSGATE
THE GARLAND

CHAPTER 5

ROSE PLANTING

The number of new roses planted in Britain each year is staggering—if set out as a single row these plants would girdle the equator! So the chances are that you will be planting new roses this year, and with care you can expect them to last for 20 years or more.

Not all rose planting is successful, because there is more to it than digging a hole, spreading out the roots and then replacing the soil. Before you even lift a spade you should have considered several things. Has the soil already grown roses for many years? Does it need improving? Is the site really suitable for roses? This chapter offers you a step-by-step guide to avoiding all the pitfalls.

Picking the right spot

PLENTY OF SUN is required to produce top quality roses, but slight shade during early afternoon is beneficial.
ROSES CANNOT STAND DEEP AND CONTINUOUS SHADE

PLENTY OF AIR is required to produce healthy plants. Bush and standard roses do not like being shut in by walls and over-hanging plants.
ROSES CANNOT STAND BEING PLANTED UNDER TREES

SHELTER FROM COLD WINDS is helpful. A nearby hedge or fence is useful, but it should not be close enough to shade the bush. Avoid planting in the lowest part of the garden if it is a 'frost pocket'.
ROSES DO NOT THRIVE IN EXPOSED, LOW-LYING SITES

SUITABLE SOIL is necessary, and fortunately this can be achieved in nearly all gardens. Ideally it should be a medium loam, slightly acid and reasonably rich in plant foods and humus. A high clay content is not necessary, and is actually harmful if not improved by adding humus. A high lime content is harmful. Soil in which roses have grown for more than 10 years is not suitable — see page 86.
ROSES CANNOT THRIVE IF THE SOIL IS POOR

REASONABLY FREE DRAINAGE is essential, so break up the subsoil if necessary.
ROSES CANNOT STAND BEING WATERLOGGED

Timing

Bare-root Plants

←————— PLANTING SEASON —————→

APR	MAY	JUNE	JULY	AUG	SEPT	OCT	NOV	DEC	JAN	FEB	MAR

Soil condition is as important as the calendar. The ground must be neither frozen nor water-logged. Squeeze a handful of soil — it should be wet enough to form a ball and yet dry enough to shatter when dropped on a hard surface.

BEST TIME in nearly all gardens, as the soil is warm enough to produce some new root growth before winter. Late October is better than November in northern counties.

BEST TIME in very heavy soils and in cold exposed areas with high rainfall.

Container-grown Plants

Can be planted at any time of the year, provided the soil condition is suitable. Spring and autumn are preferred.

Getting the soil ready

The most expensive roses you can buy will grow only as well as the soil allows. Very few soils are naturally ideal, but almost all can be transformed into a satisfactory home for roses with some spadework (especially in clayey gardens) and humus (especially in sandy soils). There is no truth in the old saying that heavy clay is essential for top quality results.

DOUBLE DIGGING is recommended to aerate the top soil and break up the subsoil. The first step is to dig out a trench 18 in. wide and 12 in. deep at one side of the bed or border and transport the soil to the other. Fork over the bottom of the trench to the full length of the prongs, working in garden compost, well-rotted manure, leaf mould or peat. Turn strip A into the trench. Fork over the trench left by the removal of A, again incorporating compost or peat. Turn over strip B and so on, until a final trench is formed which is then filled with the soil from the first one. Do not remove small stones, as they are beneficial in a dry season. Roots of perennial weeds should be removed during digging. To add major and trace nutrients, fork 4 oz of Toprose Fertilizer per square yard into the top soil, and then let the ground settle for at least six weeks before planting.

WARNING: SOILS WHICH HAVE GROWN ROSES FOR MORE THAN 10 YEARS
You may wish to replant an old rose bed or just dig up one or two old bushes and replace them with new ones. In either case the soil is likely to be rose-sick (see page 102) if the plants have been growing in the soil for more than 10 years.
The causes of rose sickness are complex and still not yet fully understood, but a well-known effect is for newly-planted bushes and standards to suffer even though the established roses were thriving before their removal.
It is therefore wise to remove the old soil, digging out a hole 2 ft in diameter and 1½ ft deep for each new plant. Dig in plenty of organic matter and use a planting mixture made up with soil from a part of the garden which has not grown roses in recent years. The old soil from the rose bed can be safely spread in the vegetable or flower garden.

DRAINAGE is all-important, and double digging will help to prevent waterlogging in wet weather. If top soil is shallow and subsoil composed of heavy clay, the simplest plan is to make raised beds with added top soil, surrounded by paths on hardcore bases which will act as soakaways.

LIMING is not usually necessary because roses prefer slightly acid soil (pH 6.0 to 6.5). Only very acid soils need liming and even then only a light dressing will be required. Avoid overliming, or weak growth will result.

WARNING: CHALK SOILS
If there is less than 1½ ft of top soil above the chalk you will have either to add more top soil or excavate a 2 ft hole at each planting site and fill with planting mixture (see page 87). Alternatively, grow chalk-tolerant Shrub Roses — Albas, Damasks and Hybrid Musks.

Getting the plant ready

IF PLANTING IS TO BE DELAYED FOR LESS THAN 10 DAYS —
Leave the package containing the bush or standard unopened in an unheated but frost-proof cellar, garage or shed.

IF PLANTING IS TO BE DELAYED FOR MORE THAN 10 DAYS —
'Heel-in' the roses by digging a shallow V-shaped trench and then spreading the plants as a single row against one side of it. Cover the roots and lower part of the stems with soil and tread down. Label with some form of permanent tag — paper labels attached by the supplier may rot away.

WHEN YOU ARE READY TO BEGIN PLANTING —
Carefully unpack and place the packing material, sacking, etc. over the roots. Then prepare bush as shown in the adjoining diagram.

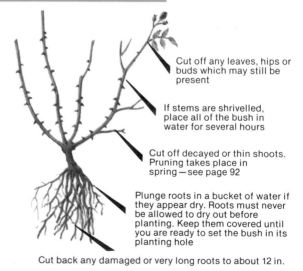

Cut off any leaves, hips or buds which may still be present

If stems are shrivelled, place all of the bush in water for several hours

Cut off decayed or thin shoots. Pruning takes place in spring — see page 92

Plunge roots in a bucket of water if they appear dry. Roots must never be allowed to dry out before planting. Keep them covered until you are ready to set the bush in its planting hole

Cut back any damaged or very long roots to about 12 in.

Planting

BUSHES

Bare-root Plants

The first step is to mark out the planting stations with canes to make sure that the bushes will be spaced out as planned. Next the planting hole for each rose must be dug, and the commonest mistake at planting time is to dig a hole which is too deep and too narrow.

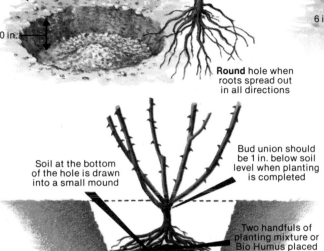

Round hole when roots spread out in all directions

Fan-shaped hole when roots run in only one direction

Soil at the bottom of the hole is drawn into a small mound

Bud union should be 1 in. below soil level when planting is completed

Two handfuls of planting mixture or Bio Humus placed on top of the soil mound

Transplanting Established Bushes

It is occasionally necessary to move a rose bush from one part of the garden to another. Do this job in late autumn or early spring — shorten stems, cut off old leaves and flowers, and then carefully remove the bush from the soil. There are two methods — two people with forks at opposite sides steadily lever up the plant or one person with a spade cuts straight down on all four sides about 9 in. from the centre of the bush and then carefully lifts it on to a wheelbarrow. Plant immediately — keep the soil ball moist and covered if there is to be any delay.

Make up the **planting mixture** in a wheelbarrow — 1 part soil, 1 part moist peat and 3 handfuls of Bone Meal per barrow load.

Spread out the roots evenly in the planting hole and work a couple of trowelfuls of the mixture around them. Shake the plant gently up and down and then firm the planting mixture with your fists. Place a cane across the top of the hole to ensure that the bud union is level with the surface.

Half-fill the hole with more of the mixture and firm it down by gentle treading. On no account should you stamp heavily — this would destroy the natural soil structure. Start treading at the outer edge of the planting hole, working gradually towards the centre.

Add more planting mixture until the hole is full, tread down once again and then loosen the surface. Spread a little more soil so that the bud union is about an inch below the surface and finally attach a weatherproof label bearing the name of the rose. The job is now finished but if frosty weather occurs after planting, refirming may be necessary.

Container-grown Plants

Never regard container-grown plants as an easy way to plant roses. If the environment surrounding the soil ball is not to the plant's liking then the roots will not grow out into the garden soil. This means that it is not enough to dig a hole, take off the container covering, drop in the plant and replace the soil.

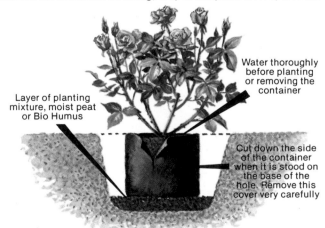

Water thoroughly before planting or removing the container

Layer of planting mixture, moist peat or Bio Humus

Cut down the side of the container when it is stood on the base of the hole. Remove this cover very carefully

Make sure that the soil is moist before digging a planting hole which is large enough and deep enough for the soil ball and a surrounding 3–4 in. layer of planting mixture. The cover of the container should be slit and then gently slid off the soil ball. Never lift up the plant to do this and never break up the compost around the roots.

Fill the space between the soil ball and the sides of the hole with planting mixture (see above) and never with ordinary soil — roots may not move from a peat-based compost into ordinary mineral garden soil. Firm down the planting mixture with your fingers or the handle of the trowel. Water regularly during dry weather in spring and summer until the plant is established.

Planting continued

STANDARDS

If bushes and standards are to be planted in the same bed, deal with the standards first.

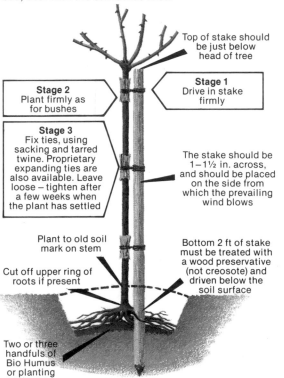

Top of stake should be just below head of tree

Stage 1 Drive in stake firmly

Stage 2 Plant firmly as for bushes

Stage 3 Fix ties, using sacking and tarred twine. Proprietary expanding ties are also available. Leave loose – tighten after a few weeks when the plant has settled

The stake should be 1–1½ in. across, and should be placed on the side from which the prevailing wind blows

Plant to old soil mark on stem

Cut off upper ring of roots if present

Bottom 2 ft of stake must be treated with a wood preservative (not creosote) and driven below the soil surface

Two or three handfuls of Bio Humus or planting mixture

CLIMBERS

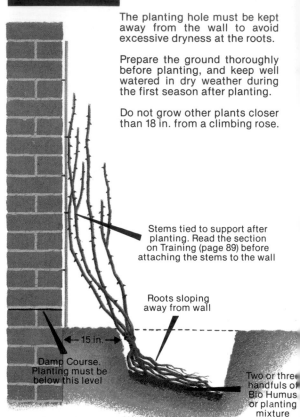

The planting hole must be kept away from the wall to avoid excessive dryness at the roots.

Prepare the ground thoroughly before planting, and keep well watered in dry weather during the first season after planting.

Do not grow other plants closer than 18 in. from a climbing rose.

Stems tied to support after planting. Read the section on Training (page 89) before attaching the stems to the wall

Roots sloping away from wall

15 in.

Damp Course. Planting must be below this level

Two or three handfuls of Bio Humus or planting mixture

Spacing

ROSE TYPE	DISTANCE BETWEEN SIMILAR PLANTS
MINIATURE ROSES	1 ft
HYBRID TEA & FLORIBUNDA BUSHES Compact varieties	1½ ft
HYBRID TEA & FLORIBUNDA BUSHES Average varieties	2 ft
HYBRID TEA & FLORIBUNDA BUSHES Tall varieties	2½ – 3 ft
LOW-GROWING SHRUBS	3 ft
STANDARDS	4 ft
SHRUBS	average 5 ft or half of expected height
WEEPING STANDARDS	6 ft
CLIMBERS	7 ft
RAMBLERS	10 ft

Bush roses should not be planted closer than 18 in. from the edge of bed or border.

CHAPTER 6

ROSE CARE

The ever-increasing popularity of the Hybrid Tea and Floribunda is no doubt due to the beauty and colours of modern varieties together with their repeat flowering habit. But the simplicity of rose care, compared to the time-consuming job of looking after some other garden favourites is also an important factor.

A number of simple and straightforward tasks have to be carried out during the rose-growing year. Some, such as hoeing and feeding, are generally understood and practised. Others, like mulching and training, are still not widely followed and countless roses suffer as a result. One feature of rose cultivation causes more arguments and concern than all the rest, and that is pruning. Finally, there is one aspect of rose care which does not appear in the textbooks — take time to enjoy your roses by sitting close to them occasionally and doing nothing!

MULCHING

A mulch is a layer of bulky organic material placed on the soil surface around plants. In the rose garden it provides five distinct benefits:

- The soil is kept moist during the dry days of summer.
- Weeds are greatly reduced.
- Soil structure is improved as humus is added to the soil.
- Plant foods are provided by some mulching materials.
- Black spot attacks are reduced.

Suitable materials are moist peat, Bio Humus, hop manure, well-rotted manure, good garden compost and leaf mould. Grass clippings are often recommended and used, but a word of caution is necessary. Do not use them if the lawn contains many weeds or has recently been treated with a weedkiller. If they are used, add only a thin layer at a time and stir occasionally.

The standard time for mulching is late April and early May. Success depends on preparing the soil surface before adding the organic blanket — remove debris, dead leaves and weeds, and then water the surface if it is dry. Apply the spring feed (see page 94) if this has not yet been done, hoe in lightly, and you are ready to apply the mulch. Spread a 2 – 3 in. layer around the roses, keeping it away from the crown of the plants. Lightly prick this dressing into the top inch of soil during October.

Mulching will greatly reduce the need for watering and hoeing, but it cannot replace the need for feeding, as the balance of nutrients in a good rose fertilizer is not generally provided by mulching materials.

Some experts believe that autumn mulching is equal to or even better than late spring mulching, as described above. If you follow this advice, apply the mulch in October before the soil has become cold.

TRAINING

Some shrubs with lax spreading stems may require some form of support after a few years. Use three or more unobtrusive stakes with a secure band or board joining the top of each stake — never rely on a single ugly pole and string.

Climbing roses must be trained from the outset to ensure that they remain attached to their supports and grow in the desired direction. This does not mean that the main stems should be allowed to grow vertically — when this happens the usual result is a mature plant which bears its leaves and flowers at the top.

To prevent this happening, train the main shoots as horizontally as possible. This interruption of the free upward movement of the sap causes lateral branches to appear. It is these laterals which grow upwards to provide both height and cover, and they bear the flowers.

Basal shoots spread out fan-wise to encourage growth of vertical laterals

Fan training is fine for a climbing rose growing against a wall, fence, or screen, but is quite impractical when a pillar or tripod is to be covered. In this case, wind the canes in an ascending spiral around the pole.

The wire ties used to attach the main stems to the supports should not be tied too tightly — these stems thicken with age and a tight tie can strangle growth.

PRUNING

A rose bush, unlike a tree, does not produce shoots which steadily increase in size every year for as long as the plant remains alive. A rose stem grows actively and bears flowers for only a few years, after which the upper portion becomes exhausted. A new shoot then appears from a bud lower down on the stem, and the part above the new shoot dies.

The result is that a rose bush left unpruned becomes a tangled and shapeless mass of live and dead wood, with poor quality blooms borne on weak and twiggy stems. The purpose of pruning is to get rid of old exhausted wood every year and to encourage the regular development of strong and healthy stems. It will not give you more flowers next year — that is the job of feeding, but it will give you a well-shaped bush which will continue to bloom freely for many years to come.

The pruning cut

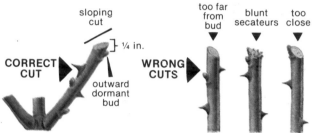

sloping cut

¼ in.

CORRECT CUT

outward dormant bud

too far from bud

blunt secateurs

too close

WRONG CUTS

All pruning cuts must be clean — pare off any ragged parts. Sharp secateurs are essential — never force them to cut through thick stems, and relegate them to ordinary garden work once the blades are dull. Cuts more than ½ in. across should be painted with Arbrex to protect them from frost and damp.

It is impossible to avoid making some wrong cuts when pruning several bushes on a cold unpleasant day. As a result snags will form above some of the new shoots which develop — merely cut these dead bits off as they appear.

The tools to use

TWO-BLADED SECATEURS will cut cleanly for many years with proper care. The cut must be made at the centre of the blades.

or

ONE-BLADED SECATEURS are easier to use and will cut at the tip of the blade, but tend to wear out more quickly than the two-bladed variety, as the anvil becomes worn.

GLOVES are necessary to protect your hands from thorns. Buy a stout and flexible pair.

LONG-HANDLED PRUNERS are essential for tall climbers and shrubs. Many gardeners prefer them to a pruning saw for dealing with thick stems.

KNEELING PAD will allow you to get close to the bush when the soil is cold and wet at pruning time. Essential for the over-fifties.

PRUNING SAW if stems over ½ in. diameter have to be cut.

PRUNING KNIFE if you are experienced in its use.

Pruning step-by-step

All bushes and standards should be tackled in the following way:

STEP 1 — Cut out completely all dead wood and all parts of stems which are obviously diseased or damaged. Test: Cut surface should be white. If brown — cut back further.

STEP 2 — Cut out completely all very thin stems, and remove any branch which rubs against another. Aim to produce an open-centred bush. Remove suckers.

STEP 3 — Cut out all unripe stems. Test: Try to snap off several thorns. If they bend or tear off instead of breaking off cleanly, the wood is too soft to be of any use.

STEP 4 — Only healthy and ripe stems now remain. Prune these to the length advised on page 92 for the type of rose in question.

Types of pruning

BEFORE	AFTER	TYPE
		HARD PRUNING *(other name: Low Pruning)* Stems are cut back to three or four buds from the base. This leaves short, sturdy stems about 5 in. high. Hard pruning is recommended for newly-planted bush roses and it is often used for established H.T.s grown solely for the production of exhibition blooms. It is no longer recommended for established roses grown for garden display although it is still used for some very weak-growing H.T.s and for rejuvenating neglected roses. Hard pruning should never be used for established Floribundas.
		MODERATE PRUNING *(other name: Medium Pruning)* Stems are cut back to about half of their length. Weaker than average stems should be reduced by more than this amount. Moderate pruning is recommended for nearly all established H.T.s growing in ordinary soils. Established Floribundas are pruned using a variation of this system (see page 92). If the roses are well cared for, you can expect exhibition-quality blooms as well as a fine garden display following the use of moderate pruning. Hard pruning is no longer considered to be essential for winning prizes.
		LIGHT PRUNING *(other name: High or Long Pruning)* Stems are cut back to about two-thirds of their length. This means that after the removal of all unwanted wood, the remaining stems are merely tipped. Light pruning is not generally recommended as it produces tall spindly bushes bearing early but poor quality blooms if used year after year. In special cases, however, light pruning is the only method to use. Very vigorous H.T. varieties such as *Peace* should be tackled in this way, and all roses growing in very sandy or smoky areas should be lightly pruned.

When to prune

BUSHES, STANDARDS & CLIMBERS

Early spring pruning is recommended for autumn- and winter-planted roses and for established plants. If the bushes or standards are to be planted in the spring, prune just before planting.

The best time to prune is when growth is just beginning. The uppermost buds will have begun to swell but no leaves will have appeared.

One of the dangers of leaving pruning until spring is the possibility of wind-rock in the winter gales. Avoid this by cutting back long shoots in November.

RAMBLERS

Prune in late summer or autumn once flowering has finished.

Prune at or before the recommended pruning date for your part of the country

- **EARLY APRIL**
- **LATE MARCH**
- **MID MARCH**

Pruning too early may result in buds breaking prematurely in a mild spell, followed by frost injury if freezing weather returns.

Despite this possibility, some rose experts prune regularly during above-freezing weather in January or February and claim they obtain earlier flowering than with the more usual March pruning.

Pruning too late results in the plant being weakened. This is because the sap is flowing freely upwards once the buds are actively growing, and pruning at this stage is bound to cause considerable loss of sap.

How to prune the roses in your garden

	NEWLY-PLANTED ROSES (Planted in previous autumn/winter or due to be planted in spring)	ESTABLISHED ROSES (Planted at least 12 months ago)
HYBRID TEA BUSHES	**Hard pruning** is required to build up a strong root system and to stimulate the growth of sturdy fresh shoots from close to the base of the bush.	**Moderate pruning** is the best method for general garden display. For show blooms hard pruning is sometimes used. In poor sites and for very vigorous varieties light pruning is recommended.
FLORIBUNDA BUSHES	Hybrid Teas should be pruned 4–6 in. from the ground, and Floribundas 6 in. In sandy soils, use moderate pruning at this stage and hard pruning the following year.	**Moderate pruning** is the basis for dealing with Floribundas, but some old stems are hard pruned to a few inches from the ground, whilst new shoots which arose from close to the base last year are only lightly pruned. In this way stems of varying lengths are retained which ensures a long period of continuous flowering.
HYBRID TEA & FLORIBUNDA STANDARDS	**Hard pruning** is recommended, but this should be less drastic than the treatment of newly planted bushes. Cut stems back to about 8 in. from the trunk.	**Moderate pruning** is used to form a properly balanced head which will produce plenty of flowers. Hard pruning should be avoided, otherwise over-vigorous shoot growth will spoil the tree. Make sure that the main branches are of approximately equal length after pruning.
WEEPING STANDARDS	**Hard pruning** is necessary, leaving branches about 6 in. long at the top of the trunk.	As for Ramblers. In autumn cut out branches which have flowered, leaving the new vigorous shoots which will flower next year. Cut off the tips of these shoots in the following March.
MINIATURE & SHRUB ROSES	No pruning is required.	Very little pruning is required. Remove dead and sickly growth and trim to shape, if necessary. Remove and burn mildewed tips. Use scissors rather than secateurs for Miniatures.
RAMBLERS	These roses are often pruned before despatch. If this has not been done, cut stems to 12 in. from the ground.	The correct pruning method depends upon the variety — see pages 52–60. **Method 1** Ideally, all the stems which have flowered should be cut out at ground level in autumn and the new stems, which will flower next year, tied into the supports. If insufficient new stems are present, retain the best of the old main stems and trim their lateral branches to about 3 in. In practice, taking down the canes may not be possible. In this case just cut back the lateral branches to about 3 in. from the main stems. **Method 2** Ideally, all flowered growth should be cut away from the main stems in autumn at a point where a vigorous new shoot has appeared. Cut back one or two old stems to about 12 in. above the ground. In practice, taking down so much wood may not be possible. In this case just cut back the lateral branches to about 3 in. from the main stems. **Method 3** Prune very lightly — merely cut out old dead wood and tip back the laterals which have flowered.
CLIMBERS	Do not prune — merely remove any dead tips which may be present.	The correct pruning method depends upon the variety — see pages 52–60. **Method 1** Little pruning is required apart from the removal of dead and exhausted wood. Withered shoot tips should be removed, and lateral branches on wood which has flowered should be reduced to about 3 in. **Method 2** Little pruning is required apart from the removal of dead and exhausted wood. Withered shoot tips should be removed.

WATERING

One of the blessings of the rose is its deep-rooting habit of growth. This means that watering of established plants is not vital in some seasons.

Unfortunately, this ability of a rose bush to remain fresh and green in summer when shallow-rooted plants have started to wilt leads many people to neglect watering. Trials have shown that during a summer with several dry spells the failure to water leads to impaired growth, small blooms and an early end to flowering even though the leaves may stay firm and green.

Some roses may need watering after only a few days of dry weather — newly-planted roses, climbers growing against walls and bushes planted in sandy soil. All roses will need water, and plenty of it, during a period of drought in late spring or summer.

A watering can is the usual applicator — use about 1 gallon for each bush or standard and 3 gallons for a climber. Never water little and often. Hold the can close to the ground and water slowly through the spout, not through a rose. Follow the experts by adding a measure of soluble fertilizer to the water.

Trickle irrigation through a perforated hose-pipe laid close to the bushes is perhaps the best method of watering. A quick and easy technique popular in America is to build a ridge of soil around each bush and then fill the basin with a hose-pipe.

HOEING

The main purpose of hoeing is to keep down weeds, such as couch grass, which are not smothered by mulching. For this purpose hoeing must be carried out at regular and frequent intervals so that the underground parts of the weeds will be eventually starved.

Hoeing must not go deeper than an inch below the surface, or rose roots may be damaged. Do not bother to hoe to keep moisture in the soil — a "dust mulch" is of very little value.

The garden fork has little place in the established rose garden. A light pricking over in spring and again in autumn can be carried out but deep soil disturbance must always be avoided.

DISBUDDING

Many Hybrid Teas normally produce more than one flower bud at the end of each shoot. If you want large specimen blooms for exhibition, garden display or indoor flower arrangement, then disbudding will be necessary. This calls for removing side buds by nipping out with the thumb and finger as soon as they are visible. This allows the stronger terminal bud to develop to its maximum size.

CUTTING

The rose is perhaps the most attractive and widely used of all cut flowers for home decoration, and an abundant supply of blooms can be obtained from June onwards from even the smallest rose garden.

A certain amount of care is necessary to avoid weakening the bushes. Do not take more than one-third of the flowering stem with the flower and always cut just above an outward-facing bud.

If the bush is not growing strongly, the flower stems removed should not bear any leaves. Cutting blooms from newly-planted roses is not generally recommended during their first season in the garden, although removal of a few blooms without leaves will do little or no harm.

DEAD-HEADING

The regular removal of dead blooms from Floribundas and Hybrid Teas is an important task. When the flowers have faded remove the whole truss, cutting the stem just above the second or third leaf down. By doing this the plant's energy which would have been lost in forming hips is conserved, and a regular succession of new flowering shoots is ensured. Faded flowers on first year roses should be removed with very little stem.

Do not dead-head once flowering roses nor varieties grown for their decorative hips.

THINNING

Following pruning, it is often found that two or more shoots have developed from a single bud. Only one of these should be retained, the other weaker or inward-facing shoots being gently removed by rubbing out with the fingers.

FEEDING

Hunger signs

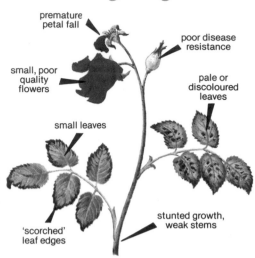

- premature petal fall
- poor disease resistance
- small, poor quality flowers
- pale or discoloured leaves
- small leaves
- 'scorched' leaf edges
- stunted growth, weak stems

Roses, like most other garden plants, make heavy demands on the reserves of plant foods in the soil. If one or more of the vital elements run short, then hunger signs appear on the leaves or flowers and both vigour and display are affected. The answer is to feed your roses every year.

Mulching, as described on page 89, will provide humus and some nutrients. But extra plant foods will be required, and the basic way to provide them is to use a proprietary compound fertilizer containing nitrogen, phosphates and potash.

Powder or granular fertilizer is the usual form, sprinkled around the plants in spring and summer. The most famous powder mixture is Tonks Formula, devised about 100 years ago. A modern version is available as Toprose Fertilizer, which contains magnesium and iron plus gypsum as well as the three major plant foods.

Liquid fertilizers are available in bottles, such as Bio Plant Food, or as boxes of soluble powder, such as Instant Bio. An excellent choice for quick and inexpensive treatment — regular repeat treatments are necessary during the season.

Foliar feeding has aroused a great deal of interest and some argument in the rose world. The specially formulated fertilizers are used to supplement and not replace soil feeding, and have the unique advantage of getting into the sap stream only hours after being sprayed on to the leaves. A favourite with exhibitors, as trials have shown that the size of blooms is increased as well as the general health of the plant.

PLANT FOOD TYPE	PLANT FOOD	WHAT IT DOES
MAJOR (required in large amounts)	**NITROGEN (N)**	Nitrogen stimulates the growth of leaves and stems and increases the size of the plant.
	PHOSPHATES (P_2O_5)	Phosphates stimulate the growth of roots and stems and speed up flowering.
	POTASH (K_2O)	Potash stimulates the production of top quality blooms. It also improves drought- and disease-resistance.
INTERMEDIATE (required in moderate amounts)	**CALCIUM (Ca)**	Calcium, magnesium, iron, boron and manganese maintain the normal green colour of the foliage so that growth and appearance are not spoilt by leaf discoloration and premature fall. Boron prevents leaflet distortion, and calcium reduces the incidence of die-back of stems.
	MAGNESIUM (Mg)	
MINOR (required in trace amounts)	**IRON (Fe)**	
	BORON (B)	The minor plant foods, or trace elements, also contribute in some way to disease prevention and the general health of the plant.
	MANGANESE (Mn)	

The Feeding Programme

STANDARD PROGRAMME

Spring treatment before leaves are fully open

Apply 1 oz (approximately one small handful) of Toprose Fertilizer around each plant when the soil is moist. Hoe in lightly.

Summer treatment in June or July

Apply 1 oz (approximately one small handful) of Toprose Fertilizer around each plant. Do not feed after the end of July or soft, frost-sensitive growth may be produced.

QUICK PROGRAMME

Monthly, from April until the end of July

Useful where a large number of roses have to be fed and where economy is an important factor. Add 1 tablespoon of Instant Bio to 1 pint of water in a Bio Hoser — apply to 250 sq.ft of bed or border.

EXPERT PROGRAMME

Fortnightly, between the two treatments of the Standard Programme

Many exhibitors and keen rose growers enrich the Standard Programme (see above) by regular foliar feeding. Use Fillip in a sprayer, taking care to wet the leaves thoroughly. Do not spray in bright sunlight.

CHAPTER 7
ROSE TROUBLES

The rose, like any other living thing, is liable to attack by harmful organisms. As a general pattern, the insect pests of spring are followed by the diseases of summer and autumn. Good cultivation is not the whole answer. A well-grown bush is able to withstand the effects of an attack much more successfully than a neglected specimen, but there is no way of completely stopping rose troubles from entering your garden.

Don't immediately assume that every disfigurement is due to an insect pest or a fungus disease — many problems are caused by the weather, lack of nutrients, weedkiller drift and poor management. Fortunately, you are never likely to see more than a few rose troubles in your own garden, and the purpose of this chapter is to show you what the rest look like as well as to list the correct control measures.

Learning to identify the symptoms of rose troubles is, of course, less interesting than learning to recognize rose varieties but it is no less important. This is because most pests and diseases can be checked quite easily if treated promptly, but may be difficult or impossible to control if left to get out of hand due to ignorance or neglect.

How to reduce the risk of troubles in your garden

● **Buy good plants.** Abundant roots and sound stems are essential — see page 73. If you live in a disease prone area choose varieties which are known to possess good disease resistance — see the A–Z guides on pages 9–46.

● **Never leave rubbish lying about.** Rake up and burn prunings and fallen diseased leaves. Pick off and destroy mildewed shoot tips.

● **Prepare the ground thoroughly.** A rose growing in poorly-drained soil is susceptible to a lot of troubles.

● **Avoid overcrowding.** Do not plant closer together than the recommended spacing — see page 88. Prune to produce an open-centred bush.

● **Feed the plants properly.** Potash is vital here, because it builds up disease resistance and accelerates the ripening of new wood. Phosphates promote a healthy root system.

● **Avoid overliming.** Too much lime in the soil will cause chlorosis — leaf yellowing due to iron and manganese shortage.

● **Plant in the proper place and in the proper way.** This will reduce the risk of problems due to drought, waterlogging, wind rock, frost damage, light deficiency, excessive suckering, etc.

● **Inspect plants regularly.** Catch problems early, when occasional insects can be picked off and diseases kept from spreading by using a fungicide.

Why roses fail to survive

A good quality rose bush planted in the manner described in this book should grow and flourish for many years. Failure to survive will almost certainly be due to one of the following causes:

Loose planting — see page 87. Test: Tug stem gently in spring after planting. If the plant moves easily, tread around the bush

Wind rock especially in exposed sites

Waterlogged soil around the roots because of poor drainage

Severe drought especially in poor soils

Severe frost — see page 96

Use of fresh manure at planting time

Hard pruning every year on Floribundas, and on Hybrid Teas in sandy soils

Dry roots at planting time

Too much lime in the soil

The fatal diseases: rust, canker and honey fungus — see pages 98 and 102

The underground pests: chafer grubs and ants — see page 99

Planting under trees can lead to death from the combined effect of root dryness, dense shade and toxic drip from the leaf canopy

Cultural Problems

NITROGEN SHORTAGE

Young leaves small and pale green. Red spots sometimes develop. Early leaf fall. Stems stunted and weak.

Apply a compound fertilizer.

PHOSPHATE SHORTAGE

Young leaves small and dark green, with purplish tints on underside. Early leaf fall. Stems stunted and weak.

Apply a compound fertilizer.

POTASH SHORTAGE

Young leaves reddish, mature leaves green with brown, brittle margins. Flowers small. Common on sandy soils.

Apply a compound fertilizer.

MAGNESIUM SHORTAGE

Leaves pale at centre, with dead areas close to midrib. Oldest leaves worst affected. Early leaf fall.

Apply a fertilizer containing magnesium (e.g. Toprose).

IRON SHORTAGE

Leaves with large yellow areas. Young leaves worst affected — almost entirely yellow.

Avoid overliming. Apply Toprose Fertilizer. On chalky soils use Sequestrene.

MANGANESE SHORTAGE

Leaves with yellow bands between veins. Oldest leaves worst affected.

Avoid overliming. On chalky soils use Sequestrene at the rate recommended on the box.

FROST DAMAGE

Affected leaves are crinkled and torn with brown markings. Yellow patches sometimes appear. In most areas of Britain this damage is not serious, and the damage to stem tips of even newly-planted roses is not likely to be a problem in an average British winter.

In northern areas where severe and prolonged frosts are frequent, some winter protection may be necessary. Cover the bush with straw and bracken, and then wrap sacking around the covered plant. Remove the protective coating after the worst of the winter frosts have passed and before the growth buds begin to open.

WATERLOGGING

Leaves with large yellow areas. Veins and central area turn yellow first. Prevent by ensuring good drainage and after heavy frosts or gales tread down all plants which have been loosened. No cure — replant in a better prepared site if growth is spindly and flowers are of poor quality.

BALLING

Buds develop normally, but the petals fail to open and then turn brown. It is usually due to the effect of wet weather on varieties with large, thin-petalled blooms. Balling is always worst in a shady spot where the buds are shielded from the drying rays of the sun. It can also be caused by a heavy greenfly attack.

LAWN WEEDKILLER DAMAGE

Leaf stalks twisted spirally, leaves narrow and twisted. Stems distorted and reddish. The cause is lawn weedkiller which has been allowed to drift on to the roses — never treat a lawn on a windy day, and never use a watering can for both weedkilling and watering roses. Cut off the affected stems — the bush will recover.

Pest and Disease Control

There are times when pests and diseases will attack, and a spray or dust will be necessary if mildew, black spot or green-fly threaten your roses.

Chemicals used to control garden troubles are called **pesticides** and are safer than the nicotine, arsenic and mercury compounds used in grand-father's day. But they still should be treated with respect and there are a few simple rules to follow.

BEFORE YOU START

● **CHOOSE THE RIGHT PRODUCT.** Insects and other small pests are controlled by **Insecticides** which are used at the first signs of attack. A **Systemic Insecticide** enters the sap stream — in this way new growth will be protected and insects hidden from the spray will be killed. **Fungicides** are designed to prevent (not cure) diseases and so spraying must start before the attack begins and repeat spraying is usually necessary. The **Systemic Fungicides,** such as Benlate, go inside the plant and have some curative effect if a few disease spots have already appeared.

● **READ THE LABEL CAREFULLY.** Follow the instructions — do not make the mixture stronger than recommended. Never use equipment which has contained weedkillers.

SPRAYING

The weather must be neither sunny nor windy

During the flowering season spray in the evening, when bees will have stopped working

Leaves should be dry

Use a fine forceful spray. It is wise to keep all sprays off the skin. Wash off any splashes

Spray the top and underside of the foliage thoroughly until the liquid starts to run off the leaves

DUSTING

Dusting is not as effective as spraying, but it is quick and easy — an excellent aid for attacking occasional pests when they are first seen

Leaves should be moist if possible — dusting in the morning after a heavy dew is ideal

Apply a fine cloud, covering each leaf with a thin, almost invisible film. Never coat the leaves thickly

Buy dust in ready-to-use puffer pack form

THE ROSE-AID KIT

Nobody wants a garage filled with a large collection of bottles, boxes and assorted brews. It is, however, a good idea to keep a small rose-aid kit for sudden emergencies — Systemic Insecticide for greenfly, Fenitrothion for caterpillars and Benlate for the common diseases. Include a Rose & Flower Pest Duster as a ready-to-use treatment when there is no time to make up a spray.

NON-CHEMICAL ROSE CARE

Some people do not like to use modern chemicals. Their fears may be groundless and they cannot expect the same degree of control from natural remedies, but they still wish to use products based entirely on organics and minerals. For greenfly and caterpillar control, use Back to Nature Insect Spray, based on derris and quassia. For mildew as well as general pest control, use Back to Nature Pest & Disease Duster, based on derris, quassia and sulphur.

AFTER YOU HAVE FINISHED

● **Wash out equipment thoroughly.** Wash your hands and face if the label tells you to do so.

● **Do not keep the spray solution.** Make up a fresh batch of spray each time you wish to treat your roses.

● **Store packs in a safe place.** Never transfer chemicals into a beer bottle or any unlabelled container and never keep old illegible boxes and bottles. Throw them in the dustbin after you have emptied the contents down an outside drain.

EXPERT ROSE CARE PROGRAMME

It is, of course, possible to keep a regular watch on your roses and then spray or dust with the appropriate pesticide when each insect appears or each disease threatens. Some keen rose growers prefer to follow a routine programme each year, and just add extra treatments as the needs arise.

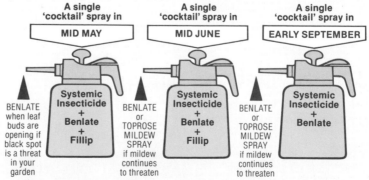

A single 'cocktail' spray in **MID MAY**

BENLATE when leaf buds are opening if black spot is a threat in your garden

Systemic Insecticide + Benlate + Fillip

A single 'cocktail' spray in **MID JUNE**

BENLATE or TOPROSE MILDEW SPRAY if mildew continues to threaten

Systemic Insecticide + Benlate + Fillip

A single 'cocktail' spray in **EARLY SEPTEMBER**

BENLATE or TOPROSE MILDEW SPRAY if mildew continues to threaten

Systemic Insecticide + Benlate

Diseases

The most serious fungal diseases are mildew, black spot and rust. Some varieties are described as "resistant to disease", which means that the bush will remain free from attack under ordinary conditions. But under epidemic conditions preventive spraying will be necessary, because these varieties are resistant, not immune.

RUST

Not common, but it is often fatal when it strikes. Rust-prone area is S.W. England. Orange swellings, which turn black in August, appear on underside of leaves. New shoots turn reddish and shrivel. Usual time for attack — July.

It is encouraged by potash shortage and by a cold spring following a dry summer and hard winter.

Use Plantvax if available. Otherwise spray with Dithane 945 every two weeks.

PURPLE SPOTTING

Not to be confused with black spot. The markings are smaller, more irregular and without a fringe. It is caused by poor growing conditions, not a fungus. It can also be caused by using a copper-based spray. It is not nearly as serious as black spot.

Improve drainage. Apply a peat mulch and a compound fertilizer.

CANKER

Usually appears as a distinct brown and sunken area close to the base of a stem. The edge of the canker may be swollen and the bark cracked.

The canker fungus enters the stem through a wound caused by insect or disease attack or mechanical damage. Be careful when hoeing!

If the canker enlarges and encircles the stem, the whole of the growth above the diseased area will be killed.

Cut out and burn all of the diseased wood. Paint large cuts with Arbrex. Dip the secateur blades in methylated spirits after use. Apply a balanced compound fertilizer, such as Toprose.

MILDEW

The most widespread rose disease. White powdery mould on leaves and buds; leaf cockling and premature fall takes place. Usual time for attack — summer or early autumn.

It is encouraged by closed-in conditions, dryness at the roots, poor feeding and by hot days followed by cold nights.

Spray with Benlate at the first signs of disease. Repeat one week later and apply further sprays if the spots reappear. It is a good idea to alternate with another fungicide such as Toprose Mildew Spray.

BLACK SPOT

S.W. England and S. Wales are worst affected areas. Less common in industrial areas. Black spots with yellow fringes spread rapidly, causing leaves to fall. Starts early; becomes clearly visible in July/August. Heavy infections spread to leaf buds and later to stems which die back. Severe defoliation may take place.

It is encouraged by potash shortage and warm, wet weather in summer.

Difficult to control. Always remove and burn fallen leaves which are diseased. Use two sprays of Benlate a week apart when leaf buds begin to open. Spray again in summer as soon as the first spots appear. Repeat as necessary.

DIE-BACK

Shoots may die back, beginning at the tip and progressing steadily downwards, for a number of reasons. Die-back is not a specific disease. It can be caused by frost damage, canker at the base of the stem, water-logging, mildew or black spot. Yellow and orange varieties are more susceptible than others.

A common cause is a deficiency in potash, calcium, phosphates and boron. Feeding is essential in spring if die-back is a problem.

Do not feed in the autumn as this leads to the production of unripe and frost-sensitive wood.

Cut off the affected shoot at a bud below the dead area.

Pests on the stem

Peach-potato aphid   Rose aphid

GREENFLY (Aphid)

The commonest and most serious of all rose pests. They can be orange, reddish and black as well as green. The first clusters of these insects can be found feeding on the sap of tender new shoots in the spring, and vigour is seriously reduced.

Growth may be stopped or distorted, and infested buds sometimes fail to open. A sticky substance (honeydew) produced by these pests is soon covered by a black fungus (sooty mould).

The best way to tackle aphids is to use Systemic Insecticide, based on the chemical dimethoate. This goes inside the plant, so foliage missed by the spray is protected, as are the leaves formed after treatment. Protection is not removed by rain.

Alternatively you can spray with a contact insecticide, which kills the aphids it touches. Choose from Malathion, Fenitrothion or Liquid Derris.

FROGHOPPER (Cuckoo-spit)

White frothy spittle on shoots in May and June. Inside this froth lives the small yellow froghopper. Affected shoots are distorted and leaves may wilt.

If only a few shoots are affected, wipe off with finger and thumb. Froghopper is susceptible to Hexyl, but before using an insecticide, spray forcibly with water to clear away froth.

ROSE SCALE

Small scurfy scales form a crust on old and neglected stems. Unsightly, and growth is weakened.

Small outbreaks can be controlled by painting affected areas with methylated spirits. Large areas will require spraying — use the modern chemical permethrin contained in Bio Flydown. Apply a forceful spray to drench the scales.

SHOOT BORER SAWFLY

A green maggot within the pith of the affected shoot. Outward symptom is withering of the tip.

Cut off and burn the branch bearing the maggot. A spray of Liquid Derris in May will prevent this damage.

Underground Pests

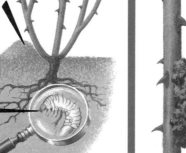

ANTS

Soil around the roots is loosened and plants may wilt and die. A pest of sandy areas.

Sprinkle Anti-Ant Powder along the runs, or use a few drops of Panant.

CHAFER GRUB

Fat, curved grub, over 1 in. long. A serious root pest which can cause death or weakening of bushes.

Kill any found during soil preparation.

Apply Bromophos and rake into soil surface before planting.

Galls

"ROBIN'S PINCUSHION"

Spongy moss-covered gall on leaves, caused by the gall wasp.

It does no detectable harm, and can be retained as a curiosity. Otherwise cut off and burn.

CROWN GALL

Very large, brown and warty outgrowth close to the base of a stem. Causes little or no harm, but can be cut off and the wound painted with Arbrex in autumn.

Crown gall is a much more serious problem when it occurs on the roots.

Pests on the leaf

COCKCHAFER (May bug)

Irregular-shaped holes in leaves in May or June may be due to this large, reddish-brown beetle.

Pick off and destroy beetles. Spray with Fenitrothion or apply Rose & Flower Pest Dust.

LEAF-MINER

White blisters on leaves, containing a grub.

Hand-pick affected leaves and burn. Fenitrothion is the recommended spray.

ROSE SLUGWORM

Skeletonised areas on leaves, as only internal tissues but not veins are eaten. Affected areas turn brown.

Greenish-yellow grub may be seen on surface. Spray with Hexyl or Systemic Insecticide.

RED SPIDER

Bronzed patches on upper surface of leaves, minute yellowish 'insects' and fine webbing on underside.

Attacks occur in hot, dry weather. Spray with Systemic Insecticide or Malathion.

CATERPILLAR

Irregular-shaped holes in leaves may be due to caterpillars —

Vapourer moth   Winter moth   Yellow tail moth   Buff-tip moth

Pick off by hand if not too numerous. All of these pests can be very simply controlled by spraying with Fenitrothion or Hexyl. Rose & Flower Pest Dust is also effective.

LEAFHOPPER

Pale mottled patches on leaves. Small yellowish insects or their empty white skins may be found on underside.

Growth is checked. Leaf fall occurs after a bad attack. Spray with Systemic Insecticide, Fenitrothion or Malathion.

LEAF-CUTTER BEE

Regular-shaped holes at sides of leaves.

Control measures are not usually necessary, but destroy nests if found.

Flower Pests

CHAFER BEETLE

Petals and anthers eaten. One-sided blooms sometimes result.

Rose chafer   Garden chafer

Pick off and destroy beetles. To prevent attack spray with Hexyl or Fenitrothion.

TORTRIX MOTH

Buds holed; brown rose maggot may be found inside, or within a characteristically curled leaf (see page 101).
Spray with Fenitrothion.

THRIPS

Petal edges blackened, flowers and leaves mottled and malformed.

Minute 4-winged flies, known as thunderflies, may become serious in a hot summer.

Spray with Fenitrothion, Hexyl or Malathion.

CAPSID

Young buds dead and withered. Small brown spots on young leaves, which become distorted. Bright green insects — which move rapidly when disturbed.

Spray plants and soil with Systemic Insecticide, Fenitrothion or Hexyl.

Hide-away leaf pests

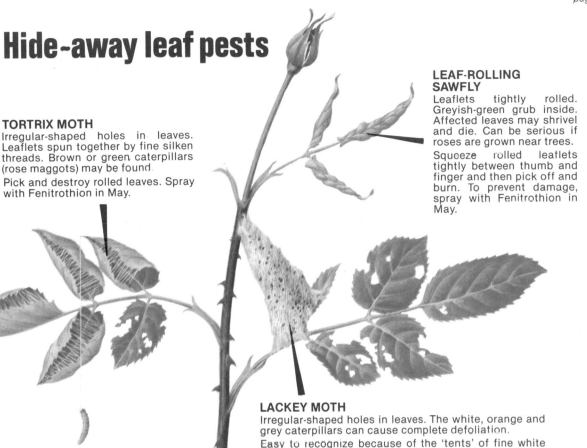

TORTRIX MOTH
Irregular-shaped holes in leaves. Leaflets spun together by fine silken threads. Brown or green caterpillars (rose maggots) may be found.

Pick and destroy rolled leaves. Spray with Fenitrothion in May.

LEAF-ROLLING SAWFLY
Leaflets tightly rolled. Greyish-green grub inside. Affected leaves may shrivel and die. Can be serious if roses are grown near trees.

Squeeze rolled leaflets tightly between thumb and finger and then pick off and burn. To prevent damage, spray with Fenitrothion in May.

LACKEY MOTH
Irregular-shaped holes in leaves. The white, orange and grey caterpillars can cause complete defoliation.

Easy to recognize because of the 'tents' of fine white threads which they spin.

Destroy 'tents'. Spray with Fenitrothion.

Virus Diseases

Fortunately, virus diseases have not become a serious problem in Britain. No drastic measures are required, but infected plants should not be used for propagation.

VEIN BANDING ROSE MOSAIC
Pale yellow or cream veining, distinct in late spring but much less so in summer. No serious effect — some regard it as decorative. Feed generously, as recommended on page 94.

LINE PATTERN ROSE MOSAIC
Yellow lines on leaf surface, sometimes forming an oak leaf pattern. Distinct in late spring, much less so in summer. Effect much more serious than vein banding rose mosaic — feed generously.

Blindness

Empty wheat-like husk instead of a flower bud on top of a mature stem. Blind shoots can occur with nearly all varieties, but some are particularly prone — *Gold Crown, Peace, Red Devil* and *Bonsoir* are examples.

Causes are many and varied — frost damage, lack of food and shortage of light have been blamed. If you are sure the shoot is blind, and not merely slow in flowering, cut it back to half its length to a healthy bud. This will then produce a shoot which should flower normally.

Weeds

It is surprising that weed control is ignored by so many books on rose growing, because weeds are certainly a major problem for millions of gardeners.

There is no single miracle cure for the weed problem — there are a number of interlinked tasks you will have to carry out. You probably already know that some weeds are annuals, and these generally can be kept in check quite easily by hoeing, mulching and spraying. The real problems are the perennial weeds — couch grass, bindweed, docks, thistles, ground elder etc. which will come up year after year if left unchecked.

At soil preparation time remove all the roots of perennial weeds that you can find. If the site is a sea of couch grass then you have a real problem. The age-old way of preparing such soil is to treat with Sodium Chlorate, but this will mean waiting for up to two years before planting. A better way is to spray with glyphosate before planting — follow the instructions carefully.

To keep weeds down among growing plants there are two basic chemical techniques. You can use a Rose Weedkiller based on simazine — if applied to weed-free soil in spring it will stop most annual weeds from germinating. Alternatively you can use Weedol later in the season as a chemical hoe to burn off all weed growth. Make sure you keep the weedkiller away from the rose leaves. If perennial weeds are present, paint their leaves with glyphosate.

Weedkillers, provided they carry a specific recommendation for roses, are valuable aids but the mainstay of weed control remains hand weeding and hoeing. Pull out or dig out perennial weeds, cut off annual weeds just below the surface, and apply an annual mulch as described on page 89.

Green slime and moss usually indicate poor drainage, surface compaction or fertilizer deficiency. Hoe regularly, and feed at least twice a year.

Suckers

Suckers are shoots which grow from the rootstock rather than from the named variety which has been grafted on to it. If nothing is done to check this growth then suckers may take over the plant completely and the bush will have reverted.

Suckering is encouraged by loose planting, severe frosts, root damage by hoeing, incorrect removal of previous suckers or the use of *R. rugosa* as a rootstock. You can easily recognize a sucker from a desirable stem by its origin below the bud union and by its different leaflet form and colour. Do not rely on the number of leaflets per leaf as your guide.

Tackle each sucker as soon as it is seen — removal is then a simple job. Trace it back to the point of origin on the root — some soil removal will be necessary. Then pull it off and replace the soil. With a recently planted rose, keep the plant firmly in place with your foot as you pull off the sucker. Snipping off suckers at ground level will only lead to an increase in sucker production.

With standards, rub off sucker growths on the stem as soon as they are seen.

Honey Fungus

A harmless-looking group of toadstools may appear next to a bush in autumn — in fact these toadstools are deadly to roses if they are the honey fungus (armillaria root rot) illustrated above.

On the roots of attacked plants you will find black "bootlaces" produced by the fungus. Remove and burn dead and dying plants with as much of their roots as possible in order to prevent the disease from spreading. Before replanting, using Armilla-tox might be a wise precaution.

Soil Sickness

So many books assume that you will always be planting your new bushes or standards in virgin soil which has never grown roses before. Unfortunately this is not always so, and if the site has grown roses for more than ten years then it is liable to be rose-sick.

This curious complaint has still not been completely explained. Exhaustion of trace elements and the build up of root diseases and rose-root poisons are all undoubtedly involved, but minute eelworms are probably the main culprits.

Oddly, the old roses growing on the site may have shown little or no ill-effect as they have adapted to the conditions. But planting a new rose in such soil can lead to poor growth ("replant disease") and for this reason the top soil should be changed (see page 86).

CHAPTER 8
GROWING ROSES AS A HOBBY

Most people who grow roses would not describe rose growing as their hobby. To them the queen of flowers is just a beautiful part of the overall garden picture.

For the rest rose growing is something more — the enjoyment of visiting rose shows and gardens, winning (or trying to win) prizes, propagating their own plants and keeping up with the latest trends and varieties. For them the study and practice of rose growing is an absorbing hobby.

Growing roses as a hobby dates from Victorian times, and one of its fascinating aspects is the way it has always cut across the various classes in our society. The workers of the Industrial Revolution were still farm hands at heart, and it was these people who set up the first flower shows. The legend is that it was a visit to a Nottingham miners' rose show which inspired Dean Hole to found the National Rose Society in 1876.

And so it is today, with people from all walks of life enjoying and succeeding in the hobby of rose growing. A rose in the buttonhole was once a badge of office for the man who was something in the City and for the man who looked after the local railway station. The ordinary gardener with a few roses has so much to learn from the hallowed names of the rose world, but it was still possible even in the 1970s for an engine driver with a tiny greenhouse to raise a new rose capable of winning the Gold Medal at Rome.

Learning more about roses

There is always something new happening in the rose world. Each year brings forth a crop of new varieties, and one or more of these may mark another step forward in the quest for perfection. *Peace*, *Super Star* and *Queen Elizabeth* stand out like milestones along the way, and no one can say what the next advance will be.

Will the Floribundas become more and more like Hybrid Teas in shape? Will the boom in Miniatures ever really take off? Will there be a new way of feeding next year? Nobody can begin to know everything about roses, and even if one did then some of the information would be out of date in a year or two. There are seven basic ways of learning more about roses. Use them all and you will surely become an expert.

Read books and journals on roses

Books and journals perform different jobs. A text book sets out to give you a sound background to the basic facts about the history, cultivation and selection of roses. The articles in gardening magazines and newspapers are usually concerned with new developments — the latest varieties, advances in feeding and pest control as well as the experiences of the writer or readers which would be out of place in a text book.

Study the latest catalogues

The catalogues of our leading rose growers are mines of information. Here you will find coloured illustrations of new varieties as well as old favourites. Essential reading for the enthusiast, but do look at the section on Rose Catalogues on page 3.

Visit nurseries in summer

An excellent way of seeing a multitude of varieties in flower — a great aid in making the right selection. In many ways a nursery visit can give the opposite view to looking through catalogues. The catalogue may give a picture that you might never achieve in your garden — the roses in the nursery are young stock which will be taller and more showy after a few years in your rose bed.

Visit the great Rose Gardens

See pages 106-107

Join your local Horticultural Society

Here you will be able to attend talks and meet fellow rose growers. Undoubtedly the greatest benefit is that you will be able to compare experiences with people who have to contend with similar conditions to your own — the same soil type, weather and air pollution. The knowledge of the long-standing members is especially helpful if you are new to rose growing or to the district.

Visit the Shows

The rose shows are the highlights of the year. You can see for yourself the beauty of the new varieties, and what experts judge to be perfect form. At the trade stands you can discuss your particular problems with a variety of knowledgeable growers and suppliers. Leading shows are:

RNRS Spring Competition, London	April
Chelsea Show, London	May
RNRS Rose Festival, Hertfordshire	July
Lakeland Rose Show, Cumbria	July
Shrewsbury Show, Shropshire	August
Southport Show, Merseyside	August
RNRS Autumn Show, London	September

Join the Royal National Rose Society

See page 104

The Royal National Rose Society

In 1876 a group of rose enthusiasts met in London to consider "what could be done to advance the interest of the rose, for in truth the Queen of Flowers has fallen on evil days." The National Rose Society was born. Its first show was held a year later — there were no Hybrid Teas, no Floribundas and very little public interest.

From these modest beginnings, with a deficit of £300 after the first year, one of the world's most important Horticultural Societies developed. In 1961 the Society moved its headquarters to Chiswell Green near St Albans and the heyday of the RNRS was reached in the 1970s. Membership passed the 100,000 mark, making it the largest specialist Society in the world of horticulture, and the prefix 'Royal' was added by command of H.M. Queen Elizabeth II.

Its awards are eagerly sought by rose breeders everywhere and its publications are important reference books. The gardens are unrivalled in Britain (see page 106) and many overseas Rose Societies have based their organization and rules on the successful British model.

The Society caters for all rose growers — the gardener with a few roses as well as the dedicated rosarian. Unfortunately the 1980s has seen a decline in membership as the cost of subscription has risen, but even at these membership rates you receive many benefits and privileges for the price you would have to pay for just a few rose bushes. Application forms are available from The Secretary, The Royal National Rose Society, Chiswell Green, St Albans, Herts AL2 3NR.

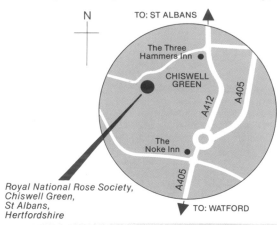

Royal National Rose Society,
Chiswell Green,
St Albans,
Hertfordshire

Benefits of Membership

FREE PUBLICATIONS

● **ROSE ANNUAL** Sent to all members each spring — 256 pages filled with up-to-date information, coloured pictures and the RNRS Analysis of reliable varieties.

● **ROSES** Sent to new members on joining — a list of over 600 varieties available in Britain, together with basic details such as colour, date of introduction and parentage.

● **ROSE BULLETIN** Sent to all members each October — the Society's magazine filled with down-to-earth articles, cartoons and items of news from the world of roses.

● **HOW TO GROW ROSES** Sent to new members on joining — a non-technical handbook containing up-to-date information on planting, pruning, problems, etc.

FREE SHOWS

Your membership card admits you to the July Rose Festival at the Society's gardens. This two day event has become a mecca for rose enthusiasts from all over the world. There are displays, living catalogues and trade exhibits. Your card will also admit you to the RNRS Autumn Show and the Lakeland Rose Show, plus many other shows in various parts of the U.K.

FREE GARDEN VISITS

The Society's Display Gardens and Trial Ground are yours to enjoy throughout the season — there is free admission for yourself and a friend. Here you can see one of the finest collections of roses in the world.

FREE ADVICE

As a member you are entitled to receive advice from the experts on all aspects of rose growing, so useful when you can't find the answer to an out-of-the-way problem. You can also use the reference library if you need more information than is available in your local library.

Awards

An award for a new variety is obviously highly desirable for both the raiser and the gardener. For the rose breeder who raised it there is valuable publicity and acclaim — for the gardener who chooses it there is the knowledge that the variety has proved its reliability for ordinary garden use to a panel of impartial experts. However, winning a high award is not a guarantee of public acceptance. Among the bi-colour Hybrid Tea group it was *Westminster* which won the Gold Medal, not *Piccadilly*. And *Whisky Mac*, one of the most popular of all Hybrid Teas, received no award at all.

The granting of an award is not an infallible guide to excellence and the absence of an award does not necessarily mean that the variety is a poor one. There are four reasons for this:

- There was no National Rose Society trials scheme before 1928, so an old variety could not possibly have received an NRS award.
- Not all new varieties are submitted for trials.
- An award-winning variety can deteriorate after a number of years.
- Foreign awards may be granted to a variety which might fail miserably under damp British conditions.

BRITISH AWARDS

A new variety sent to the Royal National Rose Society for testing is grown for two or three years in the Trial Ground at St Albans and it is assessed regularly throughout the summer by a panel of experts.

This group of amateur and professional growers looks for something more than a pretty flower. They consider many qualities, including vigour, growth habit, freedom from disease, fragrance, and freedom and continuity of flowering. If the panel feel that it should do reasonably well under most garden conditions, then a **Trial Ground Certificate** (TGC) is awarded. This is an award for reliability, not excellence, and yet only a small proportion of new varieties receive a TGC.

If in the view of the experts the variety has something more — "some novel or outstanding quality or supersedes a similar variety which has declined" then a **Gold Medal** (GM) may be awarded. This is indeed a rare honour — it is more usual for a **Certificate of Merit** (CM) to be awarded in recognition of outstanding quality.

At the top of the award ladder is the **President's International Trophy** (PIT), awarded to a variety which has received a Gold Medal and is judged to be the best new rose of the year. There is also a fragrance award — the **Henry Edland Memorial Medal** (HEMM) which is granted to the best scented new seedling of the year.

The Royal Horticultural Society can grant an **Award of Merit** (AM) to plants which show "a distinct advance on their predecessors". New varieties are often submitted for consideration but this award does not rank with the much sought-after RNRS awards.

| President's International Trophy | Gold Medal | Certificate of Merit | Trial Ground Certificate | Henry Edland Memorial Medal | Award of Merit |

The RNRS Analysis

The RNRS Rose Analysis is a useful guide to performance in gardens rather than trial grounds, and is published each year in the Rose Annual issued by the Society. All members are free to participate — volunteers are sent a questionnaire and the final placings arising from their votes are based on performance and reliability.

Obviously there are some changes in the ratings each year — new roses enter and varieties which have deteriorated drop out of the lists. But some varieties keep their place for many years — *Iceberg* was rated No. 1 in the Floribunda list in 1970, and it was also No. 1 in the 1980 Analysis.

OVERSEAS AWARDS

New roses are tested in trial grounds in many parts of the world and awards are granted on the basis of their reliability or excellence over two or more years. This method of testing roses, rather than judging them on a single day, began in the Bagatelle Gardens in Paris and was not adopted in Britain until many years later. Important European trial grounds are situated in Paris, Lyons, Geneva, Belfast, Rome, Madrid and The Hague.

In the vastness of the United States it would not be practical to rely on a single trial site — more than a score of test gardens are used to gain an overall view of the variety under widely differing climatic conditions. Roses must score highly on all features of performance for two years in order to gain the **All-American Rose Selection** (AARS) award.

| All-American Rose Selection | Gold Medal, Belfast | Fragrance Award, Belfast | Gold Medal, Geneva |

| Gold Medal, Lyons | Gold Medal, The Hague | Golden Rose, The Hague | Fragrance Medal, The Hague | Gold Medal, Rome |

| Gold Medal, Madrid | Gold Medal, Paris | Gold Medal, Baden Baden | Gold Medal, Roeulx |

Great Rose Gardens of Britain

QUEEN MARY'S GARDEN, Regent's Park, London

Britain's favourite rose garden, as it is only a few minutes' walk from Baker Street tube station. The main circular garden is surrounded by a ring of pillars which are festooned with Ramblers and Climbers. There are large formal beds as well as small secluded beds to house the 40,000 plants grown here. Queen Mary's Garden is not to be missed by any rose lover, for here you will see all types and classes —— Climbers scrambling through trees, enormous Shrubs in informal borders, formal beds of modern roses and many good examples of mixed plantings.

RNRS DISPLAY GARDENS, St Albans, Hertfordshire

From mid June until the end of September these 12 acres of gardens are open to the public for seven days a week. This display is one of the largest living catalogues in the world —— you can admire the first Hybrid Tea or an old Shrub Rose and then move to the Trial Ground where you will see varieties still unnamed but which may become tomorrow's favourites. But the St Albans gardens are much more than just an impressive display of 30,000 plants covering 1,650 different species and varieties. Here you will find many separate gardens to show you how to use roses in your own garden — sunken beds of Miniatures, large beds cut in lawns, small pillars and stately pergolas . . . and much, much more.

NEW ROSE GARDEN, Wisley, Surrey

In 1973 an area of the Royal Horticultural Society Gardens at Wisley was set aside as a New Rose Garden — a place where visitors could see how recently introduced varieties fared under ordinary garden conditions. Each year about 30 new varieties are planted. In the main gardens at Wisley there are many rose beds and borders of older varieties.

CITY OF BELFAST ROSE GARDEN, Belfast, N. Ireland

In 1964 the first roses were planted in the new Trial Grounds created in the beautiful Sir Thomas and Lady Dixon Park on the outskirts of Belfast. Since then it has become an impressive Display Garden containing over 20,000 roses.

SPRINGFIELDS, Spalding, Lincolnshire

The most famous bulb Display Garden in Britain recently joined the ranks of gardens for rose lovers. The British Association of Rose Breeders has donated an extensive collection of modern varieties to Springfields. The many thousands of plants represent a living catalogue of modern roses. Most but not all of the varieties are those holding Plant Breeders' Rights.

ROYAL BOTANIC GARDENS, Kew, London

Roses of all classes feature in our national botanical garden, but the collection is not particularly large and the displays are scattered throughout the gardens. The formal beds close to the Palm House are worth a visit, and there is also a comprehensive collection of Shrub Roses.

MOTTISFONT ABBEY, Romsey, Hampshire

Many of the gardens described on this page are designed to give the visitor an insight into newer varieties, so that he or she will not have to rely on catalogue photographs and descriptions. As a back-cloth to these modern Hybrid Teas and Floribundas there are Shrubs, Ramblers and Climbers. Mottisfont Abbey is different — it houses the National Collection of Old Roses.

PROVINCIAL DISPLAY GARDENS

Award-winning roses can be seen at the RNRS Display Gardens and Trial Ground at St Albans, but for many rose enthusiasts there is no way that they can make an annual pilgrimage to see these new varieties. To overcome this difficulty Display Gardens have been created in provincial parks so that local residents can see the award-winning varieties and information can be gained about their performance away from St Albans. Of course, these Provincial Display Gardens usually have impressive rose displays in addition to the RNRS award winners.

    SAUGHTON PARK, Edinburgh, Lothian
    VICTORIA PARK, Southport, Merseyside
    VIVARY PARK, Taunton, Somerset
    ROATH PARK, Cardiff, S. Glamorgan
    HARLOW CAR, Harrogate, N. Yorkshire
    THE ARBORETUM, Nottingham, Nottinghamshire
    HEIGHAM PARK, Norwich, Norfolk
    BOROUGH PARK, Redcar, Cleveland
    POLLOK PARK, Glasgow, Strathclyde

STATELY HOMES AND GARDENS

Virtually all of the great gardens of Britain contain roses, but some have rose displays which are either impressive or unusual enough to make this feature well worth a visit by any rose lover. Good examples are:

    ANGLESEY ABBEY, Lode, Cambridgeshire
    BODNANT GARDENS, Conwy, Gwynedd
    CASTLE HOWARD, York, N. Yorkshire
    CLIVEDEN, Maidenhead, Berkshire
    GREYS COURT, Rotherfield, Greys, Oxfordshire
    HIDCOTE MANOR, Chipping Campden, Gloucestershire
    KIFTSGATE COURT, Chipping Campden, Gloucestershire
    NYMANS, Handcross, W. Sussex
    SAVILL GARDEN, Windsor, Berkshire
    SISSINGHURST CASTLE, Cranbrook, Kent
    SYON PARK, Hounslow, London

NURSERY DISPLAY GARDENS

Your local garden centre or nursery will have maiden plants in bloom during the summer months, and a few nurseries have special Display Gardens where beds and borders of mature roses can be seen.

Great Rose Gardens Overseas

FRANCE

LA ROSERAIE DE L'HAŸ LES ROSES, Paris
Not a vast collection of plants, but undoubtedly one of the most comprehensive outdoor rose museums in the world. Here you will find beds displaying the history and development of the rose, beds containing the varieties grown at Malmaison and even a Theatre of the Rose.

BAGATELLE, Paris
The Roseraie at the Bagatelle contains many thousands of rose plants, and one of its great attractions is the multitude of neat geometric beds bearing the latest varieties. The first International Rose Competition was held at the Bagatelle, and the Gold Medal of the Concours International des Roses Nouvelles is still one of the rose world's top honours.

PARC DE LA TETE D'OR, Lyons

One of the world's great rose gardens was opened in 1964 at the birthplace of the modern rose. There are 100,000 plants in 14 acres of Display Garden — Miniatures in rockeries, Climbers on pergolas, vast seas of bushes in beds, hundreds of Shrub varieties and the trial grounds for new French seedlings.

WEST GERMANY

WESTFALENPARK, Dortmund
The original German Rosarium was founded in 1903 at Sangerhausen, and it became the most comprehensive collection of roses in the world with more than 6,500 different varieties. But Sangerhausen is in East Germany, and so in 1969 a new German National Rosarium was started. The varieties are arranged geographically, and each recognized breeder has his own plot in the area reserved for his country. Apart from these modern roses there is a large collection of old-fashioned varieties.

SWITZERLAND

PARC DE LA GRANGE, Geneva
Perhaps the loveliest rose garden of all, admired for its architecture as well as its roses. It consists of three terraces with pools and fountains. Each level is graced with many types of roses, and the whole area is floodlit during the summer months. Geneva Rose Week is the time of the International Rose Judging, and it is also the time when an open-air ballet is performed amid the 12,000 floodlit roses.

ITALY

MUNICIPAL ROSE GARDEN, Rome
This garden has the finest setting of all — a natural amphitheatre on the slopes of the Aventine Hill. In front of it are the ruins of the Palace of the Caesars. Around its edge runs a gallery of 200 climbing varieties and the central area contains Species Roses, early hybrids and popular modern varieties. An important International Rose Competition is held here each year.

DENMARK

VALBYPARKEN, Copenhagen
Opened in 1963, this large rose garden is only a few minutes away from the centre of Copenhagen. There is an extensive collection — about 20,000 plants representing 300 varieties. Danish rose breeders carry out their National Trials in Valbyparken.

HOLLAND

WESTBROEKPARK, The Hague
The rose garden in this public park was created after the war, and it has now become the largest and most important collection in the Benelux countries. More than 60,000 plants are set out in the large beds which make up the main display area of the rose garden.

SPAIN

PARQUE DEL OESTE, Madrid
A favourite argument amongst well-travelled rosarians is whether Geneva or Madrid boasts the loveliest rose garden in Europe. If variety is what you like — Miniature Roses hugging the ground near Climbers as tall as houses — statuary, fountains, cypress trees and flower-decked tunnels as well as an impressive collection of 30,000 roses then the Parque del Oeste would probably be your choice.

U.S.A.

HERSHEY ROSE GARDEN, Pennsylvania
If you had to pick just one of the countless American rose gardens to visit, then you would have to choose between the Hershey and the Park of Roses in Columbus. In the Hershey Rose Garden all rose tastes are catered for — there are thousands of modern Hybrid Teas and Floribundas as well as many hundreds of Shrub Rose varieties.

PARK OF ROSES, Columbus, Ohio
This 14 acre garden was once the home of the American Rose Society, and today it is a mecca for people who want to learn about as well as just enjoy roses. There are regular demonstrations throughout the year and the collection of over 50,000 roses covers all the various classes and types.

The New Classification

MODERN GARDEN ROSES

Roses which are neither OLD GARDEN ROSES nor WILD ROSES — as defined below

NON-CLIMBING MODERN GARDEN ROSE
A Modern Garden Rose with self-supporting stems

NON-RECURRENT SHRUB
A plant, usually taller and wider than a bush, which normally flowers only once each year

RECURRENT SHRUB
A plant, usually taller and wider than a bush, which has an extended flowering season

RECURRENT BUSH
A plant of moderate height, particularly suitable for cultivation in groups, which has an extended flowering season

RECURRENT MINIATURE
A plant with miniature flowers, foliage and growth which has an extended flowering season

CLIMBING MODERN GARDEN ROSE
A Modern Garden Rose which is climbing or rambling with long spreading or arching stems normally needing support

NON-RECURRENT RAMBLER
A climbing plant, with lax stems, which normally flowers only once each year

NON-RECURRENT CLIMBER
A climbing plant, with stiffer stems than a Rambler, which normally flowers only once each year

NON-RECURRENT CLI. MINIATURE
A climbing plant, with miniature flowers and foliage which normally flowers only once each year

RECURRENT RAMBLER
A climbing plant, with lax stems, which has an extended flowering season

RECURRENT CLIMBER
A climbing plant, with stiffer stems than a Rambler, which has an extended flowering season

RECURRENT CLI. MINIATURE
A climbing plant, with miniature flowers and foliage which has an extended flowering season

OLD GARDEN ROSES

Roses which belong to a class in common use before the introduction of the Hybrid Tea Rose

NON-CLIMBING OLD GARDEN ROSE
An Old Garden Rose with self-supporting stems

- ALBA
- BOURBON
- CHINA
- DAMASK
- GALLICA
- HYBRID PERPETUAL
- MOSS
- PORTLAND
- PROVENCE (CENTIFOLIA)
- SWEET BRIAR
- TEA

CLIMBING OLD GARDEN ROSE
An Old Garden Rose which is climbing or rambling with long spreading or arching stems normally needing support

- AYRSHIRE
- BOURSAULT
- CLIMBING TEA
- NOISETTE
- SEMPERVIRENS

WILD ROSES

Roses which are original Species, or varieties and hybrids which bear a close resemblance to Species Roses

NON-CLIMBING WILD ROSE
A Wild Rose with self-supporting stems

CLIMBING WILD ROSE
A Wild Rose which is climbing or rambling with long spreading or arching stems normally needing support

Nearly all of the Species group of Shrub Roses (see page 78 and pages 61-72) are included in this new class — examples are *Rosa rubrifolia* and *Canary Bird*.

A few of the Rambler Roses (see pages 51-60) make up this small new class — an example is *Rosa filipes Kiftsgate*.

Gardeners have grown up with the traditional classification of roses outlined on page 7, and terms such as Hybrid Tea and Floribunda have become household words. But the powers-that-be in the rose world have felt for many years that a better and more precise system is needed, and in 1971 the World Federation of Rose Societies accepted in principle the British proposals. The New Classification has now arrived, and in 1979 the RNRS began to use it in their show schedules. You will find unfamiliar terms beginning to appear in catalogues and magazines — this chart should help you to understand the new system of describing roses.

The Modern Shrub Roses plus the Rugosa Hybrids and the Hybrid Musks (see page 78 and pages 61-72) are included in these new classes of Recurrent and Non-recurrent Shrubs. Examples are *Fred Loads* and *Moonlight.*

LARGE FLOWERED BUSH
A plant with shapely buds which develop into large or medium-sized flowers of traditional H.T. form — can usually be cut as an individual bloom on a long stem

The Hybrid Teas (see pages 8-29) make up this new class — examples are *Alec's Red, Peace* and *Super Star.*

CLUSTER FLOWERED BUSH
A plant with a mass of flowers in trusses, clusters or on many stems. The blooms may be single, semi-double or double

The Floribundas (see pages 30-46) make up this new class — examples are *Allgold, Iceberg* and *Masquerade.*

POLYANTHA
A plant with small flowers, rosette in shape and carried in large clusters. The leaflets are smaller than those on a Cluster Flowered Bush

The Polyantha group of Shrub Roses (see page 78 and pages 61-72) make up this new class within the Recurrent Bush Roses. An example is *The Fairy.*

The Miniature Roses (see pages 47-50) make up this new class — examples are *Starina* and *Little Flirt.*

Some of the Ramblers and most of the Climbers (see pages 51-60) make up this large new class. Examples of the Non-recurrent climbing varieties are *Albertine* and *Mme Grégoire Staechelin.* The Recurrent climbing varieties include the Kordesii Climbers (e.g. *Dortmund*), the Climbing Floribundas and Hybrid Teas (e.g. *Climbing Masquerade*), most of the Large-flowered Climbers (e.g. *Handel*) and the Climbing Miniatures (e.g. *Nozomi*).

Colour Key to the traditional names of the new classes

Hybrid Tea Roses

Floribunda Roses

Miniature Roses

Climbers & Ramblers

Shrub Roses

Most of the Old-Fashioned group of Shrub Roses (see page 78 and pages 61-72) are included in this new class — the exceptions are the Rugosa Hybrids and the Hybrid Musks. Examples are *Old Blush, Frau Karl Druschki* and *Complicata.*

Many of the Ramblers and Climbers (see pages 51-60) are included in this new class — old favourites such as *Gloire de Dijon, Mme Alfred Carrière* and *Félicité et Perpétue.*

Naming New Roses

A new rose may bear only a code number during the trials stage, but the time comes when it needs a name. This name may be descriptive (*Allgold*), poetic (*Peace*), or it may be a famous person (*Queen Elizabeth*), a member of the raiser's family (*Ena Harkness*), or the product of a sponsor (*Typhoo Tea*).

Unfortunately this original name sometimes has little meaning overseas, and so many roses have synonyms (alternative names) — *Redgold* became *Rouge et Or* on the Continent and *Schneewittchen* became *Iceberg* when it came to Britain.

Avoiding foreign-sounding names is helpful for the purchaser but it can lead to confusion. Depending on which country you are in, *Frau Karl Druschki* can be *White American Beauty, Reines des Neiges* or *Snow Queen*, and so breeders have come up with an answer. They suggest that the 'official' variety name should always be printed in catalogues as well as the popular name, and this official name should be based on the breeder's name — *Meinatac* (*Susan Hampshire*) is a Meilland rose, *Mactru* (*Trumpeter*) is a McGredy rose and *Dicbar* (*Memento*) a Dickson rose.

The history of the rose

> ## EARLY ROSES OF THE WESTERN WORLD

About 5000 years ago Mediterranean man created a new concept — Civilization. Very quickly such basic features as writing, cities, the use of metals and the wheel appeared . . . and so did an interest in the Rose.

In Ancient Crete in 1600 BC roses were being painted on palace walls, and in Egypt a thousand years later they were portrayed on tombs. It would be wrong, however, to pretend that all ancient civilizations were fascinated by this flower — there are only two mentions of roses in the whole of the Authorized Version of the Bible . . . it may tell you to look at the Lilies of the Field, but it does not ask you to look at the roses!

The Greeks were perhaps the first to take the rose seriously. They had a good publicist — Sappho the poetess called it "The Queen of Flowers"; they also had a good technical adviser — Theophrastus wrote that roses should have their old wood removed to bear better flowers, that cuttings grow better than seeds and that success depends primarily on picking the right planting spot.

If the Greeks were the first to grow them in gardens and pots throughout the land, it was the Romans who first fell in love with them. They slept on the petals, carpeted their floors with them, imported early flowers from Egypt and raised their own blooms for winter in artificially-heated conservatories. They used them in food, wine, perfumes and medicines. The Legions took them to Britain and the other outposts of the Empire . . . and then Rome fell. The rose, now unloved and neglected, declined so that only the hardy varieties survived.

The early Christian Church rejected this floral symbol of Roman depravity, but it was back in favour by about 400 AD. Rosaries were made from the hips, medicines were made from the petals and circular windows in churches were designed on the pattern of the blooms.

We can take stock of the British garden roses as they existed in 1500. There was the most ancient cultivated rose of all — the Red Rose, **Rosa gallica.** A survivor from Roman times or brought over by the Crusaders, we can leave it to the experts to argue about its origin in the gardens of the Middle Ages.

Next the White Rose, **Rosa alba —** another very ancient rose brought over by the Romans. The fragrant **Damask Roses** came to Britain much later — modern research dates this introduction to just before 1500 rather than in the luggage of a returning Crusader as stated in many textbooks.

The red one, the white one and the richly fragrant one were all in the Tudor garden in 1500. One of the varieties was the *Autumn Damask* which had an unusually long flowering season. Not important in the early garden, perhaps, but as a parent of future generations it was destined to become one of the most important of all roses.

By 1700 other varieties had arrived. The globular and fragrant **Centifolia** or Cabbage Rose appeared in about 1550 from the Continent. Others came from much further afield. The **Austrian Yellow** had come to Britain via Vienna from Persia in 1580 and the **Musk Rose** had come at the same time from the Himalayas.

A bouquet of ancient garden roses — once flowering, limited in colour, globular in bloom and spreading in growth habit — waiting for the introduction of the roses from the Orient a generation or two later. The marriage between these Western and Oriental roses led to a bewildering array of new varieties which culminated in the modern rose of our gardens.

> ## ROSES OF THE ORIENT

Rose gardens existed in China when Western civilization was just beginning, and rose perfumes and petals were used for personal adornment and protection from evil spirits. The cultivation of roses in Japan also goes back into the mists of pre-history, but in neither country did the rose match the importance of the chrysanthemum, lotus or cherry blossom.

These ancient varieties are lost to us, but when the early 18th century traders from the East India Company arrived in China they found cultivated roses which were completely new to them. The flowers were small and without any distinct fragrance. The bushes were lanky and short of leaves, but the blooms appeared in flush after flush until the late autumn and there was a new colour — crimson. These were the **China Roses** — the first one to arrive in Europe was *Old Blush China* (see page 69) in 1752, followed by *Slater's Crimson China.*

The second wave of introductions from China occurred many years later. These were the **Tea Roses,** the first aristocrats of the rose world. Intolerant of frost and plagued with weak necks below the flowers, they still had outstanding properties — shapely buds, refined flowers, delicate fragrance and a repeat flowering habit. The first Tea Rose to arrive in Britain was *Hume's Blush Tea-Scented China* in 1810, followed by *Park's Yellow Tea-Scented China* in 1844.

Here were the ideal marriage partners for the western roses — the repeat flowering habit of the China Roses and the beautiful blooms of the Tea Roses to combine with the frost-hardiness and robustness of our own varieties.

The importance of these roses from China in the evolution of the modern rose is described in detail in every history of our favourite flower, and yet the role of the rose from Japan is often overlooked. In the 1860s **Rosa multiflora** was introduced from this relatively unknown country. The blooms of this wild Rambler would not win any prizes in a rose show — small and plain white flowers in large heads. Yet **R. multiflora** was the parent of some Ramblers and all our Floribundas.

THE MARRIAGE OF EAST AND WEST

The first east-west marriage was a chance cross in Italy between a red China Rose and *Autumn Damask*. The result was *Duchess of Portland* — the first **Portland Rose**. Between 1800 and 1850 this group became moderately popular, but its decline was rapid and very few Portland Roses are now available.

Another marriage took place across the Atlantic at about the same time — this time the partners were *Old Blush China* and the *Musk Rose*. Despite the fact that South Carolina was the site of this cross, the group was named after a French nurseryman — the **Noisettes**. Some Noisette hybrid Ramblers are still grown — *Mme Alfred Carrière* is described on page 57.

The big breakthrough came in 1818. A hybrid seedling was found at the base of a hedge containing *Old Blush China* and *Autumn Damask*. The place was Ile de Bourbon in the Indian Ocean and the tiny new rose was the first **Bourbon Rose**. Here at last was a truly successful east-west marriage — reasonably large flowers on a bush which flowered repeatedly. France was the centre of the Bourbon craze, and thousands of varieties appeared. Their popularity lasted through much of the Victorian era, and some are still listed in the catalogues.

In 1837 a new rose appeared — *Princess Hélène*. This cross between a Bourbon Rose and a Portland Rose heralded in the **Hybrid Perpetual**, and the Bourbon lost its crown as Queen of Roses. In both Europe and the U.S. rose breeders concentrated on producing more and more Hybrid Perpetuals until the end of the 19th century. Over 3,000 different varieties were introduced — in white, pink, mauve, red and purple. Some remain, led by *Frau Karl Druschki* which still keeps its place in the rose catalogues.

THE MODERN ROSE

The Victorian Queen of Roses, the Hybrid Perpetual, had its problems. The colour range was limited, repeat flowering was limited (a massive early flush was often followed by only sporadic summer or autumn blooming) and their garden use was limited — the bushes were large and rampant which meant that formal bedding in a small garden was not really practical. What was needed was the introduction of some of the elegance and delicacy of the Tea Rose. Many varieties of Tea Rose were available, but none was really winter-hardy. What was wanted was a cross between the hardy Hybrid Perpetual and the dainty Tea Rose.

There is some argument about the identity of this first **Hybrid Tea**, but the honour generally goes to *La France*, introduced in 1867. A momentous date, as this is accepted as the birth date of the modern rose.

There was no rush to buy this new rose, and the early Hybrid Teas crept in during the close of the 19th century. The acceptance of the group was accelerated by the appearance of some excellent varieties such as *Mme Caroline Testout* and *Lady Mary Fitzwilliam*, but the real breakthrough came in 1900. Pernet-Ducher in Lyons introduced *Soleil d'Or*, bred from a red Hybrid Perpetual and the *Persian Yellow* ... at last, a near-yellow flower on a bush with glossy leaves. Not truly a Hybrid Tea (it was called a Pernetiana at first), but it nevertheless enabled the Hybrid Teas to snatch the rose crown and keep it to this day.

The first pure yellow appeared in 1910 — *Rayon d'Or*. By this time the high-centred form of the Tea Rose was becoming dominant amongst Hybrid Teas — *Ophelia* (1912) was the first truly elegant pink. An impressive succession of trend-setting varieties were introduced up to the second World War — *Etoile de Hollande*, *Betty Uprichard*, *Shot Silk*, *Mrs Sam McGredy*, *Crimson Glory* and so on. Then just before the war a rose was bred in France which was to change the face of the Hybrid Tea. *Peace*, introduced into Britain in 1947, heralded in a new vigour and a new flower size.

After the war, the steady stream of exciting advances continued. In 1960 *Super Star* came to Britain from Germany — the first of the vermilion roses. Then came *Fragrant Cloud*, *Alec's Red*, *Alexander*, *Silver Jubilee* . . . and the quest for better Hybrid Teas goes on.

Hybrid Teas are not the only popular modern roses — the Floribundas are challenging them for the crown. Their story goes back to Guillot, the man who raised *La France*. In 1875 he introduced *Ma Paquerette*, which had *Rosa multiflora* and a China Rose as its parents. The small white blooms were borne in large clusters over a long flowering period on a small bush. This was the first **Polyantha Rose**, and the introduction of *Orléans Rose* in 1909 established the popularity of this group. *The Fairy* (page 71) survives in the catalogues.

But the Polyanthas needed something more — extra height and extra flower size, and here the Poulsen family in Denmark were the originators of the Polyantha x Hybrid Tea cross. These were the **Hybrid Polyanthas** or Poulsen Roses — *Else Poulsen* came first in 1924, followed by *Kirsten Poulsen* and *Anne Poulsen*. Many other varieties followed, bred in Denmark, Britain, United States, Germany and other countries, and the Hybrid Tea influence became stronger and stronger. A new name was obviously required, and the U.S. term **Floribunda** was accepted by the National Rose Society in 1952.

The colour range of the Floribundas is breathtaking — exceeding even that of the Hybrid Teas. The milestones are many, and any short list must omit numerous epoch-making roses. *Goldilocks*, *Masquerade* and *Fashion* introduced new colours in the 1940s and *Queen Elizabeth* introduced a new size and elegance in the 1950s. New shapes and colours flooded in during the 1960s, and the 1970s were marked by the growing interest in dwarfs (*Topsi*, *Golden Slippers*, etc.) and new colours such as *Picasso* (1971) and *Double Delight* (1977).

The next advance with Floribundas is just around the corner, but we cannot see it. As with all aspects of the rose, its history is still being written.

Exhibiting your roses

Decorative Classes

The roses are judged on the basis of the overall effect of the blooms together with the leaves and stems in a bowl or vase. Artistry and peak condition are much more important here than flowers which are above average in size.

Specimen Classes

The roses are mainly judged as individual blooms. The usual container is the display box (see page 113) and the quest here is for blooms which are as near perfect as possible in shape and colour and which are significantly larger than average.

You do not have to exhibit your blooms in order to be a rose lover or a rose expert. But the show-bench has a definite place in teaching you how to grow better roses, because it introduces the spirit of competition and makes you pay more attention to detail. Blooms which once were thought to be perfectly satisfactory may suddenly become second-rate when seen through the eyes of the exhibitor. The joy, of course, is in receiving an award rather than in the prize money . . . which is hardly likely to cover your expenses.

Start with your local horticultural show and don't go in for too many classes — you will soon learn that staging your exhibits takes far longer than you think. Begin by looking around this year's show — note the classes, write down the winning varieties and try to see why the winners received their awards. All of this will prepare you for your entry in next year's show. You may be puzzled by the poor standard of the First Prize display, but remember that you are seeing the exhibits *after* the judging — and judges make their awards for appearance at the time of their inspection.

If you want to take up rose showing seriously then you *must* become a member of the Royal National Rose Society. From them you will receive lists of varieties, judging standards etc., and also the right to exhibit in the RNRS classes at the shows.

HOW ROSES ARE JUDGED

Points gained

Blooms: Decorative classes — good average size for the variety. Specimen classes — larger than average size for the variety. Hybrid Teas — half to three-quarters open with a circular outline and well-formed centre. Floribundas — fully open.

Petals: Bright, firm, clean and free from blemish.

Leaves: Clean and undamaged. Adequate in quantity and size.

Stems: Straight and in proportion to flower size.

Presentation: Graceful balance, artistically arranged. Flowers neither crushed together nor too widely spaced.

Points lost

Blooms: Fewer than the average number of petals for the variety. Size not typical. Immature or blown blooms. Hybrid Teas — blooms with split or confused centres. Obvious removal of petals or obvious overdressing (see page 113).

Petals: Faded, drooping, soiled or diseased.

Leaves: Diseased or damaged. Inadequate in quantity and size.

Stems: Weak, bent, diseased or twisted.

Presentation: Untidy or lop-sided. Poor colour arrangement or an excessive display of stems and/or leaves.

GROWING PRIZE ROSES

Pick your varieties carefully

The judges will be looking for large blooms with many petals and high centres. On page 75 there is a list of H.T. varieties which frequently win prizes at local and national rose shows. Some of these are not recommended for general garden display but others, such as *Alec's Red*, *Champion* and *Pink Favorite* will give you a fine garden display as well as prizes at the show.

Keep records

Most keen rose exhibitors keep a detailed diary. In this they note the time of pruning, feeding dates and other comments so that they will know for next year what they did right . . . and wrong.

Get the timing right

One of the skills of successful showing is learning how to get a flush of blooms in peak condition just in time for the show. On average it takes about twelve weeks from pruning to the perfect bloom stage, but this can be as little as ten and as much as sixteen weeks. There is one basic way of making sure you don't miss having blooms on the vital day — try to grow as many plants as possible and prune them on different dates.

Follow the basic rules of rose care

Follow the principles of rose cultivation and soil preparation laid down in Chapters 5 and 6. Many rose exhibitors insist on hard pruning (see page 92) but this is not really necessary. Regular feeding is recommended — supplement the basic spring top-dressing with regular applications of liquid fertilizer or foliar feed (see page 94). Watering in dry weather and timely pest and disease control are vital.

GETTING READY FOR THE SHOW

About three or four days before the show you will start to get ready in earnest — at this stage you will look for blooms and stems which will be at their best on the big day. But there are several jobs, such as disbudding and covering, which will have taken place a week or two before selection, and even earlier you will have carried out one of the most important tasks of all — studying the show schedule.

Judges may mark you down or disqualify you for a minor breach of the rules — it does not have to be important. Select the class you wish to enter and make sure your exhibit will meet *all* the requirements. Does the specified number refer to blooms or stems? Is the old classification (page 7) or the new one (page 108) being used? Is wiring allowed? Are vases and bowls supplied? Clear up these and any other points well before the show.

DISBUDDING This should be carried out as soon as the side buds are big enough to handle — see page 93 for instructions. Stake the stem if the site is exposed or if the bloom is to be covered (see below).

In the case of Floribundas, some disbudding should be done about two weeks before the show. Remove the large central bud and one or two of the smallest ones from each truss, so that a large number of open and equal-sized blooms will be present on the day of the show.

COVERING A conical protector on a wooden stake above each bloom is a useful aid for the serious exhibitor. Rain is prevented from spotting delicate petals, which is vital in the more important classes.

Put the cover in position about ten to fourteen days before the show. It must be firm enough to avoid rocking against the bloom in windy weather, and it must be at the correct height to protect the bloom without shading it unduly. It must also be large enough to prevent rain from dripping down on to the petals.

TYING Many exhibitors loosely tie the centres of selected blooms with wool about three days before the show. The purpose is to lengthen the petals.

Choose half open (never fully open) blooms and use wool which is uncoloured, soft and thick. The petals must be dry at the time of tying. Secure the wool with a couple of twists and loosen slightly each day. This technique is best avoided by the novice as blooms can be damaged in unskilled hands.

CUTTING If you are exhibiting locally it is possible to cut in the early morning of the day of the show so that you can make a last-minute selection. If the selected stems have to travel some distance then cutting the night before will be necessary and many experienced exhibitors believe that cutting the previous night is the right time even for the local show. You will then have time to prepare and grade the stems properly — there will be very little time on the morning of the show.

As soon as the blooms are cut, remove the lower leaves and thorns and immerse in water to at least half the stem length. Keep in a cool and dark place.

ON THE DAY OF THE SHOW

Leave in good time and take everything you will need with you. Make a check-list — there may be a surprising number of items to carry. A typical list will contain pens, labels, scissors, secateurs, notebook, schedule, rushes, knife, camel-hair brush, house plant watering can, florist's wire and cotton wool.

TRAVELLING Cut and take double the number of blooms called for in the schedule. There are many methods of transporting them in a car, and each exhibitor has his or her favourite way. The rules are to keep the bottom of the stems wet, the blooms dry (wrap in soft paper) and the stems quite tightly packed together. If you use a bucket, put in a top layer of balls of newspaper to prevent undue splashing. If several buckets are to be carried, place them in a crate with packing material between each one.

LABELLING Do write the name of the rose or roses neatly on a card and place it alongside your display. If you do not know the name of the variety, state "variety unknown". A clearly-labelled exhibit does impress the judges.

DRESSING This is the final arrangement of the petals to secure maximum beauty. Use either your finger or a camel-hair brush to open the outside petals and partially open the second row. Never "overdress" or disturb the natural arrangement.

If an outer petal has been damaged, carefully remove it and gently press down the one above to take its place.

WIRING This is useful for roses to be arranged in vases, provided that it is not forbidden in the rules.

Push one end of the wire (obtainable from florists) into the swollen receptacle below the petals and twist the lower half around the stem. The flower can be easily broken off the stalk if this job is done clumsily, so practise on ordinary flowers from the garden before the big day.

STAGING THE EXHIBIT

3 bloom display

6 bloom display

Vases

Obtain vase from the Show Secretary on arrival. Pack with rushes before inserting the stems — make sure that lower leaves and thorns have been removed. Blooms should be close but not touching. Place the largest bloom at the base of the display. After arranging, fill the vase with water.

Bowls

Each bloom must be clear of its neighbour, but large bare gaps must be avoided. In a bowl of mixed varieties, do not have any two similarly coloured blooms next to each other. Use bright colours separated by pastel shades. If you have to supply your own bowl, make sure that it is simple in shape and neutral in colour.

Boxes

Box classes have declined in popularity. You will have to make or purchase your own specimen box for six or twelve blooms — they are not supplied by the organisers. Blooms should not touch — place the largest flowers in the back tubes which should be raised for extra display. Fill the space between the blooms with fresh green moss and label the display.

Increasing your stock

There are four ways of propagating roses — seed-sowing, layering, budding and taking cuttings. All of these methods are described in this section, but they are certainly not of equal importance. Seed-sowing and layering are rarely-used techniques for a limited number of varieties. Your basic choice, therefore, is between budding and taking cuttings.

Each of these two methods has its advantages and drawbacks. Most commercially-grown roses are raised by **budding**, which involves the insertion of a bud or "eye" of the selected variety into a T-shaped cut in the stem of a rootstock — close to the ground for a bush or some distance up the stem for a standard. It is suitable for all modern varieties, and the new plant has ready-made roots which results in quick development. But there are some disadvantages for the ordinary gardener — it calls for obtaining rootstocks and acquiring new skills.

Taking cuttings is the more popular method for the amateur — it really does mean getting new roses for nothing. The technique is child's play, but there are drawbacks. Not all roses can be propagated in this way and the new plants will take about three years before they are fully established in the garden.

BUDDING

1 Obtain rootstocks — for types available, see page 4. For suppliers — see advertisements in gardening magazines

Plant in November

Earth up stems after planting to keep the neck moist

12 in.

Neck should be barely covered, when planting

2 Bud rootstocks in the following July

Choose a cool day

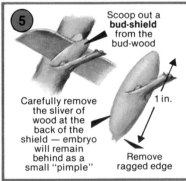

Clear soil away to expose the neck — wipe it clean with a rag

3

Cut

Select a strong shoot of the chosen variety which has just finished flowering

Cut a piece of **bud-wood** from the middle of the shoot

12 in.

Cut off leaves; retain short stalks. Keep in a plastic bag

Cut

½ in.

4

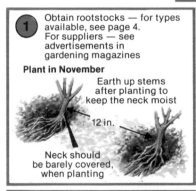

Use a budding knife to penetrate the bark of the rootstock, making a T-shaped cut

⅓ in.

¾ in.

Carefully ease back the two flaps, using the blunt end of the knife

5 Scoop out a **bud-shield** from the bud-wood

Carefully remove the sliver of wood at the back of the shield — embryo will remain behind as a small "pimple"

1 in.

Remove ragged edge

6

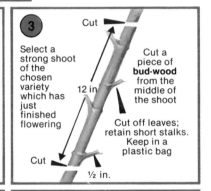

Hold bud-shield by the leaf stalk. Slide gently into the T-cut. Make sure it goes to the bottom

7

Fold back the flaps

Trim off the top of the bud-shield — the cut should be along the top of the T. Do not cut into the wood

8

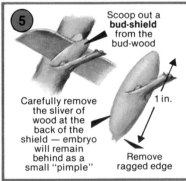

Secure (not *too* tightly) with damp raffia. Do not cover the bud

Knot on the opposite side to the bud-shield. Elastic ties are available

9

Leave ½ in., trim off later

Secure the plant with a cane

By the following February a new shoot will have started to grow. Cut off growth of the rootstock which is above it

TAKING CUTTINGS

This method is not recommended for many Hybrid Teas, especially the yellow varieties, as the root system may be too weak to transplant satisfactorily, but you can expect to succeed with Ramblers, vigorous Climbers, vigorous Floribundas and most Shrub Roses. An advantage of a rooted cutting compared to a budded rootstock is the absence of suckers — all shoots belong to the variety being grown.

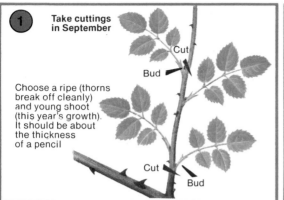

1 Take cuttings in September

Cut
Bud

Choose a ripe (thorns break off cleanly) and young shoot (this year's growth). It should be about the thickness of a pencil

Cut
Bud

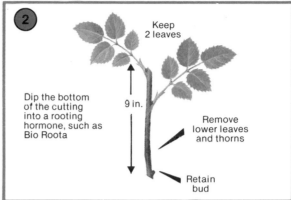

2

Keep 2 leaves

Dip the bottom of the cutting into a rooting hormone, such as Bio Roota

9 in.

Remove lower leaves and thorns

Retain bud

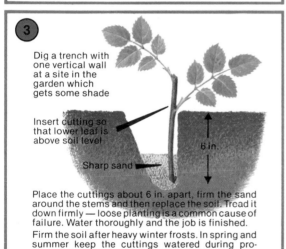

3

Dig a trench with one vertical wall at a site in the garden which gets some shade

Insert cutting so that lower leaf is above soil level

6 in.

Sharp sand

Place the cuttings about 6 in. apart, firm the sand around the stems and then replace the soil. Tread it down firmly — loose planting is a common cause of failure. Water thoroughly and the job is finished.

Firm the soil after heavy winter frosts. In spring and summer keep the cuttings watered during prolonged dry weather — remove any flower buds which may form.

By November the cuttings should be well-rooted and ready for planting.

Miniature Roses

Propagating Miniatures from cuttings has two advantages — you get more plants at very little cost and this new stock maintains its dwarf habit because it grows on its own roots.

The cuttings should be about 3 in. long — select shoots from this season's growth. Early autumn is the best time for this job — trim the cuttings to a leaf bud (see stage 2 above) and dip the bottom of each cutting in Bio Roota.

Plant firmly in pots containing Seed & Cutting Compost. A recent innovation which has proved successful for propagating Miniature Roses is the Rooting Bag — compost packed in a stout polythene bag. The method consists of cutting fourteen slits in the upper surface of the bag and then inserting a cutting through each slit.

Keep the cuttings out of direct sunlight. When new growth appears the rooted cuttings should be potted up separately into 3 in. pots. Keep indoors over winter and plant outdoors in spring or retain in pots for home decoration (see page 118).

SEED-SOWING

Raising roses from seed is usually dealt with briefly or not at all in the textbooks. There is no point in trying to raise a hybrid in this way — it will not breed true. The Species Roses will be true to type when grown from seed, but they will take years to reach a reasonable size and are much more easily raised from cuttings.

Miniature Roses are different — it is worthwhile growing them from seed and you can buy packets of various mixtures from several seedsmen. No long delays are involved — seeds sown in gentle heat in spring may be in flower by summer. Sow indoors in April in Seed & Cutting Compost. Germination is rather slow and erratic so try to sow a reasonable quantity of seeds. Prick out the best seedlings into small pots and make your selection in summer. Some of the young plants are bound to be poor and spindly — throw them away and just keep the most attractive. Repot as necessary and overwinter the plants in a cold greenhouse or on the windowsill of an unheated room.

LAYERING

Layering is an excellent method of propagating any rose which bears long and flexible stems. Of course, it is ideal for Ramblers but it can be used for many Shrub Roses as well.

In July or August work some peat into the area where the layering is to take place. Choose a stem which is mature but still flexible, and make a cut about 3 in. long on the side of the stem which will be buried in the prepared area. Place a twig in this cut and then bury this section in the ground. It should be pegged down with a forked stick.

The tip of the shoot should be secured in an upright position by tying it to a cane, and the ground should be kept watered in dry weather. Rooting will have taken place by the following March, and the new plant can be separated from the parent by cutting through the section of stem between them. Transplant the new Rambler or Shrub; do not allow it to flower during its first season.

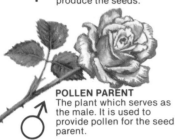

SEED PARENT
The plant which serves as the female. It is fertilized to produce the seeds.

POLLEN PARENT
The plant which serves as the male. It is used to provide pollen for the seed parent.

Breeding a new rose

Breeding roses at home is like buying a national lottery ticket — it is easy to enter but almost impossible to come up with a winner. To raise a new rose is simple — you just transfer the pollen of one variety to the stigmas of another and then sow the seeds which result. Each seedling will be unique, but the chance of one being a significant advance in the rose world is almost nil.

Professional breeders often talk about the large element of luck in the discovery of a winner, but for them it is much more than a lottery. Great care goes into the selection of parents, hundreds of thousands of seedlings are raised and a high degree of skill goes into the detection of desirable characteristics at an early stage.

None of this need worry the novice. Home-bred plants need not be world-beaters — there is great satisfaction in having a variety, however flawed, which doesn't exist anywhere else!

1 Parent selection

You will need to select a seed parent and a pollen parent for the proposed cross. Try to choose two varieties which could combine desirable characteristics to produce a unique blend — a blood-red *Peace* is a much sought-after example. Crossing Floribundas is perhaps the easiest way to start but there are no strict rules — it is very much a matter of trial and error.

If you want to be a serious hybridist then you will have to study the family trees of candidate parents — *Roses* (Jack Harkness) is an excellent guide book. Pot up the selected plants in autumn in 10 in. pots and take them into a cold greenhouse in February.

2 Pollination

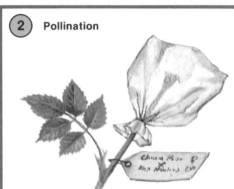

A sunny day in late May or early June is the ideal time for pollination. Prepare the seed parent. Choose a half-open flower and gently remove all the petals, taking care not to leave any bits behind. Next, pick off all the anthers with tweezers and finally place a paper bag over the emasculated flower.

Carry out pollination the following day. Snip off a flower of the pollen parent and remove or pull back the petals. Brush the anthers against the stigmas and then replace the paper bag over the seed parent. Tie a label to the stem, giving details of the parents, and continue to care for the seed parent plant as normal.

3 Seed preparation

Remove the paper bag after a couple of weeks and allow the hips to develop. Remove these swollen seed cases from the plant in autumn when they are ripe but not shrivelled. Bury them in wet peat in a flower pot, and let them stand outdoors throughout the winter — do not protect from frost. Remember to insert an identification label in the pot.

In February bring the hips indoors and squeeze out the seeds into a bowl of water. The floaters are infertile — sow the ones which have sunk to the bottom. Use Seed & Cutting Compost and when the first true rose leaves appear transplant the seedlings into small pots.

4 New rose selection

Some of these young plants will produce a bloom or two in May or June and this is the time for the first selection. One of the great skills of breeding is to spot desirable characteristics at this stage — you will have to rely on beginner's luck. Scrap all the worthless ones and transplant the promising ones into larger pots.

Carry out a second judging in August and grow as pot roses for a second season the few you wish to retain. If one shows promise you can plant it outdoors on its own roots or bud it on to a rootstock in July. You now have your very own rose variety growing in the garden.

CHAPTER 9
ROSES IN THE HOME

Half of this country's gardeners are women, and for them the rose has the added pleasure of having a place indoors. The use of cut roses for flower arranging is universal. Apart from countless garden blooms employed for this purpose, scores of millions of florist roses are sold every year.

There are many other uses for roses indoors, but the part they play in the home has declined in the sophisticated world of today. In the homes of Ancient Rome, in the refectories of mediaeval monasteries and in the kitchens of large Victorian villas you could find rose wine, rose perfumes, rose jams and so on. These are now rarities, but there is no reason why you should not try some of the old recipes which appear in this chapter.

THE ROSE AS A CUT FLOWER

It is not surprising that the favourite garden flower should be so popular for cutting. Unfortunately, as poets throughout the ages have pointed out, rose blooms are short-lived. Although you cannot expect cut roses to last as long as carnations, anemones or chrysanthemums, their life can be considerably extended if you follow a few simple rules when cutting, conditioning and arranging.

1 CUTTING

Choose a variety recommended for cutting. See list below and check in the A–Z guides (pages 9–46)

Blooms cut too early or too late will disappoint. Hybrid Teas: Sepals opened out; petals in the bud showing colour. Floribundas: Most of the flowers in the truss half-open

Cut in the evening if you can — otherwise cut in the morning

Cut just above a leaf. See page 93

Put cut blooms in a bucket of tepid water immediately

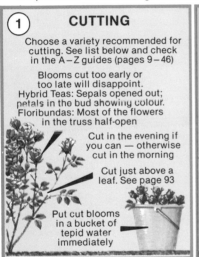

2 CONDITIONING

Remove lower leaves and thorns. Slit the bottom of each stem upwards for about 1 in. Stems should be stood up to their necks in water

Keep the bucket of roses in a cool dark place overnight

Bucket filled with water containing a dessertspoonful of sugar

If the leaves have wilted in the morning, stand ends of stems in 1 in. of very hot water for a few minutes before arranging

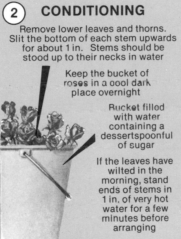

3 ARRANGING

Arrangement can be a single flower or a massed display. Roses can be grouped alone or mixed with other flowers

Keep the arrangement in good light but out of direct sunlight

Fill with tepid water — add Bio Flowerlife to extend life of blooms and keep water fresh

If plastic foam is used as the base, soak thoroughly before use and fix in position before inserting stems

Drying Roses

Dried roses will last almost indefinitely if you handle and arrange them with care. Choose semi-double blooms — cut off the stems and when quite dry lay the flowers face upwards on a layer of oven-dry fine sand in a biscuit tin. Leave about 1 in. between the blooms. Slowly add more dry sand so that all parts of the flowers are covered — avoid air pockets. Finally, cover the blooms with a 1–2 in. layer of sand and replace the lid. Seal with adhesive tape.

Store in a warm dry place for three weeks. Remove blooms gently — they should be dry and crisp. Turn each one upside down and shake out the sand — remove any remaining grains with a fine brush. Insert a piece of stout florist wire in the base of each bloom and cover with green florist tape.

RECOMMENDED VARIETIES

Hybrid Teas	Floribundas
ALEXANDER	ANNE COCKER
ALPINE SUNSET	APRICOT NECTAR
APRICOT SILK	ARTHUR BELL
BLESSINGS	CHANELLE
BLUE MOON	CITY OF BELFAST
CHAMPION	COPPER POT
DIORAMA	DEAREST
DR A. J. VERHAGE	ELIZABETH OF GLAMIS
ELIZABETH HARKNESS	ENGLISH MISS
FRED GIBSON	ESCAPADE
GAVOTTE	ESTHER OFARIM
KING'S RANSOM	GLENFIDDICH
KORP	ICEBERG
LADY SYLVIA	ICED GINGER
LOLITA	MARGARET MERRIL
MICHELE MEILLAND	MEMENTO
MISS HARP	MOON MAIDEN
MME BUTTERFLY	PADDY McGREDY
PASCALI	PINEAPPLE POLL
SILVER LINING	PINK PARFAIT
SUNBLEST	QUEEN ELIZABETH
SUPER STAR	REDGOLD
SWEET PROMISE	SEA PEARL
TROIKA	SUNSILK
VIRGO	YESTERDAY

THE ROSE AS A HOUSE PLANT

The more books you read on growing roses indoors, the more confused you will become. At one end of the scale are the British authorities who claim that the Miniature Rose is not a house plant at all. It is a garden plant, to be brought indoors when the buds start to colour and then taken out again as soon as the flowers have faded.

At the other end of the scale there are the U.S. enthusiasts who scoff at such an idea — for them the Miniature Rose is a true indoor plant, providing regular flushes of blooms every two months throughout the year.

Surprisingly, both these opposed views are correct — it depends on the care provided. If all you want to do is put the pot on the sideboard and water it occasionally then it is right to keep the plant indoors for as short a time as possible. If however you can provide fluorescent lighting above the pots and a humid atmosphere around them, then it is perfectly feasible to achieve the American all-the-year-round result.

The best compromise for most rose growers is to use the Pebble Tray technique. By this method you can have Miniature Roses in bloom by early spring in the living room, and there they can stay, producing regular flushes of flowers until late summer or early autumn.

The secret is to ensure that the plants receive **maximum light** and **adequate humidity** whilst they are indoors — see the diagram below for details.

Use rooted cuttings rather than Miniatures which have been budded on to rootstocks. In autumn transfer the pots outdoors and bring them in again in January. Prune to about half their present height and stand the pots in an unheated room for about two weeks before placing them in the heated room where they are to bloom. Avoid temperatures above 70°F. Keep a careful watch for red spider mite.

South-facing window. Screen from midday sun in summer. If possible move the pots near a fluorescent light at night in spring and autumn

Mist leaves frequently with a hand sprayer

Water liberally. Allow the pot to dry out slightly between waterings. Feed with Baby Bio each time you water

Waterproof tray about 2 in. deep

1 in. layer of gravel. Keep the bottom of this layer wet at all times, but the water level must be kept below the top of the gravel

THE ROSE IN PERFUME-MAKING

Pot-pourri

Pot-pourri is a mixture of dried flower petals and sweet-smelling oils, spices and fixatives. When the mixture has matured, it is placed in open bowls or pomanders to scent the room or placed in sachets in drawers to scent the linen.

Choose fragrant roses when they are at their prime. Cut them when the petals are dry. Spread a thin layer of petals on newspaper and place in a warm, dry room — an airing cupboard is ideal. Stir occasionally and when the petals are cornflake crisp after one or two weeks, place them in a polythene bag. Add the following mixture to the bag:

For each quart of dried petals —

    1 oz dried orris root (to 'fix' the scents)
    ½ teaspoon allspice
    ½ teaspoon cinnamon
    A few drops of rose oil

Shake thoroughly and leave the bag closed for about three weeks — then place the pot-pourri in any attractive container.

This is the basic rose pot-pourri. To vary the scent add dried orange and lemon peel, or dried aromatic leaves such as scented geranium, mint, rosemary, etc.

Rose Water

You can buy rose water from your local chemist, but if you have a plentiful supply of fragrant blooms you can try to make your own in the following age-old way:

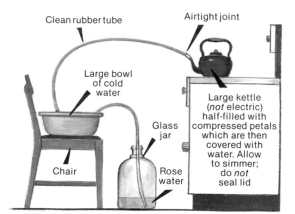

Clean rubber tube

Airtight joint

Large bowl of cold water

Chair

Glass jar

Rose water

Large kettle (*not* electric) half-filled with compressed petals which are then covered with water. Allow to simmer; do *not* seal lid

When the kettle is nearly (but not completely) dry, switch off the heat. Carefully drain the contents of the tube into the glass jar.

Rose Oil

You will not be able to obtain concentrated rose essence from your roses (it takes about 5 tons of fragrant petals to produce just one pound of attar of roses) but you can make a simple rose oil if you have an abundance of petals and time.

Place a pint of olive oil in a large bowl and add as many fragrant petals as the container will hold. Leave them to soak in the oil for two days and then squeeze through a fine strainer. Press the petals against the inside of the sieve to ensure that all the oils are squeezed out.

Repeat the process about ten times with fresh petals. Finally, decant the oil into a container with an airtight screw lid. Use the oil as a perfume or for making pot-pourri.

THE ROSE IN THE KITCHEN

The rose is not a vegetable — it is a plant to be admired for its beauty in the garden outdoors or in a vase or pot indoors. But there are recipes which call for roses, and one or two of them can be tried by the adventurous cook. If you intend to follow any of these recipes, make sure that the petals or hips are fresh and disease-free, and they should not have been recently sprayed or dusted. Petals and hips can be used in many ways, but never use rose leaves.

Rose Hip Jam

Wash and 'tail' the rose hips. Place in a large pan with an equal volume of water and cook until tender — about 15 minutes. Push the pulp through a fine strainer and to each cup of pulped hips add half a cup of sugar. Cook and stir until the mixture thickens to a jam-like consistency and then pour into sterilized jars and seal.

Rose Vinegar

Fill a large glass or glazed earthenware jar with red fragrant petals. Press them down and cover with wine vinegar. Cover the jar and leave for several weeks; then filter into screw-topped bottles.

Crystallised Rose Petals

Prepare a bowl containing beaten egg whites and another containing granulated sugar. Remove the petals gently from a dry bloom and using tweezers dip each one first into the frothy egg whites (avoid any excess on the petals) and then into the granulated sugar. Dry the crystallised petals on a lined baking tray in the airing cupboard. Store between layers of greaseproof paper in an airtight tin.

Rose Honey

Wash and 'tail' 4 oz of rose hips and boil in a cup of water in an enamel saucepan for about 15 minutes. Push the pulp through a fine strainer and add 1 lb of honey. Boil and stir the mixture until it thickens to a jam-like consistency and then pour into sterilized jars and seal.

Rose Wine

Rose wines have been made in Britain for centuries, but the methods used often led to failure. The modern techniques of home wine-making have taken the risks and guesswork out of this absorbing hobby, and both petals and hips can be used to make rose wine. You will need about 4 pints of petals or 2 pints of hips to make a gallon of wine.

There are more ingredients than just rose petals or hips plus sugar and water. The list is a long one, including yeast, nutrient tablets, Campden tablets, pectin-destroying enzyme and grape tannin. There is also special equipment — fermentation jars, airlocks, filters and the rest. Do not let this list put you off — if you have never tried your hand at wine-making you can begin with roses and a simple guide from your bookshop will give you step-by-step instructions.

If you do not wish to go to the trouble and expense of wine-making it is possible to make 'instant' rose wine. Just mix ½ lb of red fragrant petals with a pint of hot water and pulp them through a fine sieve. Add more petals until the liquor is a rich red colour and then stir in 1 lb of sugar and ½ pint of brandy.

THE ROSE AS A BUTTONHOLE FLOWER

Once the buttonhole rose was the badge of nearly every stationmaster and City gentleman, but its popularity has greatly declined. No more will you find it described in the rose books, but some men do still wear a rose in their lapel — the summer-long symbol of their hobby.

Any shapely and compact bloom will do — the ideal is a half-opened bud, pointed and high-centred with a good colour. There are varieties which have earned a high reputation as buttonhole roses — *Bloomfield Abundance*, *Cécile Brunner*, *Mme Butterfly*, *Ophelia* and *Picture*, but many other Hybrid Tea and Shrub Roses will do just as well.

Pick your buttonhole rose in the evening and stand its short stem immediately in tepid water. Leave it overnight and then prepare it for your jacket. The fashion in the early years of this century was to insert the stem into a water-filled metal tube worn at the back of the lapel, but these and the glass tubes which replaced them are now gone.

The modern way of preparing a buttonhole rose is shown on the right. As you can see, neither skill nor a special holder is called for.

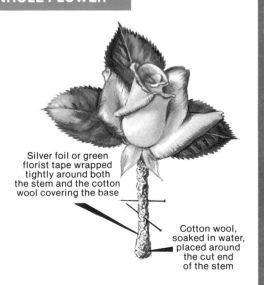

Silver foil or green florist tape wrapped tightly around both the stem and the cotton wool covering the base

Cotton wool, soaked in water, placed around the cut end of the stem

CHAPTER 10
ROSE CALENDAR

JANUARY

Frosts are likely, so there is usually little to do in the rose garden this month.

Check roses growing on supports to make sure that the ties are strong enough to hold them. Inspect autumn-planted bushes and standards to see if they have been loosened by frosts. Firm if necessary.

Planting can take place if soil is free-draining and not heavy, and if weather is dry and not freezing. Beds to be planted in March should be prepared this month.

Heating of the greenhouse containing pot roses may be required to keep the temperature at 40°–45°F.

FEBRUARY

The soil will almost certainly be wet and cold, but planting can continue in light-soil areas if the temperature is above freezing. In mild districts the pruning of vigorous Floribundas can begin at the end of the month. Stocks budded last year can be cut back.

Pot roses will now be starting to grow, and a temperature of 50°–60°F should be maintained. Spray the shoots with water to create moist conditions. Greenfly and caterpillars can cause serious damage to the new and tender shoots, so keep careful watch for these pests and spray at the first sign of attack.

MARCH

Finish planting this month. In most areas March is the best time to prune bush and standard roses. Burn all prunings.

Fertilizer may be spread around the bushes immediately after pruning and lightly pricked into the surface, but it is generally better to wait until April.

Weed beds thoroughly; apply a simazine-based weedkiller if regular hoeing is not possible.

Pot roses in the greenhouse may now be in bud. A weekly liquid feed with Bio Plant Food will improve bloom quality. Continue spraying shoots with water. Increase house temperature to 60°–65°F.

APRIL

Pruning must be completed by the beginning of the month, as roses will now be starting to grow actively. Rub out any surplus young shoots.

Apply a fertilizer, such as Toprose, which contains the main and minor plant foods needed by the rose. Keep the powder off new growth, and lightly prick into the soil surface.

Neaten bed edges with a half-moon edging iron. In areas where bad attacks of black spot are common apply two Benlate sprays a week apart as soon as leaf buds open.

Continue feeding and watering pot roses under glass, some of which will bloom this month. Spraying with water should now be directed at the paths, not on the roses. Keep watch for mildew, greenfly and caterpillar. Ideal house temperature 65°–75°F. Apply Coolglass to the panes if weather is sunny.

MAY

Garden roses will now be growing rapidly, and a mulch should be applied around the stems. Hoeing can be carried out to destroy weeds, but do not dig in the mulching material.

The first of the early-flowering Shrubs (e.g. *Canary Bird*) will now be in flower.

Greenfly attacks are likely, and a systemic insecticide which works internally is the best method of control (see page 99). A spray or dust for other insect pests or early disease outbreak may be necessary – watch for first attacks. If using a liquid fertilizer, such as Instant Bio, apply this month when soil is moist. Apply a foliar feed such as Fillip to backward plants.

Visit the Chelsea Flower Show, London.

Pot roses which have finished flowering should be moved outdoors and stood on concrete, ashes, etc., but not on earth. Water as necessary.

JUNE

Roses are now coming into flower. Hoeing, spraying and watering should continue as necessary.

Mulch with grass clippings if they are free from weedkiller. Cut flowers for indoor decoration from established plants, not from newly-planted bushes.

Disbudding of Hybrid Teas (see page 93) will ensure top-quality blooms. A summer fertilizer dressing with Toprose will keep the plants growing vigorously and help to produce a succession of flower buds. If you plan to enter your roses at a flower show, obtain show schedule as soon as possible. Continue foliar feeding for top-quality blooms.

Apply a mixed systemic insecticide/Benlate spray to keep pests and diseases at bay.

The last of the pot roses should now be moved out from the greenhouse to their outdoor quarters.

JULY

Bushes and standards should now be in full flower — July is usually the best month to enjoy your roses. Dead-head (see page 93) flower stalks when the blooms they carry have finished flowering. Apply a summer dressing of fertilizer if this was not done last month.

Hoe, disbud, mulch and water if necessary as described for June. Keep a special watch for the first signs of black spot and mildew. Spray immediately if seen.

If you are going away on holiday, remove all flowers which have begun to fade so that hips will not form during your absence.

Visit the National Rose Show at St Albans or the Lakeland Rose Show in Cumbria. Many local rose shows are held during this month.

Bud rootstocks this month.

OCTOBER

This month is the start of the rose grower's year. Tidy up beds. Hoe in the mulching material and collect up and burn leaves.

Finish preparing new beds. Nurseries start sending out their plants in October and planting can start at the end of the month. Trim off leaves and unripe wood as described on page 86 before placing each plant in its new quarters.

Inspect pot roses this month, and repot if necessary. Buy and pot up new plants. Remove shading and clean out greenhouse. Begin bringing the plants inside at the end of October.

AUGUST

The cultural techniques described for July apply this month, with the exception of fertilizer application which should stop at the end of July.

Now is the time to start thinking ahead to next year's varieties for your garden. If you can, visit the nursery of a large specialist rose grower to see the new varieties in bloom. Your local garden centre is well worth a visit. Some nurseries have special Display Gardens (see page 106). Other displays worth visiting are the RNRS Gardens at St Albans, the Provincial Display Gardens (see page 106) and the Southport Flower Show.

Send off your rose order as soon as possible, as new introductions and popular varieties are frequently sold out before planting time.

Begin the preparation of new rose beds as described in Chapter 5.

NOVEMBER

Get plants ready for winter. In exposed areas, long stems should be cut back a little to prevent wind rock during winter storms. In cold districts the stems should be earthed-up with about 4 inches of soil (remove in spring) or covered with straw (see page 96).

An excellent time for planting. If the bushes or standards arrive when the weather is unsuitable or before you are ready, leave package unopened or heel-in plants as described on page 86.

All pot roses should be placed in the greenhouse during this month.

SEPTEMBER

Roses will generally still be flowering freely, and dead-heading now will help to ensure a fine late display.

Ramblers and weeping standards should have been pruned by now (see page 92). Never leave these plants for pruning in the spring.

Carry on preparing new beds for planting in November and despatch your order to the nursery if this was not done last month.

Continue hoeing and spraying against disease if necessary. September is a good month to take cuttings of Ramblers, vigorous Floribundas etc. See page 115 for instructions.

Visit the RNRS Autumn Show in London — many local autumn rose shows are held in September.

DECEMBER

The soil will now generally be colder and wetter than last month so planting should be completed as soon as possible. Never try to plant when the soil is either hard with frost or waterlogged.

There is no work to do in the established rose garden, but work can begin on the preparation of rose beds which are to be planted up in March.

All pot roses will now be housed under glass and the temperature should be kept above freezing point if heat is available. Keep the pots fairly dry for a short time after housing, and prune at the end of the month.

CHAPTER 11

ROSE GROWER'S DICTIONARY

A

ACID SOIL A soil which contains no free lime and has a pH of less than 6.5.

ALLEN, E. F. Honorary Scientific Adviser of the RNRS since 1959, and a prolific contributor to its publications. Mr Allen is also a successful amateur breeder — his *Golden Chersonese* received a Certificate of Merit in 1970.

AMERICAN ROSE SOCIETY Started in 1899, the ARS has become one of the most active rose societies in the world. Its members receive a monthly magazine together with the American Rose Annual each year, which features the *Proof of the Pudding* survey. The headquarters are at the American Rose Center where an extensive rose garden is being created. Details of membership can be obtained from the Secretary, American Rose Society, Shreveport, Louisiana, USA.

ANTHER The part of the flower which produces pollen. It is the upper section of the *stamen*.

ARMED Bearing strong thorns.

ATTAR OF ROSES A yellowish oil distilled from rose petals which is used for making perfumes. Its production has been a major industry in the Balkans for centuries.

AXIL The angle between the upper surface of the leaf stalk and the stem that carries it.

B

BALLING The clinging together of petals in wet weather so that the bloom fails to open — see page 96.

BARE-ROOT A rose dug up at the nursery and sold with no soil around its roots — see page 73.

BASAL SHOOT A shoot arising from the neck or crown of the plant — see page 4.

BENNETT, HENRY The father of scientific rose breeding. He was a cattle breeder, and realized the need to control the pollination and keep a careful record of the crosses. In 1879 he introduced his Ten Pedigree Hybrids of the Tea Rose.

BLEEDING The loss of sap from plant tissues due to late pruning.

BLIND SHOOT A mature stem which fails to produce a flower.

BLOWN BLOOM A many-petalled bloom which has opened wide, revealing its stamens.

BLUE ROSE No true-blue rose exists, and it is extremely unlikely that one will ever be raised, because the blue flower pigment (delphinidin) is missing from the rose family. The so called "blue" roses, such as *Blue Moon, Baby Faurax* etc. are really lavender, mauve or violet.

BLUEING The transformation of a red or deep pink bloom to mauve or purple as it ages.

BOSS The ring of stamens when it is prominent and decorative.

BOX A container which bears six or twelve tubes for the display of specimen blooms — see page 113.

BRACT A small leaf-like growth on the flower stalk — see page 4.

BREAKING BUD A bud which has started to open.

BRITISH ASSOCIATION OF ROSE BREEDERS The objects of BARB are to encourage, improve and extend the introduction and growing of new roses under *Plant Breeders' Rights*. Trials are conducted, and a large rose garden has been created at Springfields (see page 106). About 250 nurseries are registered with BARB, and there is a very simple method of licensing new varieties to these growers.

BUD A flower bud is the unopened bloom. A growth bud or *eye* is a condensed shoot found in the *axil* of a leafstalk.

BUD UNION The point where the bud and the rootstock are united.

BUDDING The grafting of a bud into the neck of a rootstock — see page 114. The standard commercial method of propagating roses.

BURNING The bleaching or scorching of the petals in bright sunshine.

BUSH A growth type — see page 4 for details.

BUTTON EYE A condition found in the centre of the blooms of some old varieties — the petals are folded inwards to form a 'button'.

C

CALLUS The scar tissue which forms over a pruning cut or at the base of a cutting.

CALYX The green protective cover of the flower bud, which opens into five sepals — see page 4.

CAMBIUM A thin layer of soft tissue between the bark and the wood which allows the bud and the rootstock to unite when budding takes place.

CANE A main stem or basal shoot — a term frequently used in the U.S.

CANKER A diseased and discoloured area on the stem — see page 98.

CHLOROSIS An abnormal yellowing or blanching of the leaves due to lack of chlorophyll. See page 96 for possible causes.

CLIMBING SPORT A mutation of a bush variety which bears long canes and identical flowers to the parent.

CLUSTER A number of flowers connected by their footstalks to a single stem — see page 4.

COCKER, ALEC Scottish breeder, who began to raise roses in 1963 and died in 1977 — shortly before his great achievement *Silver Jubilee* received Britain's highest award. Earlier successes from the Aberdeen nursery were *Alec's Red, Anne Cocker, Rob Roy* and *Rosy Mantle.*

COMPOST Two meanings — either decomposed vegetable or animal matter for incorporation in the soil or a potting/cutting mixture made from peat ('soilless compost') or sterilized soil ('loam compost') plus other materials such as sand, lime and fertilizer.

CONE A conical protector used by exhibitors to prevent rain and bright sunshine from spoiling their show blooms whilst they are still on the plant – see page 113.

CONFUSED CENTRE The centre of a bloom where the petals are disarranged, giving an asymmetrical appearance.

CROCK A piece of broken flower pot used at the bottom of a container to improve drainage.

CROSS The offspring arising from cross-pollination.

CROWN The point on the bush where the basal shoots sprout from the rootstock.

CULTIVAR Short for 'cultivated variety' — it is a variety which originated in cultivation and not in the wild. Strictly speaking, all modern varieties are cultivars, but the more familiar term *'variety'* is used in this book.

CUT-BACK A bush which is one or more seasons older than a *maiden*.

CUTTING A piece of stem cut from a plant and used for propagation.

D

DEAD-HEADING The removal of faded flowers – see page 93.

DE-SHOOTING The removal of small shoots to prevent overcrowding. Another term for 'thinning' – see page 93.

DICKSON & SONS LTD The Dickson nurseries in County Down have a long and distinguished history of rose breeding. There were Dickson roses before the 20th century and *Shot Silk* (1924) still appears in the catalogues. More recent successes have been *Grandpa Dickson, Red Devil, Redgold, Mala Rubinstein* and *Precious Platinum*.

DIE-BACK The progressive dying back of a shoot from the tip – see page 98.

DISBUDDING The removal of young flower buds to allow the maximum development of the remainder – see page 93.

DOG ROSE The common wild rose found in hedgerows – so called because the Romans used it as a cure for hydrophobia.

DORMANT PERIOD The time when the plant has naturally stopped growing due to low temperature and short day-length.

DOT, PEDRO Spain's greatest hybridist. His work spanned 50 years and although he raised many noteworthy Hybrid Teas he will always be remembered as one of the world's leading breeders of Miniatures. *Josephine Wheatcroft, Pour Toi, Coralin* and *Baby Gold Star* are examples of his introductions.

DOUBLE BLOOM A flower with more than twenty petals – see page 5.

DRESSING The manipulation of an exhibition bloom in order to improve its appearance on the day of the show – see page 113.

E

EARTHING-UP The drawing up of earth around the base of a bush to protect it during a period of abnormally cold weather.

EMASCULATION A technique used in hybridising – the removal of the anthers from the seed parent to prevent self-pollination. See page 116.

EYE Two unrelated meanings – a dormant growth bud or the centre of a single or semi-double bloom where the colour is distinctly different from the rest of the flower.

F

FERTILE HYBRID A hybrid which bears viable seed capable of producing new plants. A sterile hybrid does not produce viable seed.

FERTILIZATION The application of pollen to the stigma to induce the production of seed. An essential step in hybridisation – see page 116.

FILAMENT The supporting column of the *anther*. It is the lower part of the *stamen*.

FIXED A vital feature for a new variety – it means that the new colour or growth habit is stable.

FLORIFEROUS The scientific term for *free-flowering*.

FLOWER-SHY A vague term indicating that a variety bears a below-average number of blooms during the flowering season. The opposite condition is *free-flowering*.

FLUSH The period during which the plant bears its normal complement of blooms – there may be more than one such period during the season – see *repeat flowering*.

FOLIAR FEED A fertilizer capable of being sprayed on and absorbed by the leaves – see page 94.

FOOTSTALK The pedicel or flower stalk – see page 4.

FORCING The process of making a plant grow or flower before its natural season.

FOSSIL ROSES Fossilized rose leaves have been found in rocks in Europe, Asia and North America. They are thought to be 7-30 million years old.

FREE-FLOWERING A vague term indicating that a variety bears an above-average number of blooms during the flowering season. The opposite condition is *flower-shy*.

FUNGICIDE A chemical used to control diseases caused by fungi.

FUNGUS A primitive form of plant life which is the most common cause of infectious disease – mildew, black spot and rust are examples.

G

GARNETTE ROSE A red Floribunda, similar to the variety *Garnette*, grown commercially under glass for sale as a cut flower.

GRAFTING The process of joining a stem or bud of one plant on to the stem of another.

GREGORY, WALTER One of the group of great Nottinghamshire rose growers, who began breeding new varieties in 1952. In the span of nearly 30 years before his death in 1980, he introduced *Blessings, Summer Holiday, Pink Perpetue* and his crowning glory, *Wendy Cussons*.

GUARD PETALS The outermost ring of petals.

GUILLOT, JEAN-BAPTISTE The first of the great rose breeders from Lyons. His creation in 1867, *La France*, was the original Hybrid Tea and started the era of the modern rose. In the following decade he introduced *Ma Paquerette, Gloire des Polyantha* and *Mignonette* – the first of the dwarf Polyanthas which gave rise to the modern Floribundas.

H

HARDY A plant which will withstand overwintering without any protection.

HARKNESS, JACK The family firm was established in Yorkshire about 100 years ago, and in 1892 a branch was set up in Hertfordshire to specialise in roses. It was Jack Harkness who first turned to hybridising and his successes have been outstanding – *Alexander, Southampton, Escapade, Compassion* and *Dame of Sark*. His collaboration with Alec Cocker was one of the great success stories in the world of rose breeding.

HEAD The framework of stems borne at the top of the stem of a standard.

HEADING-BACK The removal of the stems of the rootstock above the union after budding – see page 114.

HEELING IN The temporary planting of a new rose pending suitable weather conditions for permanent planting.

HEP See *hip*.

HILDESHEIM ROSE A specimen of *Dog Rose* growing at Hildesheim Cathedral in Germany. The legend is that it was planted by Charlemagne over 1,000 years ago, but it is probably 300-500 years old. Generally accepted as the oldest living rose.

HILLING U.S. term for *earthing-up*.

HIP The fruit of a rose, large and decorative in some varieties – see page 6.

HOLE, REV SAMUEL REYNOLDS Although an active churchman (he became Dean of Rochester), Reverend Hole was the dominant figure in the Victorian rose world. He amassed a collection of 5,000 varieties, arranged the first National Rose Show and was a leading figure in the formation of the National Rose Society in 1876. The Dean Hole Medal is the RNRS's highest award for distinguished service.

HONEYDEW Sticky, sugary secretion deposited on the leaves and stems by such insects as aphid and whitefly.

HURST, CHARLES C. Cambridge scientist who worked out the family history of the modern rose, as outlined on page 111.

HYBRID A rose with parents which are genetically distinct. The parent plants may be different *cultivars*, *varieties* or *species*.

I

INFLORESCENCE The arrangement of flowers on the stem.

INORGANIC A chemical or fertilizer which is not obtained from a source which is or has been alive.

INSECTICIDE A chemical used to control insect pests.

INTERNODE The part of the stem between one *node* and another.

J

JACKSON & PERKINS One of the great rose nurseries of the world. At their trial grounds in California many great roses have been raised, first by Eugene Boerner and more recently by William Warriner. Examples are *Masquerade, Goldilocks, Apricot Nectar, Aloha* and *Evening Star*.

JOSEPHINE Empress Josephine, wife of Napoleon I, bought *Malmaison* in 1799 and set out to stock it with every variety of rose grown anywhere in the world. Her passion created the world's first rose display ground, and it made the rose a fashionable flower for the wealthy to grow on their estates.

K

KNUCKLE U.S. term for *bud union*.

KORDES, WILHELM Wilhelm Kordes, until his death in 1977, ranked alongside *Tantau* as the greatest rose hybridist in Germany. The list of his introductions starts with *Crimson Glory* in 1935. Others include *Iceberg, Perfecta, Ballet, Ernest H. Morse, Peer Gynt* and *Karl Herbst*. One of his most outstanding achievements was the development of the Kordesii climbers, such as *Dortmund*.

L

LANCASTER ROSE The Red Rose of Lancaster is *Rosa gallica officinalis* (see page 69). The legend is that the first Earl of Lancaster brought it from France to England during the 13th century.

LANKY Spindly growth – a stem with a gaunt and sparse appearance.

LATERAL BRANCH A side branch which arises from a main stem.

LAWRANCE, MARY Authoress of the first book devoted entirely to roses – 'A Collection of Roses from Nature' (1799).

LEACHING The drawing away of chemicals from the soil, caused by rain or watering.

LE GRICE, EDWARD Norfolk breeder who was responsible for one of the best of all yellow Floribundas – *Allgold*. His career was a long one; in 1938 he received a Certificate of Merit for *Dainty Maid* – in 1970 he was awarded a Gold Medal for *News*. In between these two were *My Choice* and *Lilac Charm*.

LENS, LOUIS The Lens nurseries have been the most successful breeding establishment in Belgium for half a century. Louis entered the firm in 1945 and later succeeded his father, Victor. His most famous introduction was *Pascali*, which remains one of the best of all white Hybrid Teas.

M

MAIDEN A rose bush in its first year after budding.

MALMAISON A château with extensive grounds situated near Paris, famous as the first great rose garden. Empress *Josephine* stocked it with more than 200 different varieties from all over the world and new techniques for breeding and cultivation were developed. Her work at Malmaison began in 1799 – following her divorce in 1809 she move there permanently.

McGREDY, SAM Sam McGredy IV has a family tradition of rose breeding, and since taking over the nursery in 1952 in N. Ireland and then emigrating to New Zealand in 1972, he has joined the ranks of the world's great hybridists. Even his major achievements are too numerous to list in full – they include *Mischief, Piccadilly, City of Belfast, Arthur Bell, Evelyn Fison, Handel, Chanelle, Picasso* and *Priscilla Burton*.

MEILLAND François Meilland raised *Peace* just before World War II and secured an everlasting place in the Gardening Hall of Fame. Other successes included *Baccara,* but perhaps one of his greatest achievements was to secure breeders' rights for new roses. Alain now carries on his father's work – *Charleston, Papa Meilland, Susan Hampshire, Sweet Promise, Starina* and *Chorus* are a few of the products of the Antibes nursery.

MODERN ROSES The first edition of this rose variety 'bible' appeared in 1930. The eighth edition of Modern Roses, published in 1980, contains details of many thousands of varieties. It is produced by the American Rose Society, which is the international organization for the registration of rose names.

MOORE, RALPH S. Californian breeder who has revolutionised the world of Miniature Roses. He has developed Miniature Moss Roses and Miniature Climbers, and many of today's favourites are his creations – *New Penny, Easter Morning, Judy Fischer* and *Little Buckaroo.*

MULCH A layer of bulky organic material placed around the stems – see page 89.

MUTATION A sudden change in the genetic make-up of a plant, leading to a new feature. This new feature can be inherited.

N

NECK The part of the plant above the roots and below the stems.

NEUTRAL Neither acid nor alkaline – pH 6.5-7.5.

NODE The point on the stem at which a leaf or bud is attached.

NORMAN, A. An amateur rosarian, famous as an author, exhibitor and judge but above all as the raiser of two outstanding varieties — *Ena Harkness* and *Frensham.*

O

ORGANIC A chemical or fertilizer which is obtained from a source which is or has been alive.

OVARY The part of the flower which contains the *ovules.*

OVERDRESSED Petals which have been bent back to such an extent on the day of the show that the bloom has an unnatural appearance.

OVULE The part of the female organ of the flower which turns into a seed after fertilization.

OWN-ROOT A plant grown on its own roots – one that has not been budded.

P

PEACE Seedling No. 3-35-40 was raised by François Meilland at Lyons before the outbreak of World War II and a few plants were sent out on the last plane to America as France fell. He had named the plant *Mme Antoine Meilland* but it was taken to Germany as *Gloria Dei.* When the war ended the U.S. nursery which had raised his stock placed a bunch of the flowers at each seat at the Peace Conference – and the rose received its final name – Peace.

PEDICEL The flower stalk – see page 4.

PEGGING DOWN The bending over of long shoots and the retention of their tips at ground level by means of pegs.

PERGOLA An arched structure used to support climbing plants; a rose-covered tunnel.

PERNET-DUCHER, JOSEPH Born in 1858, he earned the title "Wizard of Lyons" by transforming the colour range of modern roses. His early successes included *Mme Caroline Testout,* but he is best remembered for *Soleil d'Or,* introduced in 1900, which brought yellow to bedding roses.

pH A measure of acidity and alkalinity. Below pH 6.5 is acid, above pH 7.5 is alkaline.

PISTIL The female organ of a flower, consisting of the *stigma, style* and *ovule.*

PITH The spongy material at the centre of the stem. An unripe stem is sometimes described as 'pithy'.

PLANT BREEDERS' RIGHTS Until quite recently the breeder of a new rose received no royalties from the growers who propagated and sold it. The first plant patent was awarded in the U.S. – *New Dawn* in 1930. British protection dates from 1964 (the Plant Varieties & Seeds Act). Growers pay a small royalty to the breeder for each patented rose they propagate. The payment of a royalty does not apply if you propagate roses for your own pleasure and not for sale.

POLLEN The yellow dust produced by the *anthers.* It is the male element which fertilizes the *ovule.*

POLLINATION The application of *pollen* to the *stigma* of the flower.

POULSEN The Poulsen family of Denmark have produced many great roses during the past 60 years. Svend Poulsen raised the first Hybrid Polyantha (later called Floribundas) in 1924, and he was responsible for several famous varieties, such as *Rumba.* His son Niels has carried on the tradition with *Troika, Copenhagen* and *Chinatown.*

PROOF OF THE PUDDING The U.S. equivalent of the Royal National Rose Society Analysis (see page 105). The ratings are based on the experience of members of the American Rose Society who have grown the roses in question.

PROPAGATION The multiplication of plants – see page 114.

PRUNING The removal of parts of the plant in order to improve its performance.

R

RECURRENT FLOWERING Same as *repeat flowering.*

REDOUTE, PIERRE JOSEPH French artist commissioned by Empress *Josephine* in 1805 to make a pictorial record of every rose grown at *Malmaison.* The three volumes of Les Roses portray 170 of these roses, and reproductions of these paintings are still immensely popular.

REMONTANT/REMONTANCE Same as *repeat flowering.*

REPEAT FLOWERING The production of two or more *flushes* during the flowering season — see page 6.

REVERSE The side of the petal which faces away from the centre.

REVERSION Two meanings – either a *sport* which goes back to the colour or growth habit of its parent or a cultivated variety which is outgrown by suckers arising from the rootstock.

RIVERS, THOMAS & SON LTD The oldest nursery in Britain, established in 1725. Their 'Rose Amateurs Guide' first appeared in 1837 and listed 700 varieties for sale.

ROGUE A rose supplied which was not ordered, and which is not close enough to be regarded as a *substitute.*

ROOTSTOCK The host plant on to which a cultivated variety is budded – see page 4.

ROSA The genus to which all roses belong. There are about 140 different species.

ROSACEAE The family to which roses belong, together with other plants which have rose-like flowers, such as cherry, plum, hawthorn and strawberry.

ROSE GROWERS ASSOCIATION The RGA is an association of the leading rose growers who jointly produce more than three-quarters of the roses sold in this country. They seek publicity for roses and rose growing, and to improve standards they publish rose care information. The RGA stages a major exhibit at the annual Rose Festival held at the RNRS Display Gardens.

ROYAL NATIONAL ROSE SOCIETY See page 104.

S

SANGERHAUSEN Founded by the German Rose Society in 1903, this Rosarium in E. Germany has the most extensive collection of old roses in the world.

SCION The technical term for the bud which is grafted on to the rootstock.

SEEDLING A young plant raised from seed; in the rose world it also means a mature plant raised by sowing seed rather than by budding or taking cuttings.

SEPAL One of the five green divisions of the *calyx*.

SHOOT A stem or cane. Some rose experts prefer to be more precise — a shoot is used for young growth, a stem describes mature growth.

SHOT A surface which changes colour when viewed from different points.

SIDE SHOOT Same as *lateral branch*.

SNAG A section of stem left above a bud when pruning.

SPECIES Roses which are genetically similar and which reproduce exactly when self-fertilized. The popular meaning is a wild rose or one of its near relatives.

SPIT The depth of the spade blade — usually about 9 inches.

SPORT A plant which shows a marked and inheritable change from its parent; a *mutation*.

SPOTTING The appearance of spots and blemishes on the petals during wet weather.

STAMEN The male organ of a flower, consisting of the *anther* and *filament*.

STIGMA The part of the female organ of the flower which catches the pollen.

STIPULE The small outgrowth at the base of the leafstalk.

STOCK See *rootstock*.

STRATIFICATION The breaking of seed dormancy by placing hips in a refrigerator or overwintering them outdoors in damp peat before removing seeds for sowing — see page 116.

STRIKE The successful outcome of taking cuttings — cuttings 'strike' whereas grafts *'take'*.

STYLE The part of the female organ of the flower which connects the *stigma* to the *ovule*.

SUBSTITUTE A similar variety sent out by a nurseryman if the ordered variety is not available.

SUCKER A shoot growing from the rootstock — see page 102.

SWIM, HERBERT C. Californian hybridist who has produced more All-America Award winners than any other breeder. His successes include *Sutter's Gold, Helen Traubel, Mojave, Circus, Pink Parfait, Royal Highness* and *Mister Lincoln*.

SYSTEMIC A pesticide which goes inside the plant and travels in the sap stream.

T

TAKE The successful outcome of budding — grafts 'take' whereas cuttings *'strike'.*

TANTAU The father and son partnership of Mathias Tantau and Mathias junior has produced such world-famous roses as *Super Star, Fragrant Cloud, Fountain* and *Topsi*. The first Tantau rose from the N. German nursery was *Beauty of Holstein* (1919). Since then the list has been outstanding — *Stella, Duke of Windsor, Whisky Mac, Blue Moon, Prima Ballerina* and many more.

THORN A characteristic spine or prickle, usually found on the stems but occasionally on the backs of leaves and on hips.

TRANSPLANTING Movement of a plant from one site to another.

TREE ROSE U.S. term for a standard rose — see page 4.

TRUSS A number of flowers connected by their footstalks to a single stem — see page 4.

TUDOR ROSE The royal badge of England, combining the Red Rose of Lancaster with the White Rose of York. It was adopted as our national emblem when Henry Tudor (Henry VII) married Elizabeth of York in 1486.

U

UNDERSTOCK See *rootstock*.

UNION See *bud union*.

V

VARIETY Strictly speaking, a naturally occurring variation of a species (see *cultivar*). The popular meaning in the rose world is any distinct type of rose which bears one or more unique features.

W

WEEPING STANDARD A Rambler budded on to a tall standard stem — see page 4.

WHEATCROFT, HARRY Until his death in 1977, Harry Wheatcroft was 'Mr Rose' to millions of British gardeners. His nursery at Edwalton, Nottinghamshire, produced two million plants a year, but he will be best remembered for his personal appearances and his introduction to Britain of such great roses as *Super Star, Peace. Fragrant Cloud* and *Queen Elizabeth.*

WILLMOTT, ELLEN Authoress of 'Genus Rosa' published between 1910 and 1914 with illustrations painted by Alfred Parsons. This book is regarded as one of the milestones in rose literature, rivalling the work of Redouté.

WORLD FEDERATION OF ROSE SOCIETIES The rose societies of 17 nations belong to this worldwide organization which held its first meeting in New Zealand in 1971. It meets every two years, and its objects include establishing common standards for judging and classification, granting international awards, avoiding confusion over the naming of new roses and encouraging research.

WORLD'S FAVOURITE ROSE Competition run by the *World Federation of Rose Societies* in which each member society sends in its nomination. Winners have been *Peace* (1975) and *Queen Elizabeth* (1979). A winning rose is not allowed to stand again.

Y

YORK ROSE The identity of the White Rose of York is not known for certain. It was probably *Rosa alba semi-plena,* but it may have been *R. arvensis.*

CHAPTER 12

ROSE INDEX